Y0-CCN-326

Reinterpreting
Urban School Reform

Reinterpreting Urban School Reform

Have Urban Schools Failed, or Has the Reform Movement Failed Urban Schools?

EDITED BY

Louis F. Mirón
and
Edward P. St. John

State University of New York Press

Published by
State University of New York Press, Albany

Printed in the United States of America

For information, address State University of New York Press,
90 State Street, Suite 700, Albany N.Y. 12207

Production by Diane Ganeles
Marketing by Patrick Durocher

Library of Congress Cataloging-in-Publication Data

Reinterpreting urban school reform : have urban schools failed, or has the reform movement failed urban schools? / edited by Louis F. Mirón and Edward P. St. John.

p. cm.

Includes bibliographical references and index.

ISBN 0-7914-5707-9 (alk. paper)—ISBN 0-7914-5708-7 (pbk. : alk. paper)

1. Education, Urban—United States. 2. Educational change—United States. I. Mirón, Louis F. II. St. John, Edward P.

LC5131 .R45 2003
371.'00973'091732—dc21

2002075789

10 9 8 7 6 5 4 3 2 1

Contents

Introduction: Rethinking Urban School Reform

Louis F. Mirón and Edward P. St. John

The desegregation of Little Rock, Arkansas, schools, after the *Brown v. Board of Education* decision, unleashed nearly a half century of externally generated reforms of urban schools. At the turn of the century, the array of education reforms that have been attempted in urban schools are extensive, their effects controversial, and the cumulative knowledge limited. Although the context has changed, the effects of reform on urban schools have arguably been remarkably consistent: the intended effects have largely remained unrealized. This raises a vital concern. Have urban schools failed *or* has educational reform failed urban schools?

The New Global Context of Urban School Reform

In the early history of urban school reform the embedded social context was fairly straightforward: urban schools mirrored the political economy of the city. Funding for urban school districts ebbed and flowed in proportion to the local tax base.

Now the political economy of urban school districts is situated much more globally. As Julius Wilson, Gary Orfield, and others have consistently pointed out, urban schools are resegregated, underfunded, and perhaps somewhat academically weakened largely because of the waves of poor and uneducated immigrants, the disappearance of work in the inner city along with the concomitant rise in low-paying, part-time jobs, and the rise of high-tech industries that call for a highly educated labor force. These sociodemographic changes have spurned a passive resistance in high school students, who perceive that public schooling in the inner city is no longer relevant to their needs. In brief, the plight of urban school reform is now tied not only to the economic and social health of the city but indeed to rapid changes in the world economy. The justifications for current school reform efforts are similar to previous ones in that elites are in need of a skilled labor force in the cities. However, the discourse surrounding current reform efforts now pays more attention to the "performances" of school systems and their capacities to "produce" students as lifelong and constructivist learners. This appears to be a transformation in the societal conversations about school reform linked to the "mode of information" (see Poster 1989, 1990; also see Castells 1996). This transformation, unlike the early history of urban schools, is globally situated. By "globalization" we mean here those social, economic, and technological processes largely confined to urban centers characterized by "de- and reindustrialization, automation, revenue losses, brought on by middle-class taxpayer flight, and the emergence of new and urban multi-ethnic majorities." (see Valle and Torres 2001, 102)

The Reformers in Context

A wide array of proponents of urban school improvement has initiated reforms that have had major influences on urban schools. Many of the reforms have both advocates and detractors, who interpret the reforms, their rationales and consequences, very differently. Therefore, there is a need to take a fresh look at urban schools. In this volume we propose to reinterpret urban school reform through what we call a *critical-empirical* review. The major sections of the book provide critical reviews of the evidence of the impact of four types of reform. These are discussed briefly below.

The Courts and Urban School Reform

Both the federal and state courts have played a direct, yet external, role in urban school reform. The federal courts have influenced urban schools through school desegregation litigation, whereas state constitutions and state supreme courts have influenced urban schools through legal challenges of school finance formulas.

The U.S. Supreme Court's decision in *Brown v. the Board of Education* initiated a wave of reforms in urban communities. Although desegregation influenced nonurban schools as well, the impact of desegregation in urban schools was more substantial than in other types of school communities. The citywide remedies ordered by the courts spurred massive bussing as well as widespread resistance, especially among white enclaves in local urban residential neighborhoods.

Desegregation hastened white flight from urban schools and the concentration of poverty in inner cities. Further, the newer centers of global technologies are now usually located in suburban areas, rather than in urban centers, creating a further distance between the cities and the suburbs and the increasingly technologically linked world. In the early twentieth century, America's cities represented the focal point of culture and technology, whereas the American metropolis now runs the risk of having its citizens, and especially its youth, become isolated. (see Valle and Torres 2001)

Yet the nationwide efforts to desegregate urban schools also influenced a wave of educational innovation in urban schools. For example, the Boston school desegregation case introduced the concept of magnet schools that would provide specialized educational opportunities that might induce desegregation through informed choice.

These contradictory aspects of the new urban school reform efforts are inexorably linked to a set of forces set in motion by desegregation. Indeed, the unintended consequences of desegregation—the new racial and economic isolation of urban youth—may help offset innovations in education, the results of which may further undermine the hard-fought legal remedies.

The state courts also play a hand in school reform through their role in helping to ensure equity in school finance. In the recent Ohio case, for example, the urban schools joined with the rural schools in litigation on the adequacy of funding (see Theobald, chapter 2 of this volume). The intersection between litigation on school equity and school finance reform has been systematically examined only sparingly.

Two of the chapters in this volume examine issues related to the role of the courts in urban school reform. In chapter 1, Richard Fossey examines how well evidence about the impact of desegregation strategies supports the claims of those advocating the remedies in the first place. After decades of court ordered remedies to alleviate de jure and de facto segregation in urban schools, a number of questions have surfaced about the extent to which these remedies have resulted in educational improvement and contributed to the new pattern of metropolitan resegregation. Fossey's analysis adds substantially to our collective understanding of the role of the courts in desegregation and sets the stage for the analysis of the impact of reforms in urban schools.

In chapter 2, Neil Theobald develops an approach to informing policymakers about equity issues in school finance. He examines the cases of the states of Washington, Indiana, and Ohio, with a specific focus on the ways in which equity for urban students has been dealt with in the policy debates about school finance. His analyses provide insight into the role school finance reform plays in improving urban schools, as well as providing insight into a process-oriented approach to policy development.

Federally Initiated, External Reforms

The federal role in education began to take shape after the Soviet Union launched Sputnik and Congress passed the *National Defense Education Act* of 1958. This action initiated four decades of federal efforts to improve education. There have essentially been three major waves of federal reform, each of which has had distinct impacts on urban schools.

The first wave of federal reform involved introducing major new programs aimed at improving education and equalizing opportunity. The programs that were targeted at improving educational opportunities for the "disadvantaged" had the most substantial influence on urban schools because of the increasing concentration of poverty in urban communities. Two types of federal programs have had a substantial influence on urban schools. First, Title I of the *Elementary and Secondary Education Act* has subsidized efforts to provide compensatory education to children from disadvantaged backgrounds. Second, the federally funded special education programs provided supplementary services to students with special learning needs.

The efforts to provide compensatory opportunities through Title I have had mixed success and have gone through multiple iterations. Initially Title I functioned as a "pull out" program for reading instruction, but the early evaluations did not demonstrate that students who were pulled out made as much progress as students who stayed in the classroom. Rather than catching up with their peers, many fell further behind. Over time Title I was reformed to encourage schoolwide approaches in schools with high concentrations of poor children.

Special education, too, has gone through several iterations. Initially the emphasis was on pulling children out and placing them in a special classroom of students with similar learning problems, but these programs are in the midst of a massive shift toward "inclusion," which places special-needs students and teacher aids in regular classrooms. These basic federal programs and their iterations have had profound effects on the learning environments in urban schools. We will explain the major effects in this volume.

The second wave of federal reform involved a rethinking of the federal role and consolidating of educational programs. The "wall charts," the *Education Consolidation and Improvement Act* of 1980, and the publication of the *A Nation at Risk* ushered in a period of "reforming the reforms," that is refocusing federal efforts on educational outcomes rather than on equalizing opportunity.

The "excellence movement" brought a new wave of scientific methodology to educational governance. What the reforms did was to connect tests and measures to managerial processes of governance as a means of regulating and controlling students and curriculum. In this new model, states became the instruments for implementing the new scientific reform designs. The new standardized models did not fit urban centers well, creating an image of school failure, when in fact the reforms themselves may have failed urban schools, exacerbating inequality in the process.

The third wave of federal reform is just now emerging, with the creation of the *Comprehensive School Restructuring Demonstration Project*, the *Reading Excellence Act*, *Gear Up*, and the pending *America Counts Act*. These new federal programs reinvolve the federal government in funding new initiatives that aim at improving educational practice. They do so with a different orientation than the prior waves of reform: they encourage states to select school improvement methods that have a research (empirical) basis.

This newest wave of federal reform creates a potential opening for university researchers. Indeed, new models of restructuring, reading, and other approaches to educational improvement that had been pioneered by university researchers lead the new lists of approved reforms. However, this new silver cloud also may have a dark lining: the escalation of lists of approved reforms could further eliminate the opportunity for local innovation, especially in urban contexts.

Three of the chapters in this volume take a critical look at the role of government as a reformer. In chapter 3, Kenneth Wong critically examines the history of Title I. Since its inception, Title I funding and programs have been concentrated in urban schools. An implicit purpose of this Great Society program was to lift urban children out of poverty by raising their academic achievement. Wong's analysis provides insight into the reasons why over time Title I program changed the methods it promotes, which helps illuminate the issues that face researchers and policy in the future.

In chapter 4, Genevieve Manset and Sandra Washburn examine the impact of state mandated graduation tests on special education students in Indiana, with a focus on urban schools. Their analyses reveal a potential conflict between the goals of federal special education programs and the new efforts to require tests for graduation. The federal and state efforts to implement inclusive approaches to the education of children with special needs intersect with other educational policies in complex ways. The implementation of graduation tests complicates the impact of processes that mainstream special-needs students. The Indiana study reveals the contradictory impact of these policies on urban high schools in Indiana and suggests a need to rethink the convergence of these policies.

In chapter 5, Barry Franklin examines the issues of external efforts to reform schools from a different vantage: What happens when federal and state effort appear to fail? In some instances mayors have taken over urban schools systems. Recently the state took over the public schools in Detroit in an attempt to salvage a system that was perceived to be failing. Barry Franklin examines this move in light of past attempts to improve Detroit public schools. He analyzes interviews with reformers, testimony at state hearings, and newspaper editorials. He considers the impact of the takeover on schools and school children.

Independently Adopted, Research-Based Reforms

In the newest wave of school reform, a greater emphasis is being placed on the implementation of research-based reform models. Currently, federal funding has promoted research based reforms in reading and comprehensive school reform. However, private vouchers initiative, implemented as "experiments," are now being used as evidence to support federal legislation that promote vouchers, or opportunity grants, for urban schools.

Many of the new research-based reforms originated from reform efforts situated in universities or independent foundations. Frequently they involved working in partnership with schools. Activist university faculty sought support from private foundations and other sources of funding to experiment with new approaches to school reform. These efforts are especially important to urban schools, because many originated as efforts to target urban schools.

Many university-based reading reforms, such as *Four Block and Reading Recovery*, follow a model of reading advocated by universities. Many of these reforms are gaining support as part of states' response to the *Reading Excellence Act*. These reforms have not been as widely adopted in urban schools as they have in suburban schools, which raises questions about the consonance between these reforms and the needs of urban schools.

Also, many of the widely known comprehensive school reforms followed this university-based model. Restructuring movements that initially focused on urban schools included Comer's *School Development Project*, Levin's *Accelerated Schools Project*, and Slavin's *Success for All*. These and other initiatives involve the entire school in a process of reconceptualizing the school. Comer's project involves both community mental health and school improvement, Levin's involves the school community in a Deweyian reform process, and Slavin's focuses on integrating cooperative education with research-based methods of teaching. These and other reforms were initiated by universities and mostly funded by national and local corporations. Although these efforts have recently come into the educational mainstream with schoolwide Title I and CSRD, their impact on urban schools has not been systematically examined.

Another set of independently funded, internal reforms are now underway in the area of school choice. In New York City, Washington, D.C., Dayton, Indianapolis, San Antonio, and other cities, private groups have funded massive experiments with need-based vouchers. These independent reforms, along with information from the public reforms in Cleveland and Milwaukee, have ignited a wave of federal efforts to reform urban education. In particular, these reforms open the way to the choice of whether to attend private schools for a larger percentage of the urban population.

Three of the chapters in this volume focus on the impact of these new research based reforms. In chapter 6, Edward P. St. John and his colleagues at the Indiana Education Policy Center examine the impact of recent reading reforms on schools in Indiana. This chapter includes a critical review of the designs of a select group of reading reforms (e.g., *Reading Recovery*, *Four Block*, *First Steps*). Then it uses a data base on urban schools to assess the effects of these reforms on student educational progress. They find that comprehensive, cohesive reform approaches can potentially improve educational outcomes for urban school children.

In chapter 7, St. John and his colleagues examine the impact of implementing comprehensive school reform (CSR) models on educational improvement in high poverty schools in Wisconsin. This analysis reveals that some types of reform induce improvement in the learning outcomes.

In chapter 8 Carolyn Ridenour and Edward St. John examine the impact of a newly implemented voucher scheme on students in an urban school system. Most of the research on the new wave of privately funded urban school choice schemes has focused on student achievement and parent satisfaction. More recently researchers are focusing on the effects these reforms have on urban public and private schools. This chapter examined how one of these programs influenced the behavior and attitudes of teachers parents in one of these schools systems. This analysis not only reveals that choices are constrained for urban schools children, but that these new schemes add substantially to the complexities of teaching in urban schools in both public and private systems.

Community-Based Reforms

A fourth strand of independent urban school reform can be characterized as furthering the goal of community development (see Crowson 2000). Here the institutional boundaries between public schools and city government apparently blur (see Mirón 1998; Baum 1998), and both institutions work interactively to promote shared community values and local economic development. With a few exceptions (see Crowson 2000) this is an area of reform that is both new and underinvestigated. In section IV, we attempt to develop an understanding of community-based reforms as an alternative to the more structured approaches that receive wider public attention.

In chapter 9, Kathy Nakagawa examines parent involvement in the Chicago school reform. She examines the outcomes in Chicago of the Chicago School Reform Act (1988, 1995) that created the Local School Councils, considering whether parents and other community members "enabled" reform or were substantive partners.

In chapter 10, Louis Mirón examines collaborations between urban schools and local governments. This chapter provides comparative case studies of "joint ventures" (see Mirón 1998) between school districts and cities in Santa Ana, California and New Orleans, Louisiana. The new ventures in urban cooperation were intended to foster school improvement and local economic development.

Finally, in chapter 11, Leetta Allyn-Haynes and some of her colleagues examine how the African-American education tradition can inform efforts to reform urban schools. They first review the research literature of this tradition, focusing on some of the underlying moral questions. Then they explore two case studies of schools engaged in the Accelerated Schools Project from this perspective. Based on this review they explore how the African-American tradition might inform future efforts to reform urban schools.

Critical-Empirical Review Approach

Given that all of these reform efforts have proponents who construct rationales for the reform, and who engage in research to document their effects, it is difficult to build a shared understanding of urban school reform. In this book the authors undertake a critical-empirical review of a selected group of reforms that have affected urban schools. The critical-empirical review method was developed in a study of higher education desegregation (St. John and Hossler 1998). The authors in this volume will extend this approach to build a new interpretation and understanding of urban school reform. The critical-empirical review approach generally involves:

1. reviewing the historical context for a reform (how it came about);
2. examining the ideologies that guide the reformers and their critics, as a way of discerning how politics informs the reforms;
3. identifying the theoretical claims about processes and outcomes (both intended and unintended consequences) that inform both the design of the reforms and the critiques;
4. assessing the research relative to the ideological and theoretical claims; and
5. building new understandings of the meaning of the reforms based on the review.

In this critical-empirical review of urban reforms we asked the chapter authors to consider four questions related to the reform efforts.

1. *How is the reform situated historically?* Each of the authors in the analytic chapters of the volume will examine a specific reform. They will start their inquiry by situating the reform historically, then apply this historical context to a specific reform initiative.
2. *What ideologies drive the reform?* Most reforms have both proponents and critics. The authors in this volume will review the ideological positions of proponents and critics to build an understanding of the use of information in building arguments, the claims about program

effects embedded in their rationales, and the other unintended consequences overlooked by advocates and pointed to by critics.

3. *What theories underlie the success claims embedded in the reform?* Theories underlie the ideological claims of reform proponents and their critics. These implicit theories rest on assumptions of truth about social systems, student learning and development, and leadership. For example, the new market theory argues that schools are more innovative and students learn more when market competition is unfettered. Critics point to gaps in this logic or to unintended consequences of removing students from public schools. However, both positions are based on a construct of social and economic theory. The authors of this volume will discern divergent theoretical claims embedded in the argument of the advocates and proponents of specific reforms.
4. *How does the research evidence support the claims? (And what are the unintended consequences?)* With the critical perspective generated from the review of claims, it is possible to reconstruct the alignment between the evidence in research studies and the rationales used to argue for and against specific reform measures. The review of research studies can then be constructed to provide an empirical "test" of the truth claims (of a political, theoretical, and practical nature) that are embedded in rationales and critiques. In other words, the purpose of the review of quantitative and qualitative studies is to discern whether the truth claims of various reform advocates hold up to empirical scrutiny.

Each of the authors of the chapter described above considered these questions in their students. Their review methods varied widely, however, so the degree of emphasis each question received varied across the chapters. However, in totality, these chapters provide a set of research studies as a means of adding the empirical aspects of their critical-empirical perspectives. The purpose of a critical-empirical review is not to develop a new synthesis or universal claim, but rather to reveal the complexities and nuances of the problem in a way that can inform a theory of action and a new generation of reform activists. From these studies, as editors we have tried to develop a more informed understanding of the role of reform initiatives in urban schools. From looking across these chapters, we attempt to provide insights that might inform educators and students of education, as well as policy makers and researchers.

In chapter 12, we use the critical-empirical perspective to reach an understanding of the ways research can inform policy and practice about urban schools. We provide a summary chapter that attempts to build new critical understandings by examining the findings reached by the authors of this volume. We examine the claims made by various types of reformers and consider the findings from these studies in relation to those claims. We conclude this chapter by considering the role policy research can play in improving practice and reforming the policy process.

Finally, in chapter 13, we consider the implications for educational leadership. This chapter synthesizes the intermediate reflections gleaned from the previous chapters and the implications of a critical-empirical approach for educational leadership and school administration. It will focus on new partnerships between federal and local governments and independent, nonprofit organizations that have risen to reconnect schools with their communities.

References

Baum, H. S. 1997. *The organization of hope: Communities planning themselves*. Albany: State University of New York Press.

Castells, M. 1996. *The Rise of the Network Society*, Vol. 1 from *The information age: Economy, society, and culture*. Oxford: Blackwell.

Lewis, D. A. 1995. *Race and educational reform in the American metropolis : A study of school decentralization*, ed. Dan A. Lewis and Kathryn Nakagawa. Albany: State University of New York Press.

Mirón, L. F. 1996. *The social construction of urban schooling*. Cresskill, N.J.: Hampton Press.

Poster, M. 1989. *Critical theory and poststructuralism: In search of a context*. Ithaca, N.Y.: Cornell University Press.

Poster, M. 1990. *The mode of information: Poststructuralism and social context*. Chicago: University of Chicago Press.

St. John, E. P., A. I. Griffith, and L. Allen-Haynes. 1997. *Families in schools: A chorus of voices in restructuring*. Portsmouth, N.H.: Heinnemann.

St. John, E. P., and D. Hossler. 1998. Higher education desegregation in the post-*Fordice* legal environment: A critical-empirical perspective. In *Race, the courts, and equal education: The limits of the law*, ed. R. Fossey. Reading on Equal Education, vol. 15. New York: AMS Press.

Valle, V., and R. D. Torres. 2000. *Latino Metropolis*. Minneapolis: University of Minnesota Press, pp. 7–8.

Wilson, W. 1987. *The truly disadvantaged: The inner city, the underclass, and public policy*. Chicago: University of Chicago Press.

Part I

The Courts and Urban Schools

Chapter 1

School Desegregation Is Over in the Inner Cities: What Do We Do Now?

Richard Fossey

"The mark of the age," novelist Walker Percy wrote, "is that terrible things happen and no evil is involved." Surely Percy's observation rings true when we ponder racial isolation in our nation's inner-city schools. In *Brown v. Board of Education* (1954), the Supreme Court ordered an end to racially segregated public education. Tragically, in spite of hundreds of federal court orders and the efforts of the U.S. Justice Department, the NAACP, and legions of fair-minded educators, hundreds of thousands of African Americans still attend school in racial isolation. Demographic trends suggest that racial isolation in the schools will grow worse, not better, in the years to come.

Overwhelming evidence is all around us. In many of the nation's urban districts—Cleveland, Detroit, New Orleans, and Washington, DC, to name a few—African Americans comprise 70, 80, and even 95% of the total student enrollment (National Center for Educational Statistics 2000). In Los Angeles, the nation's second largest district, non-Hispanic whites make up only 15% of the school population. In Miami, the nation's fourth largest district, the figure is just 13%. According to a study by the Harvard University's Civil Rights Project, American schools are rapidly resegregating (Orfield and Yun 1999). As Gary Orfield and Susan Eaton (1996) wrote in *Dismantling Desegregation*, the nation's schools appear to be returning to the *Plessy v. Ferguson* era of "separate but equal," when segregated schools were taken for granted in many states and upheld by the courts.

Desegregation litigation continues in many urban school districts, but lawsuits and desegregation strategies have not stepped the outflow of white students. In Baton Rouge, Louisiana, for example, a school desegregation lawsuit has been ongoing for 46 years, but demographic projections predict the district will be nearly all black within the next few year (Caldas and Bankston 2000). This scenario appears to be the future for many urban districts all over the United States.

In fact, it is time for civil rights advocates and desegregation experts to confront reality. School desegregation is over in the inner cities. No desegregation strategy now in place or likely to be put in place will change these facts: most minority school children in the inner cities attend racially isolated schools and will do so for the foreseeable future.

How Did This Happen?

How could this have happened? How did the bright and tangible promise of *Brown v. Board of Education* dissolve into an "arid abstraction" in the core cities (Carter 1995, p. 626), devoid of power or meaning for African American school children?

Mountains of books, articles, and papers have tried to answer this question, but basically they all point to three possible explanations.

The Supreme Court's Milliken Decision

First, some scholars blame the Supreme Court itself for making a promise in *Brown* and then snatching it away in later decisions. Specifically, they point to the Court's decision in *Milliken v. Bradley* (1974), in which the Court struck down a trial court's desegregation plan for metropolitan Detroit (Orfield and Yun 1999). This plan would have required about 50 predominately white suburban communities to participate in desegregating the Detroit district's overwhelmingly black schools. In the trial court's view, a metropolitan plan that would force suburban white children into contact with Detroit's black children was the only feasible way to attack racial isolation in the Detroit system.

In perhaps its most important desegregation decision since *Brown*, the Supreme Court rejected the trial court's cross-district desegregation plan, ruling that such strategies are only permissible when there is evidence that school district boundaries were drawn for the purpose of racial segregation. In addition, the Court expressed skepticism about the creation of a "super school district" that would diminish the powers of more than 50 local school boards and perhaps create a logistical nightmare.

Without a doubt, *Milliken* stopped most cross-district desegregation proposals in their tracks. Thus the Court virtually guaranteed the demographic picture that now exists in urban areas: a racially isolated inner-city school district surrounded by a ring of largely white suburban school systems.

This pattern is particularly prominent in the Northern industrial cities where school systems were organized without regard to racial makeup, foreclosing any argument that district boundaries were drawn to promote segregation. For example, many of the suburban towns around Boston were organized in the seventeenth and eighteenth centuries, when Massachusetts was still a British colony. Today, the schools of modern Wellesley, Newton, and Concord are overwhelmingly white, while the majority of students in nearby Boston are black, Hispanic, or Asian. No one can rationally argue, however, that these municipal subdivisions were intentionally organized to promote racially segregated schools.

In addition, *Milliken* affected Northern cities more than Southern cities because many urban school systems in the North are geographically small compared to the countywide systems that are common in the South. Looking at a map of the Boston metropolitan area, it is apparent that white parents can conveniently work in Boston without putting their children in Boston's schools. It is only a short drive from Boston's city center to the affluent and overwhelmingly white communities of Brookline, Newton, or Waltham.

Critics of the Supreme Court may be right to say that *Milliken* contributed to the transformation of urban school systems into racial ghettos. Still, it is by no means certain that the demographics of the core cities' schools would be any different had the Supreme Court approved the Detroit cross-district desegregation plan that was at issue in *Milliken*.

Specifically, the logistics of managing metropolitan-wide desegregation plans would be overwhelming, as the U. S. Supreme Court pointed out in *Milliken*. The Detroit plan that the Supreme Court considered in *Milliken* would have involved three-quarters of a million students; and, if implemented, would have put enormous strains on transportation, municipal taxing systems, and traditional notions of local control. It seems highly unlikely that federal courts would mandate many desegregation remedies of that magnitude even if the Supreme Court were to allow them to do so.

Segregated Housing Patterns

A second explanation for *Brown's* failure in the core cities has to do with the nation's housing patterns, whereby African Americans are still largely contained within all black residential districts. Until

African Americans and white families live together in integrated neighborhoods, some commentators argue, no meaningful desegregation will occur in urban schools.

This observation is surely correct. In fact, school desegregation has been most successful in rural districts and the smaller cities, where blacks and whites generally live in closer contact than in the large metropolitan areas. For example, Louisiana's West Feliciana Parish, where I lived for a time, is a rural community where blacks and white live in close proximity to one another, and which was successfully desegregated many years ago. The school system has a school population of about 1200 students, almost evenly split between white and black. Since the district has only one high school, all high school students are assigned to it without regard to race, a simple desegregation strategy that probably incorporates what the Supreme Court intended in *Brown*. Such a strategy would not be adequate, however, in an urban district of 100,000 students where white families and black families typically live in different residential sections of the city.

Unfortunately, those who explain racial isolation in urban schools by pointing to segregated housing patterns have no realistic solutions for changing this situation. No federal law or court-articulated constitutional right compels adult citizens to be assigned to residences by race. As a political matter, it seems unlikely that such a law will ever be enacted. Indeed, an effective integrated housing policy is probably more unlikely than a decision by the Supreme Court to overrule the *Milliken* decision. Thus to speak of *Milliken* or housing as core reasons for *Brown's* failure is to offer very little that is helpful in the search for a solution to racial isolation in urban schools.

Underestimating the Impact of "White Flight"

There is, however, a more useful explanation for the racial isolation of inner-city school children, and it is this. During the 1960s and early 1970s, most of the major players in the school desegregation process—judges, attorneys, political leaders and policy makers—failed to recognize the overwhelming impact of "white flight" on school desegregation plans. In fact, many of the people most involved in school desegregation refused to admit that middle-class families were fleeing urban school districts in such massive numbers that they were fatally undermining judicial efforts to enforce the *Brown* decision. Furthermore, because they refused to admit this fact, they failed to craft solutions that might have counteracted the mass flight of middle class families out of the cities.

One of the first policy scholars to address white flight forthrightly was James S. Coleman, the eminent social scientist and author of the Coleman Report. In a *Phi Delta Kappan* article that appeared in 1975, and which was subsequently reprinted (1979), Coleman pointed out what now seems obvious: racial isolation of urban school children was increasing even as segregation within school districts was on the wane.

> This increase in between-district segregation, as I have said, results principally from the movement of whites to districts with fewer blacks. Its increase is not checked by any policies of desegregation of central-city districts; yet it is clear that segregation of the future in metropolitan areas of the U.S. will be of this sort: central-city schools nearly all black, suburban schools largely white. (Coleman, 1979, p. 124)

Furthermore, Coleman suggested, the desegregation process might actually be counterproductive. "[D]esegregation in some large cities is certainly not solving the problem of segregation," Coleman wrote. "Ironically, 'desegregation' may be increasing segregation. That is, eliminating central-city segregation does not help if it increases greatly the segregation between districts through accelerated white loss" (1979, p. 126).

Coleman's article was widely criticized for its research methods, its findings, and its conclusions. Perhaps his harshest detractors were Thomas Pettigrew and Robert Green, who blasted Coleman in the pages of the *Harvard Educational Review* in 1976. (The piece was reprinted in a 1979 collection of essays.) Pettigrew and Green described Coleman's desegregation piece as methodologically flawed and "an unprecedented campaign by a sociologist to influence public policy" (p. 133). Most damningly, they charged that Coleman's conclusions about desegregation were derived more from his personal beliefs than his research. Although smoothly written and accompanied by tables and graphs, Pettigrew and Green's essay had a harsh and jarring tone. Their underlying theme was that Coleman's conclusions were not only incorrect, they were irresponsible.

Other prominent scholars joined in criticizing Coleman's white flight thesis. Gary Orfield delivered a paper at a Brookings Institute symposium in which he stated, "It is impossible now to demonstrate that school integration, in itself, causes substantial white flight (quoted in Pettigrew and Green 1979, p. 153). Christine Rossell (1979) also challenged Coleman's desegregation research, writing that "school desegregation causes little or no significant white flight, even when it is court ordered and implemented in large cities" (p. 225). (Rossell later amended her views to acknowledge that desegregation plans did lead to significant white flight under some conditions.) Stanley Robin and James Rosco, two scholars from Western Michigan University, weighed in as well, arguing that Coleman's research was "seriously flawed" (1976, p. 56). Roy Wilkins and Kenneth Clark also attacked Coleman's work (Ravitch, 1979, p. 239), and Robert Crain (1976) of the Rand Corporation wrote that white flight from desegregation was not as serious as Coleman had argued.

Finally, Charles Willie, a Harvard professor who has written and consulted on school desegregation issues over a period of many years, rejected the argument that there might soon be too few white children to effectively desegregate urban public schools. "It is my contention," Willie wrote, "that there are enough whites in central cities now, and there will be in the future, to achieve meaningful desegregation of their public school systems" (1981, p. 126). By 1981, when this statement was published, any Boston parent could have told Willie that this statement was wildly incorrect, at least in the metropolitan area where Willie taught and resided.

A quarter of a century after Coleman's article was published, it is difficult to comprehend why Coleman's observations about white flight from inner city schools were so controversial. In retrospect it seems clear that Coleman was basically correct in attributing some white flight to coercive desegregation plans. The Boston experience alone should have told Coleman's critics that he had identified an important problem. In 1971, before Boston was subjected to a federal court's desegregation order, there were 57,000 white students in the district. By 1977, the number had dropped to 29,000. David Armor (1980) estimated about three-fifths of this loss (16,000 students) was attributable to desegregation activities (p. 205).

Indeed, data gathered by Christine Rossell, one of Coleman's earliest critics, would have confirmed Coleman's central thesis had it been interpreted in a reasonable way. Less than a year after Coleman's *Phi Delta Kappan* piece appeared, Rossell presented findings that flatly contradicted Coleman, and which concluded that mandatory desegregation plans had minimal impact on white flight. However, as Diane Ravitch, explained in a 1978 issue of *The Public Interest* (reprinted in1979), Rossell had "selected a statistical method that [would] show small declines even in the face of large absolute movements."

For example, Rossell reported that San Francisco, which was put under a desegregation order in 1971, experienced relatively minor white enrollment losses in the years immediately before and immediately after the order was imposed. In the four years prior to the order, white losses as a percentage of total school population were −2.9%, −1.2%, 0%, −4.1%, and .2%. In the two years after the plan was enacted, white losses were −3.0 and −2.1. Rossell used these figures to support her conclusion that San Francisco had experienced "no significant white flight" as a result of desegregation (quoted by Ravitch 1979, p. 241).

However, if one examines San Francisco's white enrollment losses in absolute terms during the years immediately before and after its desegregation plan went into effect, it becomes apparent that the city experienced very significant white flight. In 1968, San Francisco had 38,824 white students. Four years later, only 26,067 remained, a loss of 12,757 students, or about one third of the 1968 white enrollment. As Ravitch pointed out, any statistical method that would declare such a loss to be insignificant "is, at the very least, not very useful" (p. 248).

Ravitch then went on to report the white and minority enrollments for the 29 largest school districts in the country for the years 1968 and 1976. All 29 districts had experienced significant declines in white enrollment during those years, ranging from 16.2% in Jacksonville to 78.3% in Atlanta. By 1976, only 8 of the districts were majority white (pp. 250–251). Ravitch admitted that it is impossible to determine with certainty how much of this white flight was a reaction to desegregation. Nevertheless, she argued, it was "unsupportable to claim that there [was] no effect whatsoever" (p. 253).

In short, Rossell, along with several other respected scholars, used sophisticated statistical techniques to discredit Coleman's white flight thesis, even though any American who possessed the urban school enrollment figures and had eighth grade arithmetic skills could easily discern that Coleman was correct. Why, then, was Coleman so bitterly attacked?

As Ravitch pointed out, the Coleman "white flight' controversy symbolized the struggle over the future direction of school desegregation policy. "Coleman [was] urging a cautious and deliberate approach that takes into account the possibility of 'white flight' and resegregation" (p. 253). Coleman's critics were committed to racial balancing in the schools, without much regard for what the racial makeup of a school district might ultimately be.

Looking back, it is hard to escape the conclusion that Coleman's critics lost an important opportunity to reevaluate school desegregation strategy when they rejected his concerns about white flight out of hand. Coleman rightly predicted that the desegregation strategies then being used would ultimately lead to a new form of segregation—

a form in which nearly all black inner city districts would be surrounded by suburban schools that are mostly white.

Sadly, 47 years after the Supreme Court's *Brown* decision, thousands of minority school children still attend schools in racial isolation as if the Supreme Court had never spoken. As we begin the twenty-first century, *Brown's* promise remains unfulfilled. The question before us then is this: What do we do now?

Facing the Truth About Urban Schools

Before answering that question, it is useful to review the status of urban public education in the opening years of the twenty-first century. Any honest review will show that urban school systems are not healthy organisms with a few minor aches and pains. On the contrary, they are deeply and seriously dysfunctional. We must face that reality before we can decide what to do about the endemic racial isolation of public schools in the inner cities.

Governance and Leadership Problems

First of all, many inner-city school districts have serious governance and leadership problems. In too many cities, school board members are driven, not by the needs of children, but by racial and ethnic politics (Applebome 1996), patronage, and naked political ambition (Harris 1996, McAdams 2000).

David Rogers's study of the New York City school system, published in 1968, described the New York City Board of Education in terms that might apply to many urban school boards even today. In Rogers's words, the New York City board had shaped a "politics of futility" that allowed it to function in inefficient, unprofessional, and undemocratic ways.

> It has an almost unlimited capacity [Rogers wrote] for absorbing protest and externalizing the blame, for confusing and dividing the opposition, "seeming" to appear responsive to legitimate protest by issuing sophisticated and progressive policy statements that are poorly implemented, if at all, and then pointing to all its paper "accomplishments" over the years as evidence both of good faith and effective performance. (p. 13)

In fact, urban school governance has been so bad in recent years that some respect commentators have recommended an end to democratic control of urban schools (Chubb and Moe 1990: McAdams 2000). In city after city, alternative governance structures have been tried to bring more professionalism to urban school boards. In Boston, for example, the city replaced a system of elected school board members with members appointed by the mayor. Some cities have tried to decentralize power in order to reduce school boards' mischief-making ability. Several states have passed so-called "academic bankruptcy" provisions, permitting state agencies to take over districts that are mismanaged or that have records of substandard student performance. In order to discourage patronage, several states limit school boards' authority over the hiring process.

Thus far, however, legislative efforts to improve urban school governance have had little impact on day-to-day school operations. As one commentator (McDermott 2000, p. 87) pointed out:

> In theory, it makes sense to replace the boards of education that currently oversee failing school systems. In practice, the boards themselves often do not control administrators so much as they are controlled by them, and it is difficult to see how replacing one source of top-down oversight with another will improve matters much.

In addition to dysfunctional school boards, many inner-city school systems are shackled with ineffective executive leadership. Urban school superintendents, as Orfield and Eaton (1996) pointed out, seldom keep their positions for more than two or three years. Often they arrive at a school system touting a "brand-new" school reform plan. Too often, these executive educators resign their posts before they can be held accountable for results, frequently forced from office by a capricious school board (Parker 1996).

Public disappointment with traditional urban school administrators has caused many urban systems to look outside the ranks of professional educators for effective leadership (McAdams 2000, p. 255). Los Angeles, for example, the second largest school district in the nation, recently appointed Colorado's former Governor Roemer to be its new superintendent. In the year 2000, the chief executive of the San Diego schools was Alan Bersin, an attorney; and another attorney, Harold Levy, was recently appointed to head the New York school system (Lewin 2000). A least two large urban systems—Seattle and New Orleans—recently chose former military men to be their school superintendent.

Both trends—briefer tenure for urban school executives and the search for leadership outside the education profession—illustrate the problems urban systems are having in finding competent and effective executive leadership. This problem, along with a trend toward volatile, racially divisive, and politically motivated urban school boards, are major contributors to the phenomenon of increasingly dysfunctional urban school governance.

Incompetent, Poorly Trained, and "Burned Out" Teachers

Second, a great many of the educators who staff our urban schools are incompetent, uninspired, or indifferent. Linda Darling-Hammond, who wrote about her early teaching experience in Camden, New Jersey, described an urban teaching environment that is not atypical. As a new teacher, Darling-Hammond "found a crumbling warehouse high school managed by dehumanizing and sometimes cruel procedures, staffed by underprepared and often downright unqualified teachers, an empty book room, and a curriculum so rigid and narrow that teachers could barely stay awake to teach it" (1996, p. 7).

As Darling-Hammond has noted, perhaps a quarter of the teachers hired each year are underprepared for their assignments, "and they are assigned disproportionately to schools and classrooms serving the most educationally vulnerable children" (p. 6). Often our best teachers avoid the inner-city schools or transfer out of them as fast as they can.

Those who remain behind often experience workplace "burnout," a condition in which the teacher experiences feelings of alienation, helplessness, meaninglessness, depersonalization, and emotional exhaustion (Dworkin 1987; Maslach and Jackson 1981). Urban teachers are more likely to experience burnout than suburban teachers. LeCompte and Dworkin (1991), assessing various studies, estimated that between one-third and two thirds of inner-city schoolteachers may be burned out (p. 98).

The reasons for this are plain enough. Inner-city schools have large numbers of socially and economically disadvantaged students. Poverty, racial tension, violence, drugs, and fragmented family life are every-day realities for many of these children; and these conditions make it more difficult for them to learn (LeCompte and Dworkin 1991, p. 108). Teaching such children can be extraordinarily stressful, and teachers are often dissatisfied with the learning outcomes they achieve. Thus it is not surprising that inner-city teachers have especially high burnout rates.

In addition, teachers who are racially isolated in their school setting tend to experience high levels of burnout. Typically, such teachers are found in inner-city schools. In particular, many inner-city school systems operate according to desegregation plans under the supervision of federal courts. Often these plans require teachers to be assigned to schools by race, in approximately the same proportions as the racial makeup of the district as a whole. Generally, such orders require some white teachers to teach in schools with predominately black student populations. In these situations, teachers may experience mistrust, feelings of isolation, and sense of being unwanted (LeCompte and Dworkin, 1991, pp. 104–105).

Too often, urban administrators practice sloppy recruiting procedures (Murnane et al. 1991) and simply refuse to document and address poor teaching practice. Susan Moore Johnson's classic case study, "The case of Edna Wiley," (1978) is an almost unbelievable description of one urban school system's tolerance of a tenured teacher's bizarre and dysfunctional behavior over a period of many years.

Hand-in-hand with the problem of underprepared, unskilled, and burned out teachers is the "backwardness of curriculum policy" in schools for the poor (Darling-Hammond 1996, p. 7)—in other words, the schools that many African American children attend. "Because of the capacities of their teachers," Darling-Hammond wrote, "most classrooms serving poor and minority children continue to provide students with significantly less engaging and effective learning experiences."

Several scholars have written convincingly about the need for "culturally relevant teaching methods" when teaching African American children (Ladson-Billings 1994; Delpit 1995); and we now have good scholarship on this topic. But a new curriculum, even a culturally relevant curriculum, will not increase learning in an environment where skilled teachers and motivated students are in short supply. In such environments, Richard Elmore wrote, "[s]trict curriculum mandates would seem to hold little promise of increasing student learning, except to reinforce adult influence against a hostile or indifferent clientele, or possibly to tell teachers whose knowledge and skill were low what to teach" (1987, p. 70). Or, as Thomas Sergiovanni (1992, p. 4) put it, too many policymakers, school administrators, and academics have emphasized process over substance—satisfied if they implement the "right method," regardless of whether those methods produce better outcomes for children.

General Malaise and Indifference to Children

Finally, and most disturbingly, many urban school systems seem infected by a general malaise, difficult to describe in a few words, but characterized by the dilapidated condition of urban school buildings, an inattention to the welfare of students, and an overall climate of indifference. I was struck most forcefully by this phenomenon in 1996, when I inspected school facilities in New Orleans at the request of the American Civil Liberties Union, which had brought a lawsuit against the state of Louisiana in an effort to get more financial resources for several poorly funded Louisiana school districts. My job was to visit randomly selected New Orleans schools, document the state of the schools' physical facilities, and determine whether teachers had proper credentials and adequate textbooks and supplies.

What shocked me the most, as I went from one New Orleans public school to another, was the condition of the restrooms, particularly in the high schools and middle schools. Almost without exception, restroom facilities were unfit for human use. In general, they were unventilated, dirty, smelly, poorly lighted and vile. Students had no privacy while in the restrooms, because toilet doors and stalls had been removed. In most cases, hand-washing sinks and ventilation fans were nonfunctional; and soap, towels, mirrors, and toilet paper were almost always missing. At several schools, officials told me the students simply did not use the school restroom facilities; most preferred to endure physical discomfort rather than enter these truly hellish restrooms.

Not surprisingly, other school conditions were bad as well. Some teachers did not have enough textbooks for their students, and others were using out-of-date books. In school after school, science laboratories had become virtually inoperative due to lack of running water, functioning ventilation hoods, equipment, chemicals, and supplies. Many schools had leaky roofs and broken windows; few were air conditioned or adequately wired for the proper use of computers and instructional technology.

Some of what I saw in New Orleans schools can be explained, at least in part, by a lack of money; but some cannot. Obviously, the city of New Orleans has sufficient resources to provide school children with toilet paper, restroom stalls, soap, and clean, well-ventilated bathrooms. In my mind, the fact that New Orleans did not provide these things has only one explanation—indifference and a lack of respect for the human dignity of a school child.

Of course, one person's observations in a single urban school district cannot stand as an indictment of American urban education in general. But my observations are consistent with what others have observed and described in urban schools across the country. Jonathan Kozol's (1991) descriptions of schools in East Saint Louis,

Chicago, and New York, for example, are wholly consistent with what I saw in New Orleans.

Not only are conditions bad in many inner-city schools, but many urban school leaders seem unable to admit this simple fact. Several of the New Orleans schools I visited had posted cheerfully optimistic posters, prepared by the school district's central office, boasting about lowered dropout rates and improved standardized test scores. These representations were totally inconsistent with the squalid conditions I encountered and with what state education records revealed about the district's on-time graduation rates.

What Do We Do Now?

Ideas about how to improve urban schools are plentiful. Hundreds of books, research articles and scholarly papers have addressed the topic. There are research centers and scholarly journals devoted entirely to urban education. It is fair to say that we have gathered sufficient research on urban school reform; indeed, we may have accumulated more than we need.

It is not the purpose of this essay to add to this list of nostrums for fixing inner-city schools. Instead, I suggest that we examine urban schools from a new perspective—a perspective of cold, stark realism, and that we then attack urban school problems from this new perspective.

First of all, it is time to admit that school desegregation in many urban districts is over. James Coleman's concerns about white flight—made in the early 1970s—were perceptive and accurate. The nation ignored Coleman's warnings and listened to his detractors—Gary Orfield, Christine Rossell, Charles Willie and others; and we need only stroll the corridors of an inner-city high school to see where that decision brought us. In urban districts where white students are substantially in the minority, policymakers, attorneys and judges should quit tinkering with desegregation strategies and let school officials educate students without regard to maintaining racial balance.

I am not suggesting that we retreat from the moral principles of the *Brown* decision. *Brown*'s simple holding—that American school children deserve equal educational opportunities regardless of race—is the nation's supreme moral statement of the twentieth century. Moreover, many of the strategies that were developed to implement *Brown*—flawed though some of them turned out to be—still have application in the nation's new large school districts, where a high percentage of white children go to school with minority school children. Most of these districts are in the South and the West.

Nevertheless, in cities like Atlanta, Dallas, Detroit, Memphis, New Orleans, Washington, DC and a string of other cities, we must admit that most black children attend school in racial isolation and that this reality is not going to change in our lifetimes. In those communities, the job of the schools is to prepare children who live and study in racial isolation for the opportunities that exist in the larger world.

Second, we must face another stark reality about inner-city schools. Outside the selective, magnet-style schools, education in the minority-dominated urban districts is on the verge of collapse. Educational researchers tend to portray urban schools as basically sound educational environments, which only need a bit of policy advice and guidance to function at a higher level of adequacy. This is not correct. Jonathan Kozol's *Savage Inequalities* paints a true portrait of the typical inner-city school; and it is a picture of squalor, chaos, and indifference to children's needs. Any researcher or policymaker who offers a rosier picture is not providing useful or accurate information.

Finally, we must face a third stark reality about urban education: school desegregation failed in the inner cities for essentially one reason: many of the people who implemented it—judges, attorneys, court-appointed experts, school board members, union officials, and professional educators—never intended to disturb the status quo of public education. Thus, the long years since *Brown v. Board of Education* are a history of mechanical and ineffective remedies—forced busing, magnet schools, race-based staffing ratios, special intervention programs for "at risk students," etc.—while African American children continued to huddle in racially isolated schools where they could not even decently go to the bathroom. During all this time, the teachers' unions, urban school boards, state education departments, and affluent suburban school districts continued doing business as usual.

Paulo Freiere's work, *Pedagogy of the Oppressed* (1970), which is based on his experience with repressive Latin American regimes, is useful for understanding why fifty years of school desegregation has been so ineffective. According to Freire, the oppressors (in this case the education industry's various special interest groups) can never be relied upon to liberate the oppressed.

> The oppressors, who oppress, exploit, and rape by virtue of their power, cannot find in this power the strength to liber-

> ate either the oppressed or themselves. . . . Any attempt to "soften" the power of the oppressor in deference to the weakness of the oppressed almost always manifests itself in the form of false generosity; indeed, the attempt never goes beyond this. In order to have the continued opportunity to express their "generosity," the oppressors must perpetuate injustice as well. An unjust social order is the permanent fount of this "generosity," which is nourished by death, despair, and poverty. (p. 44)

Thus, school desegregation became "an instrument of dehumanization," which began with the "egoistic interests of the oppressors" and which made the oppressed the objects of paternalistic humanitarianism (p. 54). (In fact, false generosity probably explains why liberal minded social scientists reacted so negatively to James Coleman's accurate observation in the early 1970s that school desegregation was simply not working.)

In Freire's view, the liberation of the oppressed can never be achieved through the "false charity" of the oppressor. It can only be achieved when the oppressed recognize the reality of their oppression and begin working toward the transformation of the world, of themselves, and of their oppressors. For Freire, this transformational work by the oppressed is an act of love that restores not only their own humanity, but also the humanity of their oppressors as well (1970, p. 56).

Obviously, Freire's work is deeply moral. It is not surprising that his work has found expression in liberation theology, which has greatly influenced Catholic thought, particularly in Latin America. Is it possible that Freire's vision of liberation for the oppressed could be introduced into school desegregation policy? More specifically, is it possible, that education policy makers might allow inner-city families to take control of their children's educational destinies themselves, instead of being forced to rely on the "false generosity" of the courts and the special interest groups that have controlled the school desegregation process throughout its 50-year history?

It seems unlikely. Indeed, most mainstream educational scholars and policymakers recoil from any proposal that would radically alter the basic status quo in public education. This view largely explains the deep resistance of educational constituencies to voucher proposals, which are seen as an insidious plot to undermine the public schools.

This is unfortunate, because school desegregation has been a disaster in the inner cities. False generosity—court-imposed desegregation remedies, advice from so-called desegregation experts, and the policies implemented by various education agencies—have left the inner city school schools racially isolated and dysfunctional. To solve this calamity, the oppressed themselves must have the power to throw off oppression—and this includes the power to choose an alternative to public education.

In other words, the transformation of inner-city education depends, and depends quite heavily, on the adoption of some form of vouchers and family choice. In particular, inner-city families should have access to Catholic parochial schools—institutions that recognize the humanity of oppressed children as an act of faith.

So far, public opinion is hotly divided about voucher programs that include religious schools; and the courts have not offered much encouragement. Indeed, Justice Clarence Thomas, in *Mitchell v. Helms* (2000), bluntly suggested that the courts' hostility to public funding for religious education is based not on high-minded concerns about the separation of church and state, but anti-Catholic bigotry.

But the public and judicial climate may change. After all, Canada permits government support of church-sponsored schools, and no one can seriously argue that Canadian education has been hurt by that practice. Two things are certain: the status quo is not an option for public education in the inner cities, and current desegregation strategies have not worked for inner city children. We are now faced with two choices—we can continue to engage in false generosity—implementing a failed school desegregation policy while refusing inner-city families any alternatives to the public education's status quo. Or we can insist on decent education for racially isolated inner-city school children. If we choose the second option, it is time for American education policy to become more welcoming to vouchers, family choice, and religious schools.

References

Applebome, P. 1996, June 27. Bitter racial rift in Dallas board reflects ills in many other cities. *New York Times*, p. 1.

Armor, D. J. 1980. White flight and the future of school desegregation. In W. G. Stephan and J. R. Feagin (Eds), *School desegregation past, present, and future*. New York: Plenum Press.

Caldas, S. J., and Bankston, C. L., III. 2000. East Baton Rouge, school desegregation, and white flight. Unpublished manuscript.

Carter, R. L. 1995. The unending struggle for equal educational opportunity. *Teachers College Record, 96*, 619–626.

Chubb, J. E., and Moe, T. M. 1990. Politics, markets, and America's schools. Washington, DC: The Brookings Institution.

Coleman, J. S. 1979. Racial segregation in the schools: New research with new policy implications. In N. Mills (Ed.), *Busing, U.S.A.* (pp. 21–131). New York: Teachers College Press.

Crain, R. L. 1976. Why academic research fails to be useful. In F. H. Levinsohn & B. D. Wright (Eds.), *School desegregation, shadow and substance* (pp. 31–45). Chicago: University of Chicago Press.

Darling-Hammond, L. 1996. The right to learn and the advancement of teaching: Research, policy, and practice for democratic education. *Educational Researcher, 25*, 5–17.

Delpit, L. 1995. *Other people's children: Cultural conflicts in the classrooms.* New York: New Press.

Dworkin, A. G. 1987. *Teacher burnout in the schools: Structural causes and consequences for children.* Albany: State University of New York Press.

Elmore, R. F. 1987. Reform and the culture of authority in schools. *Educational Administration Quarterly, 23*, 60–78.

Freire, P. 1970. Pedagogy of the oppressed (30th anniversary ed.). New York, NY: Continuum International.

Johnson, S. M. 1978. The case of Edna Wiley. Harvard Graduate School of Education (typewritten case study).

Ladson-Billings, G. 1994. The dreamkeepers: Successful teachers for African American children. San Francisco: Jossey-Bass.

Kozol, Jonathan. *Savage inequalities: Children in America's schools.* New York: Crown Publishers.

LeCompte, M. D., and Dworkin, A. G. 1991. *Giving up on school: Student dropouts and teacher burnouts.* Thousand Oaks, CA: Corwin Press.

Lewin, T. 2000, June 8. Educators are bypassed as school system leaders. *New York Times*, p. A1.

McAdams, D. R. 2000. *Fighting to save our urban schools . . . and winning! Lessons from Houston.* New York, NY: Teachers College Press.

McDermott, K. A. 2000. Barriers to large-scale success of models for urban school reform. *Educational Evaluation and Policy Analysis, 22*, 83–89.

Murnane, R., Singer, J., Willett, J., Kemple, J., and Olsen, R. 1991. Who will teach? Policies that matter. Cambridge, MA: Harvard University Press.

National Center for Educational Statistics (2000). *Characteristics of the 100 largest public elementary and secondary school districts in the United States: 1998–1999.* Author: Washington, DC.

Noddings, N. 1984. *Caring: A feminine approach to ethics and moral education*. Berkeley, CA: University of California Press.

Orfield, G., and Eaton, S. E. 1996. *Dismantling Desegregation: The quiet reversal of Brown v. Board of Education*. New York: Free Press.

Orfield, G., and Yun, J. T. 1999. Resegregation in American schools. Cambridge, MA: Harvard University Civil Rights Project.

Parker, P. Superintendent vulnerability and mobility. *Peabody Journal of Education 71*, 64–77.

Pettigrew, T. F., and Green, R. L. 1979. School desegregation in large cities: A critique of the Coleman "white flight" thesis. In N. Mills (Ed.), *Busing U.S.A.* (pp. 132–190). New York: Teachers College Press.

Purpel, D. E. 1989. The moral and spiritual crisis in education. Bergin and Garvey.

Ravitch, D. 1979. The "white flight" controversy. In N. Mills (Ed.), *Busing U.S.A.* (pp. 238–256). New York: Teachers College Press.

Rogers, D. 1968. *110 Livingston Street: Politics and bureaucracy in the New York City School System*. New York: Vintage Books.

Rossell, C. H. 1979. School desegregation and white flight. In N. Mills (Ed.), *Busing U.S.A.* (pp. 214–238). New York: Teachers College Press.

Sergiovanni, T. J. 1992. *Moral leadership: Getting to the heart of school improvement*. San Francisco: Jossey-Bass.

Willie, C. V. 1981. The demographic basis of urban educational reform. In A. Yarmolinsky, L. Liebman, and C. S. Schelling (Eds.), *Race and schooling in the city* (pp. 126–135). Cambridge, MA: Harvard University Press.

Legal Cases

Brown v. Board of Education, 347 U.S. 483 (1954).

Plessy v. Ferguson, 163 U.S. 537 (1896).

Milliken v. Bradley, 418 U.S. 717 (1974).

Mitchell v. Helms, 530 U.S. 793 (2000).

Chapter 2

The Need for Issues-Driven School Funding Reform in Urban Schools

Neil Theobald

The previous chapter in this volume demonstrates the crucial roles that both federal and state governments have played since the 1950s in regulating the operation of urban schools. This chapter focuses on the impact of school finance reform on urban districts during this period. Therefore, it necessarily focuses on state—rather than federal—actions. Although the federal government in the last twenty years has often used "bully pulpit" pronouncements (Jung and Kirst 1986) to enforce its agenda for urban schools, its role in paying for these initiatives is quite limited. The federal share of total public school revenue peaked in the late 1970s at 9.8 percent and currently stands at less than 7 percent (National Center for Education Statistics [NCES] 2000, 174). An attempt by an urban school parent to force a more substantial involvement by the federal government in K–12 funding was blocked by the U.S. Supreme Court in *San Antonio v. Rodriguez* (1973), which held that education is not a fundamental right under the U.S. Constitution.

States, though, play a much more central role in public education. Each of the fifty state constitutions recognizes that public schools are the responsibility of state government. Thus, it has always been clear that state governments have had the legal power to regulate the operations of urban schools in their states. Yet, for much of our nation's history, states delegated all executive power and even many legislative powers (e.g., the power to tax property) to local school boards.

The last two decades of the twentieth century, though, marked a major change in this general pattern of limited state involvement in the operations of public schools. Although states have publicized decentralization policies, they have added significantly to the volume of regulations imposed on schools in what Mazzoni (1994, 53) describes as an "extraordinary eruption" of policy activity. In the years since 1980, "state after state, usually led by their governors, enacted significant legislative reforms to their public schools" (Bull 1998, 194). This shift in initiative, away from local school boards and towards state-level institutions, has been particularly stark in the school finance arena.

A host of factors contribute to this move by states to take on a greater role in the funding of public schools. One is the "new federalism" that pushed much of the educational responsibility that the federal government had collected in the 1960s back to the states. Also, the publication of *A Nation at Risk* in 1983 "connected the American public's worries about the nation's economic future to the performance of its schools" (Bull 2000a, 108). Driven by this widely perceived linkage between high quality schooling and a state's economic growth,

> Many states asserted their interest in domains that had been the province of individual schools and school districts or professional organizations. States chose to hold schools accountable to *state-articulated* standards through an array of monitoring and sanctioning tactics such as publicizing test scores, labeling and ranking schools, issuing bonuses to "high performing" schools, placing struggling schools on watch-lists, and threatening reconstitution or privatization. (Malen and Muncey 2000, 217)

The pivotal factor, though, has been school finance litigation. Although state constitutions create a state-level duty to support public education, allowing local funding of public schools has resulted in significant funding disparities among many states' public schools. Persons disadvantaged by these funding disparities have challenged state funding systems based on local wealth, resulting in significant litigation. Since 1975, state courts have struck down the school funding systems of seventeen states. As we enter a new century, twelve states have school funding litigation pending at some level.

Yet, despite these decades of court-ordered funding remedies, the most needy children continue to be concentrated in schools without a corresponding concentration of the resources necessary to meet those children's needs (Kantor and Brenzel 1992; Kozol 1991). This chapter traces the impact of school finance reform on urban districts in three states that implemented new funding systems during different phases of the evolving federal reform context of the late twentieth century. The state of Washington rewrote its school funding formula in the mid-1970s during a wave of federal reform that emphasized equalizing opportunity. Indiana followed suit fifteen years later, following the publication of a considerable body of research evidence describing the unique educational problems of poor and minority students (Fordham and Ogbu 1986; Weinberg 1986; Wilson 1987). At the end of the century, Ohio developed a school-funding plan that reflects the refocusing of federal attention on educational outcomes. How have these reforms impacted the lives of urban children? Why have such reforms often proved unsuccessful in breaking the nexus between student background characteristics and school resources?

This chapter first provides a brief review of the historical context in each state to help explain how the selected reforms came about. It then examines the ideologies that guide the reformers and their critics, as a way of discerning how politics informed these new funding policies. The next two sections identify the theoretical claims about processes and outcomes (both intended and unintended consequences) in the reforms and the critiques and assess the research relative to the ideological and theoretical claims. The concluding section outlines an alternative hypothesis based on this review that seeks to assist policymakers in tying their school funding systems more closely to the goals and aspirations they hold for their state's schools.

Historical Context

Washington

Washington historically maintained a relatively high level of state financial support for K–12 public schools. In the early 1960s, school districts nationally received about 40 percent of their revenue from state sources, whereas Washington school districts generated more than 60 percent of their revenue from state coffers (NCES 1965, 55). During the next decade, however, the mix of state and local revenues used to support Washington's public schools shifted dramatically. Local revenue sources increased in importance and dependence upon state money dropped so that, by the early 1970s, Washington's schools received barely one-half of their revenue from state coffers (NCES 1975, 61).

In 1977, Washington's school finance system was declared unconstitutional because of this increased reliance on local property taxes to provide basic education. The school funding package approved in 1977 by the Washington legislature sought to equalize opportunities across school districts by funding all districts based on statewide averages. The Washington formula contains no adjustments for local socioeconomic characteristics (e.g., variations in the percentage of poor students) or for the local costs of living. This relatively uniform, statewide system, which has now been in place for almost twenty-five years, continues to raise concerns about its impact on urban schools (Theobald 1994; Theobald 2000; Theobald and Hanna 1991).

Indiana

Indiana, on the other hand, had historically maintained a relatively low level of state financial support for K–12 public schools. In 1973, in a precursor to what was to occur in California two years later, Indiana froze local property tax levies. Although the 1973 legislation succeeded in lowering property taxes (Indiana Fiscal Policy Institute 1994), critics charged that the state made only marginal progress in narrowing revenue disparities among school districts (Johnson and Lehnan 1993).

In 1987, five Indiana school districts filed a lawsuit challenging the school funding system's constitutionality (*Lake Central et al. v. State of Indiana et al.* 1987). *Lake Central* argued that allowing property-rich school districts to generate more revenue than property-poor districts violated the equal protection clause of the state constitution and that the state was not meaning its constitutional duty to provide for a general and uniform system of schools. Five years later, the state reached an out-of-court settlement with the *Lake Central* plaintiffs that called for additional state funding for property-poor districts.

In addition to this goal of eliminating the effect of a school district's property wealth on its operating revenue, though, the school funding formula that passed the Indiana General Assembly in 1993 also explicitly sought to provide higher funding to school districts with more disadvantaged students. Theobald (2001) shows that in the 1990s, Indiana's new formula increased the share of school revenues being provided to Indiana school districts educating large percentages of minority students and maintained the per-pupil funding advantage that exists for districts educating large numbers of poor students.

Ohio

Ohio, like Indiana, historically had maintained a relatively low level of state financial support for K–12 public schools. Yet, the property tax freeze that significantly increased the state share of revenue in Indiana did not occur in Ohio. As a result, concerns about the level of property taxes have remained coupled to discussions of school funding throughout the state's twenty-five-year search for a formula that is fair both to taxpayers and to children. The Ohio Supreme Court ruled against a constitutional challenge raised by the Cincinnati school board in 1979, basing their decision on the principle of local control of schools: "We conclude that local control provides a rationale basis supporting the disparity in per pupil expenditures in Ohio's school districts" (*Cincinnati School District Board of Education v. Walter* 1979).

Discontent, though, continued to grow and in 1991 a coalition of school districts sued the state, claiming that the current school funding system failed to meet Ohio's constitutional requirement for a thorough and efficient system of common schools. In 1997, the Ohio Supreme Court found in favor of the plaintiff school districts (*DeRolph v. State* 1997).

In the current outcomes-oriented reform context, the Ohio General Assembly devised a new school funding process based upon average expenditures of school districts that are deemed effective in meeting state-specified performance indicators. However, in 2000, the Ohio Supreme Court ruled this response to be insufficient to meet the requirements of their earlier decision. The Ohio Supreme Court stated that proficiency tests "Need, most importantly, to be accompanied by a thoughtful, comprehensive, sustained strategy for strengthening the capacity of teachers, principals, and other education professionals to change their practice, and a commitment to provide extra resources and support to students and schools who start out furthest from the goal line" (*DeRolph v. State* 2000, 76–77). According to the plaintiffs in the case, "standards must necessarily include reference to the additional needs of pupils residing in conditions of poverty, both in the cities and in the rural areas of Ohio" (Equity and Adequacy Coalition 2000, 5). The Ohio General Assembly is required to submit a new school finance package for Supreme Court review by June 15, 2001.

Ideologies

For most of our country's history, the balance between state regulation and local control tilted heavily towards the latter. In retrospect, observers often cite financial considerations as one of the major forces in explaining this tilt. Until the twentieth century, local sources provided all or nearly all school revenue. As late as the 1929–30 school year, local taxes accounted for 83 percent of total public school revenue (NCES 2000, 174). In such an environment, it is easy to see how a strong tradition of local control of schools would naturally develop.

It is unclear, though, whether high levels of local funding forged the preference for local control or whether high levels of local funding were simply a manifestation of America's long-standing and deeply embedded fear of large government. Our noncentralized, federal system of government is based on the Founding Fathers unwillingness to trust central government with the supervision of the people's liberties. In a like fashion, a noncentralized, local system of school funding could find its basis in Americans' unwillingness to trust central government with the supervision of their children's education. Local people clearly believed they knew the community and its children the best. High levels of local funding for schools kept locals—and not the state—as the primary decision makers with regard to their children's education.

Contemporary observers, though, did not cast local control strictly as a matter of "those who pay the piper call the tune." Organizational theorists joined in the support of local control by contending that the practice allowed schools to adapt to the diverse conditions they faced in the communities in which they were located. According to this view "a large measure of local control is necessary if the public school system is to fulfill its function in a dynamic society" (Holmstedt 1940, 45). The primary value of this organizational structure was that it permitted variety and flexibility in school systems. "There must be freedom in the school system to experiment, invent, and adapt, and these are possible only when external restraints are absent" (46).

Throughout the United States, though, state governments in the last two decades have moved into new terrain, especially with regard to urban schools, by limiting local taxation, mandating high stakes testing of students, and by creating charter schools. These assertive actions reflect more than incremental adjustments of long-standing views. They mirror a competing conception of the appropriate balance between state regulation and local autonomy. Whether viewed historically, legally, or politically, this competing ideology resurfaces directly as part of governance debates and judicial interpretations in each of these three states.

In Washington, a report issued by a former state budget director (Miller 1975) blamed efforts by "wealthy school districts" to reduce class size, expand course offerings, and provide "disproportionate salary increases" for causing Washington's school funding problems. At this time, the national agenda for public schools centered around the Serrano principle—educational spending should not be a function of the wealth of the local community, but instead should be a function of the wealth of the state as a whole. Thus, the centerpiece of school finance reform in Washington became teacher salary controls. Proponents of limits on teacher salaries argued that the legislature should place restrictions on teacher salaries in order to ensure that "wealthy" districts did not "continue to pass high levies, improve programs, and continue to increase the diversity among districts. This was the opposite of what the Legislature wanted" (Reff 1982, 58–59).

Critics of this reform effort point out that the wealthy districts targeted by school finance reform in Washington were primarily urban school districts. In order to attract and retain quality teachers into these urban districts, they paid salaries that were above the state average. As a result of school finance reform, though, average salaries for teachers in urban districts in the 1980s fell below the state average. Critics cite evidence that, at least partially as a result of these lower salaries, teachers were significantly more likely to leave teaching positions in urban school districts during the 1980s than they were elsewhere in the state (Theobald 1990). Novice teachers in urban districts, which are predominantly in the Puget Sound region, continue to receive salaries that provide 11–14 percent less purchasing power than salaries paid in school districts in other, less costly regions of the state (see Table 2.1).

School finance reform in Indiana, on the other hand, was driven much less by national reform agendas. Instead, state legislative staff developed eight explicit goals for school finance reform: (1) increase school revenue per pupil; (2) provide higher funding to school districts with more disadvantaged students; (3) equalize school revenue per pupil across school districts; (4) increase the share of school revenue provided by the state; (5) eliminate the effect of a school district's property wealth on its operating revenue; (6) make a school district's general fund property tax rate depend on the revenue it receives per pupil; (7) limit increases in property tax rates; and (8) equalize property tax rates across school districts.

Critics of this reform point out that suburban schools, whose relatively high per pupil revenue levels at the beginning of the 1990s were based on their relative high property wealth (see Goal 5 above), received funding increases in the 1990s that were one-third less than other schools in the state. In addition, rural and town schools, whose general fund property tax rates were well below the state

TABLE 2.1
Purchasing Power of Total Novice[a] Teacher Pay[b] in Seven Washington Communities 1998–99 School Year

School District	*1998–99 Novice Teacher Total Salary*	*1998–99 Relative Novice Total Purchasing Power*	*Difference in Relative Purchasing Power*	*Percentage Below Highest*
Kennewick	$25,134	$25,414	$0	0.0%
Tacoma	$25,856	$24,879	−$534	−2.1%
Spokane	$25,127	$23,908	−$1,506	−5.9%
Wenatchee	$24,534	$23,344	−$2,070	−8.1%
Everett	$25,944	$22,698	−$2,716	−10.7%
Vancouver	$23,568	$22,088	−$3,326	−13.1%
Seattle	$24,597	$21,519	−$3,894	−15.3%

[a]One year of teaching experience and a baccalaureate degree.

[b]Estimated using sum of actual base salary and the district's average supplemental contract per FTE Certified Instructional Staff for additional time-related certificated assignments (duty suffix 2) and not time-related certificated assignments (duty suffix 1).

average (see Goal 8 above), saw sizable tax rate increases during the decade. Supporters of the reform initiative are usually quick to observe that urban schools, whose general fund property tax rates were well above the state average, have seen tax rate decrease during the decade.

School finance reform in Ohio has occurred under a very different ideological framework than either Washington or Indiana. Although the plaintiffs' lawsuits in Ohio (*DeRolph v. State* 1997; *DeRolph v. State* 2000) dealt with similar equal opportunity issues as had been decided earlier in Washington and Indiana, it is clear from interviews conducted with nearly sixty stakeholders in Ohio that schooling outcomes, and not financial inputs, are seen as "the best measure of the state's success in meeting its constitutional obligation" (Theobald and Bull 2000, 30).

This approach has led to an ideological clash between state policy makers and parents, who are criticized by state officials for not being "on board" with the state's program. The disconnection between the views of state-level leaders and parents seems to be based primarily on the opposite perspectives these two groups have of K–12 schools. As one state official put it, the state's focus is on "What am I getting for my money, and if you want more, what more am I going to get? And how are you going to measure that in a way that I can understand it, that's tangible, that I can see it" (Theobald and Bull 2000, 28). Parents, on the other hand, tended to focus much more on local views. They worried that "the outcomes that the test makers think are important will trump the values that the community, which supports the schools, thinks are important. If we aren't careful here, we could end up cutting programs that the local community [supports]" (Theobald and Bull 2000, 28). The type of "tangible" outcomes parents tended to emphasize were much more related to the quality of students' experiences. Their goals for the state's schools focused more broadly on how responsive the schools were to their children's social, emotional, and academic needs.

Theoretical Claims

Garms, Guthrie, and Pierce (1978), Boyd (1984), and Monk (1990) treat equity, efficiency, and liberty "as the basic and fundamental goals that societies pursue when resources are allocated for education" (Monk 1990, xvi). Although it is too simplistic to argue that school finance reform seeks to further only one of these aims, Mitchell and Encarnation (1984) find "a strong historical tendency for states to pursue only one goal at a time, neglecting or suppressing the others" (9). One way to distinguish between different states' school finance reforms, therefore, is to see them as implicit endorsements of one of these three competing values.

Liberty-Enhancing Structures

Traditionally, the states' focus in school finance has been to promote local autonomy. By leaving funding decisions to local school boards, states sought to provide freedom for school districts to adapt to the diverse conditions they face in the communities in which they are located. Critics, though, point out that although liberty-enhancing structures provide freedom to choose, they include the freedom to choose incorrectly. From the critics' perspective, the externalities generated by potentially poor local decisions (e.g., "disproportionate salary increases" in urban districts, insufficient focus on student performance) outweigh Americans' long-held preference for local control of schools. State regulations are seen the most cost-effective way to achieve higher levels of student performance and therefore the economic and social benefits that are thought to come in the wake of improved student performance.

Defenders of these liberty-enhancing structures counter that state regulations often attempt to engender equal treatment for people who may, in fact, be very different from each other. For example, funding based on state-wide averages may produce the semblance of equality, but this equality is purchased by severely restricting the capacity of school districts to respond flexibly to unique local conditions. As Comer (1988) pointed out, the ability of schools to respond flexibly to students' needs is particularly important in educating poor minority youth.

Equity-Enhancing Structures

Equity-enhancing school-funding structures initially emanated from school finance litigation in the 1970s. By centralizing school funding decisions at the state level, these reforms attempt to equalize the ability of school districts to raise funds and provide more equal opportunities for students. Observers point to the experiences of states that have centralized their school-funding systems and argue that the resulting reform legislation tends to disadvantage urban schools (Theobald and Picus 1991). Legislators from mostly white, middle-income districts can focus their energy on passing school funding measures that benefit children and teachers within their legislative districts, whereas legislators from predominantly urban areas have greater difficulty organizing themselves around a single issue because, more than their suburban and rural counterparts, they must constantly balance the needs of the public schools against funding for extremely popular social and criminal justice programs. To garner sufficient legislative support for the noneducational programs that are of great importance to urban voters, large city legislators are seen as being under pressure to accept school funding packages that place large city districts at a disadvantage.

In addition, intrastate acrimony toward urban communities, driven by a wide variety of economic and sociological factors, can play a significant role in highly centralized funding systems. Theobald and Picus (1991) point-out, "thinly veiled anti-Seattle or anti-Los Angeles school funding measures have been implemented in the Washington and California legislatures; both are widely popular throughout the remainder of their respective states. In a situation where very little local funding leeway is permitted, the impact of such measures on the education of inner city students is immediate and noticeable" (5).

Proponents of equity-enhancing school-funding structures point out that school attendance is compulsory. By requiring children to spend more than a tenth of their expected life span in school, it is argued, a state incurs a moral and legal obligation to support schools in ways that are congruent with its ideals. Although a state's responsibility for many aspects of children's lives is at best indirect and limited, its constitutional obligation for providing an equitable system of public schools is both direct and clear. For these individuals, the tradeoffs cited by critics are reflections of social prejudice. "In retrospect, it probably should have been recognized that the structural, political and fiscal forces that gave rise to inequitable distributions were not going to be easy to reverse, even with reform" (Berne 1988, 173–74).

Efficiency-Enhancing Structures

Efficiency-enhancing initiatives are based on the belief that a state's school funding system should simultaneously increase demands on the K–12 education system, reduce discretion of decision-making parties within the system, and hold schools more responsible for performance. Critics of this approach charge that reducing local discretion highlights a fundamental dissimilarity between local school boards and state legislatures. Although the constituents served by school boards are the same people who elect them, strict state regulation creates finance systems that expect legislators to put the interests of all of the state's children ahead of the interests of only those children in their particular legislative district. If they do not, local school districts are powerless to generate the incremental dollars needed to address emerging local needs.

Proponents of efficiency-enhancing reforms press the need to alter incentives to make performance count in urban schools. "Altering incentives responds to the fact that the school finance system historically has operated almost in isolation from educational performance, in that educational goals and desired outcomes have seldom been reflected in pay for teachers or budgets for schools" (National Research Council 1999, 9).

Assessing the Research Relative to the Claims

The desirability of school-finance reforms enacted in the last two decades of the twentieth century are subject of strong disagreement because core societal values such as liberty, equity, and efficiency are at stake. In addition, commonly held assumptions about which levels of government hold the comparative advantage in promoting these values have not always proven to be accurate. Galvin (2000) shows that both states and local schools have worked to extend educational opportunities and perpetuate ingrained inequities; both have a place in the press for efficiency; and both have worked to protect and restrict individual and institutional freedom.

In addition, neither state governments nor local school districts have mobilized on behalf of policies that might tackle some of the underlying causes of educational problems. For example, efforts to redistribute wealth, expand the scope of promising interventions, or otherwise confront the life-conditions as well as the learning opportunities of children are few and far between (Anyon 1997; Edelman 1987; Schorr 1988; Tyack and Cuban 1995).

What is clear, though, is that these school finance reforms reflect a power shift from schools to the state. This shift is both noticeable and consequential. In the traditional pattern, schools had considerable latitude in terms of the educational revenues they could raise and the particular programs and priorities they could pursue. They were accountable to their local constituents in that they recognized the importance of cultivating positive sentiments toward and public confidence in public schools. Although scholars regularly questioned whether local schools were really open to lay influence and whether they operated as responsibly and efficiently as proponents of "liberty-enhancing" school-finance models suggested, this arrangement prevailed in many states (e.g., Boyd 1976; Burlingame 1988; First and Walberg 1992; McDermott 1999; Ziegler and Jennings 1974).

With the onset of the extensive state activism in school finance in the last twenty years of the twentieth century, the dynamics changed markedly. Relying primarily on their regulatory and their purse-string authority to craft mandates and incentives, state governments adopted a more aggressive and intrusive stance. States have become more prescriptive about both "the purposes for which the school funds available to localities are to be used and the education means by which those purposes are to be pursued" (Bull 2000b, 22).

The move by state policymakers in Ohio to introduce vouchers in Cleveland clearly reflects a second trend that is evident in school reform in the last two decades of the twentieth century: greater reliance on market mechanisms to encourage efficiency. Ohio has also joined most other states in intensifying its use of bureaucratic controls through the imposition of "high stakes" testing programs, school report cards, and other publicly disseminated indicators of organizational performance. As a result, thrity-nine school districts in Ohio, including nearly all urban districts in the state, have been deemed "Academic Emergency" districts and are subject to tighter state control.

As states move towards these accountability-driven, efficiency-oriented reforms, other social values, such as equity and liberty, receive less attention. Issues of excellence and economic growth often superseded issues of equity and liberty in recent educational reform efforts (Boyd 1988; Howe 1991). Through regulations at the state level, and "bully pulpit" pronouncements at the federal level, both levels of government seemed to be seeking dramatic and inexpensive ways to foster efficiency even if the mechanisms they employed were ignoring, jeopardizing or, in some cases trumping, efforts to foster equity and protect liberty (Clark and Astuto 1986; Howe 1991).

Further, states' willingness to consider policies that might break up public education, augmented by the federal government's endorsement of choice experiments, challenged the status of public schools and signaled a change in the values emphasized and the mechanisms used to deliver educational programs and services. Some of the multiple school choice plans and charter-school proposals tried to preempt equity concerns in the rhetoric if not the design of their initiatives. Nonetheless, the primary appeal appeared to be that altered incentives will force schools to become more efficient in the production of services.

These and other indicators suggest that states have emphasized efficiency-oriented policies. Reflecting this emphasis, states used their funding systems to leverage marked changes in the governance of urban districts as well as to focus attention on desired changes in performance. For instance, states have withheld funds, pending the negotiation of "state-local partnerships" that substantially alter governmental roles and relationships in select urban areas (Henig et al. 1999; Orr 1999). Overall, states have put the focus on financial (as well as reputational) incentives and sanctions rather than fiscal and programmatic entitlements.

Although governmental actions at any level of the system defy precise prediction, it seems that state activism in school finance may well be here to stay. In addition, the high economic and educational stakes now attached to school-funding reform suggest that states are likely to continue their focus on performance and efficiency. Given the challenge urban districts face in demonstrating significant gains on test-based accountability measures, the frustration that comes with reports of "flat" or "declining" scores, the embarrassment that accompanies exposes on various schemes devised to artificially and dishonestly increase test scores, and the impatience that smolders as policy elites await the results they seek, school finance reform may actually become more aggressive and more punitive.

Yet, attempts in Ohio to follow this national pattern have found state policy makers frustrated by "the inability of the state to have parents follow through at home to enhance their children's performance on state proficiency tests. A prominent legislator holds that "our greatest failure is engaging parents" (Theobald and Bull, 28). If the schism found in Ohio is typical, states clearly face a great challenge in moving down the current path of refocusing school-finance reform on educational outcomes. Proficiency tests provide an answer to the business community's queries of "what are we getting for this extra spending?" Parents, though, who are seen as the linchpin for success, place much greater emphasis on schools that are caring and responsive to student total needs.

An Alternative Hypothesis

In many states, school finance reform in the last two decades has been driven by national networks, coalitions, and advocacy groups that explicitly seek to exert agenda-setting influence on state legislatures around school-finance issues (Kaplan and Usdan 1992; Mazzoni 2000). To the extent that these efforts are successful, state policymakers face the risk of being prematurely pushed to the "solution stage" of their state's school-funding process without ensuring that the proposed reform synchronizes with their state's goals and aspirations. Although the agenda put forward by a national organization may sometimes be applicable in a state, the experiences of Washington, Indiana, and Ohio suggest that one-size-fits-all solutions can lead to unintended consequences, particularly for urban schools, that can be remedied by a more issues-driven school-funding reform approach. As state legislatures are forced to respond to agendas set on the national stage, policymakers face a continual need to ensure that the solutions proposed target the highest priorities that they and their constituents hold for their states' K–12 schools.

In order to tie school-funding reform better to state goals, there is a real need to develop *two* sets of capacities. First, states need to be able to gather critical information about the definition and nature of the state's school-funding problems, as well as possible solutions. In this way, policymakers can begin to build a consensus across the education, government, and business communities about what the state wants to achieve through its school funding system and, how best to work together to achieve these goals. Second, states need to develop a process for monitoring the overall effects of changes it makes to the state's school-funding system. This capacity enables legislatures in these states to modify continuously their funding systems in order to achieve the general goals for which they are enacted. In addition, states need information on the unintended side effects of legislative actions so that legislators can reassess the value of achieving those goals in light of other consequences.

Lacking a focused issues-driven approach—in the current environment where states are increasingly being called upon to fund school-funding "solutions" that are part of a national education agenda—policymakers could find themselves allocating limited state dollars to school-funding reforms that relate only tangentially to state needs. An issues-oriented approach instead encourages policymakers not to rush toward solutions until they have carefully answered the question, "What is this a solution for?" Then a "solution" can be crafted around the particular issues, concerns, and values of that state's citizens. Goals must precede solutions.

This approach is currently being used in the very different political contexts of Indiana and Ohio. The goals that result from these two processes (Theobald 2000; Theobald and Bull 2000) reflect quite different policy concerns. Despite the elements of disagreement—or more accurately, *because* of the elements of disagreement—policymakers in both states found the process described in this report very helpful. The divergence in the destinations sought by Indiana and Ohio underscores the difficulty of responding to local hopes, dreams, and realities with a one-size-fits-all agenda put forward by parties outside the state. Instead, policymakers in these two states emphasize the critical importance of driving school-finance reform by focusing on the issues of greatest importance in their own states. The wide differences in the school funding issues facing these two midwestern states reinforce the necessity of goals preceding solutions.

By identifying a consensus about goals for a state's system of school funding, the issues-driven process is intended to provide an objective, nonpartisan basis for the logical next step, which is to determine specific funding proposals that lead to the achievement of the goals that make up the consensus agenda. This process is designed to shield decision makers from being rushed prematurely towards crafting solutions. Instead, it allows policymakers to undertake the systematic analysis and deliberation needed to understand the nature of the challenges facing them and to reach agreement about what would constitute satisfactory progress in overcoming these challenges. Moreover, this approach provides the basis for an ongoing process. A funding strategy that meets state objectives adequately at a particular point in time is likely to be inadequate at some future time.

At least two caveats must be considered in this process, though. First, it must be recognized that the information generated by an issues-driven process will be used in the larger political context of a state legislature. A dominant view in policy research is that policymakers fasten upon information that affirms their convictions and use it to advance their goals and preferences. The alternative process described here does not attempt to substitute information for politics. Instead, it attempts to integrate politics into the information-generating process by seeking to ascertain points of consensus among policymakers and interest groups regarding key pieces of the debate over how best to finance the schools.

Second, it is possible for individual points of consensus to be inconsistent with one another. Experience suggests that as long as the debate is highly abstract, it is relatively easy to "paper-over" differences in points of view with lofty rhetoric. However, when attention turns to the design and implementation of real-world policy, the ability to finesse underlying differences in the point of view can decline, and disagreements can become quite sharp.

The process outlined in this chapter has evolved since 1994 to recognize and attempt to address these realities. Central to our evolving understanding of state school funding is that no definitive solution exists for the funding questions in any state. The lack of a definitive answer, though, does not preclude deducing on principled grounds a viable direction in which to proceed. Once a direction has been set, this process has been very useful in monitoring the results carefully. This approach is necessarily an iterative process with the results of the monitoring being used to further inform the various parties as they undertake further debate and further action.

References

Anyon, J. 1997. *Ghetto schooling: A political economy of urban educational reform.* New York: Teachers College Press.

Berne, R. 1988. Equity issues in school finance. *Journal of Education Finance* 14: 159–180.

Boyd, W. L. 1976. The public, the professionals and education policymaking: Who governs? *Teachers College Record* 77: 539–577.

———. 1984. Competing values in educational policy and governance: Australian and American developments. *Educational Administration Review* 2: 4–24.

———. 1988. How to reform schools without half trying: Secrets of the Reagan Administration. *Educational Administration Quarterly*, 24, 299–309.

Bull, B. 1998. School reform in Indiana since 1980. In *Hoosier schools: Past and present*, ed. W. J. Reese. Bloomington: Indiana University Press.

———. 2000a. National standards in local context: A philosophical and policy analysis. In *Educational leadership: Policy dimensions in the 21st century*, ed. B. A. Jones. Stamford, Conn.: Ablex.

———. 2000b. Political philosophy and the state-local power balance. In *Balancing local control and state responsibility for K–12 education*, ed. N. D. Theobald and B. Malen. Larchmont, N.Y.: Eye on Education.

Burlingame, M. 1988. The politics of education and educational policy: The local level. In *The handbook of research on educational administration*, ed. N. Boyan. New York: Longman.

Clark, D., and T. Astuto. 1986. The significance and permanence of changes in federal education policy. *Educational Researcher* 15(7): 4–13.

Comer, J. P. 1988. Educating poor minority children. *Scientific American* 259(5): 42–48.

Edelman, M. W. 1987. *Families in peril: An agenda for social change*. Cambridge, Mass.: Harvard University Press.

Equity and Adequacy Coalition. 2000. *Action plan for implementing DeRolph*. Columbus, Ohio: Author.

First, P., and H. Walberg, eds. 1992. *School boards: Changing local control*. Berkeley, Calif.: McCutchan.

Fordham, S., and J. U. Ogbu. 1986. Black students' school success: Coping with the "burden of 'acting White.'" *Urban Review* 18: 176–206.

Galvin, P. 2000. Organizational boundaries, authority, and school district organization. In *Balancing local control and state responsibility for K–12 education*, ed. N. D. Theobald and B. Malen. Larchmont, N.Y.: Eye on Education.

Garms, W. I., J. W. Guthrie, and L. C. Pierce. 1978. *School finance: The economics and politics of public education*. Englewood Cliffs, N.J.: Prentice-Hall.

Henig, J. R., R. C. Hula, M. Orr, and D. S. Pedescleaux. 1999. *The color of school reform: Race, politics and the challenge of urban education*. Princeton, N.J.: Princeton University Press.

Holmstedt, R. W. 1940. *State control of public school finance*. Bloomington: Indiana University, Bulletin of the School of Education, vol. 16, no. 2.

Howe, H., III. 1991. America 2000: A bumpy ride on four trains. *Phi Delta Kappan* 73(3): 192–203.

Indiana Fiscal Policy Institute. 1994. *Local property tax limitations in Indiana*. Indianapolis: Author.

Johnson, C. E., and R. G. Lehnen. 1993. Reforming Indiana's school finance formula, 1973–1990: A case of unanticipated outcomes. *Journal of Education Finance* 18: 264–80.

Jung, R. and M. Kirst. 1986. Beyond mutual adaptation, into the bully pulpit: Recent research on the federal role in education. *Educational Administration Quarterly* 22(1): 80–109.

Kantor, H., and B. Brenzel. 1992. Urban education and the "truly disadvantaged": The historical roots of the contemporary crisis, 1945–1990. *Teachers College Record* 94: 278–314.

Kaplan, G. R., and M. D. Usdan. 1992. The changing look of education's policy networks. *Phi Delta Kappan* 73(9): 664–72.

Kozol, J. 1991. *Savage inequalities: Children in America's schools*. New York: Crown.

McDermott, K. A. 1999. *Controlling public education: Localism versus equity*. Lawrence: University Press of Kansas.

Malen, B., and D. Muncie. 2000. Creating "a new set of givens"? The impact of state activism on school autonomy. In *Balancing local control and state responsibility for K–12 education*, ed. N. D. Theobald and B. Malen. Larchmont, N.Y.: Eye on Education.

Mazzoni, T. L. 1994. State policy-making and school reform: Influences and influentials. In *The study of educational politics*, ed. J. D. Scribner & D. H. Layton. New York: Falmer Press.

———. 2000. State politics and school reform: The first decade of the "education excellence" movement. In *Balancing local control and state responsibility for k-12 education*, ed. N. D. Theobald and B. Malen. Larchmont, N.Y.: Eye on Education.

Miller, W. G. 1975. *Common school financing and reform*. Olympia, Wash.: Miller and Associates.

Mitchell, D. E., and D. J. Encarnation. 1984. Alternative state policy mechanisms for influencing school performance. *Educational Researcher* 13(5): 4–11.

Monk, D. H. 1990. *Educational finance: An economic approach*. New York: McGraw-Hill.

National Center for Education Statistics (NCES). 1965. *Digest of education statistics*. Washington, D.C.: U. S. Government Printing Office.

———. 1975. *Digest of education statistics*. Washington, D.C.: U. S. Government Printing Office.

———. 2000. *Digest of education statistics, 1999*. Washington, D.C.: U. S. Government Printing Office.

National Research Council. 1999. *Making money matter: Financing America's schools*. Committee on Education Finance, H. F. Ladd and J. S. Hansen, ed. Commission on Behavioral and Social Sciences and Education. Washington, D.C.: National Academy Press.

Orr, M. 1999. *Black social capital: The politics of school-reform in Baltimore, 1986–1998*. Lawrence: University Press of Kansas.

Reff, D. F. 1982. Ample provision for education: A study of school finance reform in Washington State. Unpublished manuscript.

Schorr, L. B. 1988. *Within our reach: Breaking the cycle of disadvantage*. New York: Anchor Press.

Theobald, N. D. 1990. An examination of the influence of personal, professional, and school district characteristics on public school teacher retention. *Economics of Education Review* 9: 241–250.

———. 1994. Financial roadblocks to renewing and enhancing Washington's public schools. In *The political economy of school finance*, ed. C. Herrington. Tallahassee, Fla.: Learning Systems Institute.

———. 2000. Listening, not telling: The need for issues-driven school funding reform. *NCREL Policy Issues* 5: 1–8.

———. 2001. Indiana's performance in meeting its school funding goals. *Journal of School Business Management* 13(2): 27–31.

Theobald, N. D., and B. Bull. 2000. *Ohio's goals for school funding: Objective measures for informing policy debate and action*. Oak Brook, Ill.: North Central Regional Educational Laboratory.

Theobald, N. D., and F. Hanna. 1991. Ample provision for whom?: The evolution of state control over school finance in Washington. *Journal of Education Finance* 17: 7–32.

Theobald, N. D., and L. O. Picus. 1991. Living with equal amounts of less: Experiences of states with primarily state-funded school systems. *Journal of Education Finance* 17: 1–6.

Tyack, D., and L. Cuban. 1995. *Tinkering toward utopia*. Cambridge, Mass.: Harvard University Press.

Weinberg, M. 1986. *The education of poor and minority children*. Westport, Conn.: Greenwood Press.

Wilson, W. J. 1987. *The truly disadvantaged: The inner city, the underclass, and public policy*. Chicago: University of Chicago Press.

Ziegler, H., and M. K. Jennings. 1974. *Governing American schools*. Scituate, Mass.: Duxbury Press.

Legal Cases

Cincinnati School District Board of Education v. Walter. 1979. 58 Ohio St.2d 368, 387, 12 O.O.3d 327, 338, 390 N.E.2d 813.

DeRolph v. State (1997), 78 Ohio St.3d 193.

DeRolph v. State (2000), 89 Ohio St.3d 1.

Lake Central et al. v. State of Indiana et al., Newton County Circuit Court, Indiana, Cause No. 56 Col-8703-CP-81 (filed 1987).

San Antonio v. Rodriguez (1973), 411 U.S. 1.

Part II

Government Initiated, External Reforms

Chapter 3

Federal Title I as a Reform Strategy in Urban Schools

Kenneth K. Wong

In public education, the federal government has focused on social redistribution by promoting racial integration, protecting the educational rights of the handicapped, assisting those with limited English proficiency, and providing supplemental resources to children who come from at-risk backgrounds. By far the largest federal program in elementary and secondary education is Title I of the Elementary and Secondary Education Act (ESEA), which was originally passed in 1965 at the height of the civil rights movement and social reforms. Despite several revisions and extensions, ESEA Title I continued to adhere to its original redistributive goal of federal assistance to learning-deficient children from low-income families. As declared in the 1965 Act, ESEA Title I was designed "to provide financial assistance to local educational agencies serving areas with concentrations of children from low-income families to expand and improve their educational programs . . . which contribute particularly to meeting the special educational needs of educationally deprived children." (U.S. Congress 1965, Sec. 201)

Thirty years later, the 1994 Improving America's Schools Act (IASA), which reauthorized Title I, sharpened the focus on academic accountability in Title I schools. In 2002, Congress again took on the task of reauthorization. These latest, bold legislative extensions of Title I constitute a new phase in the policy development of Title I during the course of its thirty-five year history. In this chapter we will not only synthesize the lessons learned from the current literature but also trace the major phases of policy development

Table 3.1
The Broadening Agenda in Title I Reform and Implementation

	1960s–1980s	*1988–Present*	*1994–Present*
Dominant Policy Paradigm	• Antipoverty	• Antipoverty • Reduce regulatory compliance	• Antipoverty • Reduce regulatory compliance • Improve achievement
Programmatic Mechanisms	• Categorical funding • Targeting aid to eligible students	• Schoolwide as experiment for high-poverty schools • Targeted assistance for other schools	• Assessment standards to measure accountability • Adequate yearly progress • Schoolwide in full-scale expansion • CSRD—adoption of knowledge based practices
Issues in Implementation	• Local noncompliance	• Pull-out of students remains dominant • Coordination of curriculum/ instruction as a challenge	• Quality of student data-driven measurements • Mixed student performance as basis for extensive reform (including vouchers and district/state direct intervention)

that the federal policy has gone through over the last thirty-five years. To avoid confusion, we have used Title I throughout this paper even though the program's label was changed during the 1980s.

For analytical purposes, we differentiate three phases in the development of Title I policy over time. Each of these phases, though interrelated, is connected to a particular policy challenge, faced with a distinct set of political factors, and involved with new institutional practices. Rationales behind these changes are also discussed. As shown in Table 3.1, the policy agenda in Title I has expanded from its original intent to address poverty in the 1960s to include instructional coherence and student achievement in the 1990s. The first policy phase (1960s to 1980s) involved intergovernmental accommodation on targeting federal Title I funds on low-income children. Much of the research on Title I during the first ten to fifteen years focused on local response to federal direction in Title I as a "categorical" program. During this phase, local control was being challenged by federal antipoverty objectives. The second phase emerged during the late 1980s when policymakers and educators began to pay greater attention to the quality of instruction and curriculum in the Title I program. With the passage of the 1994 Improving America's Schools Act, the schoolwide program gained prominence as a leading reform strategy to reduce "fragmentation" between Title I and the regular classroom in schools with high concentrations of poor children. Indeed, the number of schoolwide programs increased from about 1,300 in 1990 to over 9,000 in 1998, or a jump from 10 percent to 50 percent of the eligible schools. The third phase began around the mid-1990s when competing visions shaped the agenda to raise student performance in Title I schools. Frustrated by the lack of significant academic progress in most Title I schools, reformers made serious attempts to restructure Title I in three different directions, namely, whole school reform, district-based support, and consumer-based or voucher program. Taken as a whole, Title I has reduced its focus on regulatory compliance but increased its emphasis on outcome-based accountability.

This chapter will examine the issues, the politics, the knowledge base, and the institutional practices in the development and implementation of federal Title I policy in each of the three phases. We will synthesize the literature and, where appropriate, we will draw on our own research on Title I. Based on our synthesis of Title I research in all three phases, we will explore policy implications upon accountability and equity issues.

Phase One: Managing the Tension between Federal Anti-Poverty Direction and Local Control 1960s–1980s

The 1965 Elementary and Secondary Education Act (ESEA) marked a significant turning point in the federal role to address education and social issues. At the time of the enactment of ESEA, the federal government declared "War on Poverty" and launched the Great Society programs. Federal activism in social issues followed the 1954 landmark U.S. Supreme Court decision on *Brown v. Board of Education* and the congressional enactment of the 1964 Civil Rights Act. Hundreds of federal categorical (or single-purpose) programs were formulated to provide supplemental resources for local agencies to combat social and economic problems in poor communities. The passage of ESEA and other federal programs contributed to a significant increase in intergovernmental transfers. By 1980, there were approximately 500 federal categorical programs, including such major antipoverty programs as Aid to Families with Dependent Children, Medicaid, food stamps, low-income housing, bilingual education, school desegregation grants, and compensatory education (Title I).

The literature on federalism has looked for structural sources to explain why social redistribution is more likely to come from the national government. The federal government enjoys a broader revenue base in which taxes are raised primarily on the ability-to-pay principle and represents a constituency with heterogeneous demands (Lowi 1964; Peterson 1981; Wong 1990). In other words, it has both the fiscal capacity and the political resources (often facilitated by interest groups) to respond to social needs. In contrast, localities are more limited in their ability to address social needs because their most active voters come mostly from the middle class, they compete with one another for investment in an open system in which businesses and labor can move freely, and they have a restricted tax base (namely, reliance on land values as a major source of income). Consequently, both incentives and regulations are necessary in order to alter local practices.

The incentive for local government to meet antipoverty objectives lies in the way federal funds are distributed. The territorial impact of federal grants has contributed partly to the popularity of Title I in Congress over time. For example, in 1990, the federal grant provided supplemental resources to 64 percent of all the schools in the nation, covering virtually every congressional district. Clearly, big city districts are not the only beneficiaries of compensatory education funds. Indeed, over 20 percent of federal aid goes to districts with fewer than 2,500 students (Millsap et al. 1992). Districts with enrollments between 2,500 and 25,000 receive almost 45 percent of the funds. Because there are Title I programs in almost every congressional district, partisan conflict has generally been limited during the appropriations process.

To ensure its redistributive focus, Title I policy maintains federal direction to counteract the local tendency of antiredistribution. Designed to alleviate poverty and create opportunities for the underrepresented, Great Society programs required local governments to reformulate the way services were delivered. Because revenues in antipoverty programs mostly came from the U.S. Congress, the federal government imposed numerous complicated guidelines upon local schools. These regulations were intended to make certain that disadvantaged pupils directly benefited from federal dollars.

In the case of ESEA Title I, extensive local misuses of federal resources prompted the federal government to write tighter regulations during the 1970s. Most notably, a study conducted by the NAACP Legal Defense Fund during the first years of the program found that federal funds were being used for "general school purposes; to initiate system-wide programs; to buy books and supplies for all school children in the system; to pay general overhead and operating expenses; [and] to meet new teacher contracts which call for higher salaries" (Martin and McClure 1969). Consequently, throughout the 1970s, the program acquired a well-defined set of rules and guidelines that many state and local officials had difficulty putting in place. In Title I, local districts were required to use federal funds in schools with the highest concentration of poor students, to use federal dollars as a supplement instead of supplanting local revenues in Title I schools, to spend as many local dollars on these schools as any other school in the district (i.e., comparability requirement), and to commit at least the same level of local resources as they provided in previous years (i.e., maintenance of efforts requirement). During the 1970s and the early 1980s, Title I required the formation of advisory councils composed of parents of children participating in the program. Typical of a federal categorical program, only eligible students would receive federally funded Title I service.

As expected, there was local resistance to federal targeting on special needs populations. In a comparative study of four major federal education programs in four urban districts, Peterson, Rabe, and Wong (1986) found that local districts were tempted, to a greater or lesser extent, to divert funds away from these redistributive programs to other purposes. Title I funds, for example, were used for general operating purposes that tended to benefit the entire school population during the 1970s and the 1980s.

With the passage of time, a tendency towards increasing intergovernmental accommodation seems to have emerged in Title I policy. This shift from intergovernmental conflict to regulatory accommodation has been facilitated by several factors. At the district and school level, a new professional cadre more identified with program objectives was recruited to administer special programs, and local officials became more sensitive to federal expectations. At the federal level, policymakers began to doubt whether detailed regulations, tight audits, and comprehensive evaluations were unmixed blessings. With the state agency serving as an active mediator, appropriate changes and adjustments were made. By the 1980s, administrators developed program identifications that transcended governmental boundaries and a commitment to a coordinated effort gradually emerged.

To be sure, the pace of moving towards federal-local cooperation in the management of special programs has not been uniform. There are significant variations among districts (McLaughlin 1990). Wong found that local reform in Title I services depends on the district's fiscal conditions, political culture, and the policymaking autonomy of the program professionals (Wong 1990). More severe and prolonged conflict is likely to be found in districts with a weak fiscal capacity and a program apparatus that is subject to strong patronage-based local practice. A combination of these fiscal and political circumstances hinders local reform towards redistributive goals. At the other end of the continuum are districts with strong fiscal capacity, autonomous program professionals, and most of all, teacher commitment to policy.[1] These local conditions facilitated the transformation from the conflictual to the accommodative phase in Title I programs. This institutional process of adaptation (e.g., targeting resources to the eligibles) is a necessary condition for instructional and academic improvement in disadvantaged schools.

Phase Two: Schoolwide Reform to Reduce Fragmentation, 1988–Present

As fiscal auditing requirements became more manageable, improvements in teaching and learning for disadvantaged students

---

[1]On linking site-level variables to the design of macro policy, see objectives (McLaughlin 1987; Elmore 1980; McLaughlin and Berman).

emerged at the top of the policy agenda. Concerns with student performance are in part due to global competition and in part to the dissemination of a more comprehensive assessment of our educational system. Based on a national survey of ECIA Chapter 1 district-level coordinators in 1990, a major evaluation study found that federal requirements on funding compliance—supplement not supplant, maintenance of efforts, and comparability provisions—are all ranked as far less burdensome than procedures that affect instructional practices. Indeed, evaluation procedures, needs assessment, and student selection are viewed as the three most burdensome federal regulations that govern Chapter 1. For example, few districts develop reliable procedures for assessing the educational needs of students who remain in compensatory education for more than two years (Millsap et al. 1992).

In light of these concerns about classroom practices, the federal government and local school professionals began to look for ways to improve program effectiveness. A key strategy has been to improve instructional and curricular coordination, a policy goal that is frequently undermined by the categorical nature of Title I. Fragmentation is nothing new and it was found to be counterproductive in meeting the educational needs of disadvantaged pupils. Schools that receive Title I funding often "pull out" the program participants for special instructional purposes as a way to meet the accounting requirements. A 1983 survey of district-level program coordinators found that 73 percent of the respondents used pull-outs mainly to comply with auditing regulations. More often than not, "pull out" sessions offer inferior instruction and students are held accountable to low standards. "Only 18 percent of district administrators who used a pullout design indicated they believed it was educationally superior to any other mode of delivery" (Smith 1988, 130).

In the context of increasing public concern abcut competitiveness and reform, policymakers and local school professionals are beginning to shift their focus from administrative compliance to program effectiveness. As Michael Kirst observed, federal publication of "A Nation At Risk" has renewed concerns for blending Chapter 1 with a core academic curriculum (Kirst 1988, p. 110). Indeed, the Commission on Chapter 1 urged that the federal program be redesigned in ways that would strengthen the school's overall organizational capacity in developing more comprehensive (instead of fragmentary) strategies toward the disadvantaged (Commission on Chapter 1 1992; Timar 1994). To paraphrase the Commission's central argument, federal policy should promote "good schools" and not merely provide good programs.

The argument to improve the instructional quality of an entire school is further supported by research that found "concentration effects" of students, including those who come from nonpoor families, in neighborhoods where the incidence of poverty is very high (Wilson 1987). According to a national assessment of Title I, educational performance is just as adversely affected by living in a low-income neighborhood as by coming from a poor family. As the report pointed out, "[S]tudents were increasingly likely to fall behind grade levels as their families experienced longer spells of poverty, and . . . achievement scores of all students—not just poor students—declined as the proportion of poor students in schools increased[d]." (Kennedy, Jung, and Orland 1986, 107) In other words, if both factors are present—a child comes from a poor family and lives in an impoverished neighborhood—the incidence of educational disadvantage is approximately twice as high as when neither factor is present. Similarly, a 1992 GAO report found that schools with a high concentration of poor children "have disproportionately more low achievers than schools with fewer children in poverty." (U.S. General Accounting Office 1992)

To reduce fragmentation within schools and to build up the overall capacity of Title I schools, the Congress approved the schoolwide concept on an experimental basis in 1988 and then on a full scale in 1994. We will first discuss the 1988 legislation and its impact on Title I schools and then examine the 1994 policy change.

Lessons from the Early Implementation of Schoolwide Programs

In 1988, Congress adopted the Hawkins-Stafford Amendments. The legislation required coordination of Chapter 1 with the regular instructional program, encouraged parental involvement, allowed schoolwide projects in schools with a high concentration of poverty children (without asking for local matching funds), and directed the district to take steps to address ineffective programs. Most importantly, the Hawkins-Stafford Amendments in 1988 allowed for schoolwide projects in schools that have at least 75 percent of students enrolled falling below the poverty level. This new flexibility doubled schoolwide programs within the first two years (Millsap et al. 1992). High poverty schools were now permitted to use federal funds to reduce class size, develop staff training, support parent involvement, and recruit new professional support personnel. A review of the literature during this early phase suggests the following patterns of implementation.

Title I funding at schoolwide program schools has been frequently used to hire additional staff to reduce class sizes. Reduced class size was identified by principals in slightly more than half of schoolwide program schools during the 1991–92 school year. Schools reported that the average reduction in school class size was from twenty-seven to nineteen children. The addition of new staff has not been limited to teachers or instructional aides. Counselors, social workers, school-family coordinators, and schoolwide program coordinators have also been hired to support schoolwide program services in efforts to strengthen the relationship between the school and families, for example (Millsap et al. 1992). The schoolwide reform has also facilitated district activities to promote parental involvement. Between 1987 and 1990, more districts reported "disseminating home-based education activities to reinforce classroom instruction," and using liaison staff to coordinate parent activities (Millsap et al. 1992).

Moreover, principals reported that staff development activities had been implemented or significantly strengthened in over three-fourths of schoolwide program schools. During the first years of implementation, a majority of districts reported that staff development at schoolwide program schools was more inclusive of teachers and involved more total hours than regular Title I schools. Staff development activities in schoolwide program schools have included training in reading/language arts instruction, instruction for low achieving students, and mathematics instruction (Schenck and Beckstrom 1993). According to principal reports, a teacher at a schoolwide program school received an average of twenty-nine hours of staff development, which is six hours more than that received by the average teacher in a Title I school without a schoolwide program (Schenck and Beckstrom 1993; Millsap et al. 1992).

The schoolwide program option encourages increased teacher input into decisions affecting the school, emphasizing teacher input into decisions about assessments. Based on reports by principals in one major urban school district, the majority of teachers had some level of input into decisions about assigning students and teachers to classrooms, hiring staff, and selecting materials or purchasing hardware. Teachers, however, had the greatest input in decisions about selecting materials or purchasing hardware and had the least input in decisions about teacher assignment and replacement (Winfield and Hawkins 1993). In-depth case studies, however, suggested that a school's change to a schoolwide program tended to be accompanied by a high degree of teacher control and site-based management arrangements (Stringfield et al. 1997).

A central component of the schoolwide program is the provision of Title I activities and services to all students in the school. One indicator of a program's inclusiveness is the extent to which Title I services cannot be distinguished from services offered for all children (e.g., one that lacks "pull-out" programs that serve only a subset of students). Sixty percent of schoolwide program school principals reported that their schools operated programs in which Title I services are indistinguishable from services for all children. Among those schools in which Title I services were distinguishable from the regular program, the most common distinction was the provision of additional services to educationally disadvantaged students who would have received Title I services in a traditional, targeted program. Only 12 percent of schools reported using a "pull-out" model (Schenck and Beckstrom 1993). In one major urban district, principal reports indicated that schoolwide program schools were in transition toward the provision of Title I services to all children during the first years of implementation, with higher percentages of schools reallocating resources to provide instruction to all students each year (Winfield and Hawkins 1993).

Perhaps the most critical components of schoolwide programs are those which have the potential to directly influence what takes place in the classroom. Schoolwide program principals reported having introduced or significantly strengthened the following components related to curriculum and instruction: computer assisted instruction (over three-fourths); provision of a coordinated and integrated curriculum and supplemental instruction (two-thirds); and provision of an extended school day (less than one-fourth) (Schenck and Beckstrom 1993). Schoolwide program schools have adopted a range of programs and curricula, such as "Reading Recovery" or "Success for All," as part of their schoolwide programs (Millsap et al. 1992; National Association of State Coordinators of Compensatory Education 1996). In fact, the majority of "Success for All" schools are Title I schoolwide programs (Slavin et al. 1996).

It is difficult to obtain a clear picture of the particular ways in which the schoolwide program option actually impacts classroom instruction. Nonetheless, in-depth case study analysis begins to inform this question. For example, case studies of schoolwide programs identified a common theme of individualizing instruction to the needs of particular students (Stringfield et al. 1997). Additional evidence indicates that schoolwide programs have increased the capacity of schools and teachers to provide instructional services more flexibly, as particular student needs arise; whereas traditional Title I "pull-out" programs have typically required a more formal process of student selection (Millsap et al. 1992).

In addition to the components described above, schoolwide programs are frequently reported to have adopted practices associated with effective schools. State Title I coordinators reported that 62 percent of schoolwide programs in their states incorporated components of effective schools programs as a main feature of their programs (Turnbull, Zeldin, and Cain 1990; U.S. Department of Education 1992). Title I district coordinators reported that a number of effective schools components were implemented as part of schoolwide programs through activities such as needs assessment, staff development, changes in classroom instruction, and changes in school management (Millsap et al. 1992). The presence of characteristics associated with effective schools may, reciprocally, impact the successful implementation of schoolwide programs, in that the factors that make good schools may also facilitate innovation and change. Case studies suggested that factors that facilitate innovation include strong principal leadership and management skills; meaningful, universally agreed upon goals; a nurturing school culture; well-qualified staff; and organizational mechanisms to support schools' problem-solving (Stringfield et al. 1994).

An Illustration of Schoolwide Implementation in a Big-City Setting

Although schoolwide reforms have become more popular in high-poverty schools, coordination between Title I and the regular curriculum remains a challenge in most Title I schools. In most schools, coordination relies almost entirely on informal meetings, and staff planning sessions rarely occur. Further, local districts remain largely uncertain about student needs assessment and program evaluation, areas where federal and state agencies can provide crucial technical assistance.

The ongoing challenge of improving the effectiveness of schoolwide programs can be illustrated by our research in Minneapolis (Wong, Sunderman, and Lee 1994; Wong, Sunderman, and Lee 1997). This study makes comparisons between the schools with a Title I schoolwide program and the district as a whole to show how Title I students are distributed and what resources are available to service them. In analyzing the data collected from the district office and the schoolwide programs in Minneapolis during 1993–94, three emerging trends were observed: (1) school and classroom practices are, to some extent, shaped by recently adopted policies at the district-wide level; (2) variation in instructional practices exists between the schoolwide programs; and

(3) these variations in practices may explain some of the differences in student outcomes.

Let us briefly consider each of the findings from Minneapolis. First, several recent district-wide policies have reinforced the intent of the schoolwide program, granting greater flexibility and programmatic autonomy in the high poverty schools. These include (1) efforts toward site-based management that, among other things, enable schools to select their own text books; (2) an increase in local tax revenues to reduce class size; and (3) a push for a collaborative services model that encourages coordination of services between regular program staff and other special needs program staff. District policies therefore support schoolwide programs in Minneapolis.

At the school site level, variation in instructional practices between the schoolwide programs was found. In Schoolwide Program 1, the school was 100 percent pull-out for Title I students in 1986. Beginning in 1989, the school began to experiment with collaborative services and team teaching in which the Chapter 1 teacher worked in the classroom. Over the past two and a half years, the staff creatively used the computer lab to promote individualized instruction, accommodate students' different ability levels, identify each student's strengths and weaknesses, and place a focused emphasis on academic skill building. These instructional efforts seem to have produced reasonably good outcomes. Analysis of School 1 shows that student performance in vocabulary and reading is generally positive with incremental gains over the years. Although "poor" students are performing at a lower level than the "nonpoor" students, the former group has made measurable progress over a four-year period. There is no significant difference in achievement scores between African-American and white students in School 1. Overall, this schoolwide program has had "an equalizing" effect upon the impact of race and poverty.

In contrast, Schoolwide Program 2 has not brought about substantial restructuring. Practices and organization that began during the 1980s have been left largely intact staffing assignments, team teaching, and ability grouping within the classroom. Teachers have not given much attention to curricular changes, student assessment, or instructional practices that integrate the at-risk student populations. The only major change that came with the schoolwide project was the flexibility of teachers to work with any student in the building. This change, however, has not been enough to effect student performance. Indeed, students' gains in reading scores at School 2 tended to remain stable over time, whereas significant losses in math occurred. It should be noted that the lack of progress may also be related to the school size (with 1,000 students, the largest of the four schoolwide projects in the district) and its physical organization (it has no walls and uses white dividers to designate classrooms).

To sum up, although the schoolwide initiative began to attract national attention in the late 1980s, research continued to lag behind during the early and mid-1990s. Evaluation of schoolwide programs in the initial years has shown some potential. On the one hand, findings suggest that, as a group, Title I students in schoolwide programs performed better than their peers in the more traditionally organized service programs, such as pull-out instructional settings. On the other hand, nationwide evaluations suggest that schoolwide programs have continued to encounter a wide range of implementation difficulties. These challenges have included the need for assessment of student progress and a general lack of high-quality professional development activities. Further, the data base on the implementation and outcomes of Title I schoolwide projects is scanty (Wong and Wang 1994; Wang and Wong 1997; Wong and Meyer 1998). An extensive review of the literature examining Title I programs since the 1988 Hawkins-Stafford amendment suggests only thirteen major empirical studies on the implementation of Title I schoolwide programs (Wong and Meyer 1998). Clearly, there is an empirical need to further understand whether the schoolwide strategy is affecting school performance.

Scaling-Up Schoolwide Reform

The 1994 Improving America's Schools Act established an ambitious agenda for systemic improvement in schools with a high concentration of students with at-risk backgrounds. For the first time in the history of federal involvement in public education, students receiving federally funded compensatory services (Title I) are no longer left at the margin of school reform. Two of the provisions in the 1994 legislation have significant implications for schooling opportunities. The first mandates that district-wide performance standards must apply to all students including those receiving Title I services, as indicated in the administration's proposal that "Title I, bilingual education, and dozens of other federal programs must become integral to, not separate from, state and community education reforms that center on high standards" (U.S. Department of Education 1993, 3). The second provision included in this legislation promotes schoolwide initiative in Title I schools with at least 50 percent low-income students.

The schoolwide programs create an opportunity for high-poverty schools to allocate Title I resources with fewer restrictions in order to meet the legislative expectations of academic performance as set forth in the 1994 legislation. The 1994 Act encouraged the adoption of schoolwide programs by lowering the eligibility threshold for schoolwide programs to schools with 50 percent low-income students beginning in the 1996–97 school year. Schoolwide programs are expected to reduce the historically fragmented or categorical character of Title I programs, improve the effectiveness of Title I programs, and improve the effectiveness of entire schools, rather than targeting services to meet the needs of the most disadvantaged subpopulations. In other words, schoolwide programs are designed to replace regulatory compliance with instructional coherence and organizational coordination. Encouraged by the IASA legislation, the number of Title I schoolwide programs grew almost seven-fold between 1990 and 1998, representing an increase from about 10 percent to 50 percent of the eligible schools.

Further, schoolwide reform is facilitated by additional federal resources with the passage of Public Law 105-78 in November 1997. Known as the Obey-Porter legislation, the 1997 law appropriated an additional $145 million to support the Comprehensive School Reform Demonstration Program (CSRD) in Title I schoolwide programs. The 1994 and 1997 laws provide a set of legislative expectations that research suggests is essential to any high-functioning school. These expectations include:

1. A comprehensive assessment of student performance in relation to state/district subject-area content and assessment standards. Measurable goals and benchmarks for meeting the goals must be developed.
2. An instructional program that is grounded in effective, research-based methods and strategies.
3. High-quality professional development for teachers, aides, and other support personnel to enable all students to meet the state/district performance standards.
4. The development and implementation of strategies to increase parental and community involvement.
5. Strategies to identify how resources from federal, state, local, and private sources will be utilized to coordinate services to support and sustain the reform program.

These legislative expectations have the potential to transform Title I from its categorical and isolated character into an integral part of systemic reform, coherent with core academic standards. Together, the IASA and the Obey-Porter legislation provide a unique opportunity for high-poverty schools to raise standards and to raise student achievement. The first set of studies of the implementation of IASA suggests that the more effective schoolwide programs are more likely to meet legislative expectations. Based on a national study of thirty-two schools in nine urban and three county-wide districts during 1997–98, Wang, Wong, and Kim (1999) reported that higher performing schoolwide programs show strong implementation of student performance goals, academic standards and assessments, enriched curriculum, student-centered instruction, and evaluation of student performance. This study also identified the importance of a district-wide academic accountability framework to support schoolwide implementation.

Phase Three: Competing Approaches to Raise Student Performance in Title I Schools, 1994–Present

Although the IASA and the Obey-Porter legislation depict bipartisan agreement over Title I, there is another side to the debate on the future of Title I. There are, indeed, competing visions of how Title I should be improved to raise student performance. For one thing, the mid-1990s was punctuated by a brief period of highly visible partisan contention over redistributive educational programs. To be sure, during the 1980s the Reagan administration succeeded in terminating several small categorical programs, slowing down funding support in others, and consolidating various categorical programs into broadly defined block grants. However, the Emergency School Aid Act (ESAA) Title VI for desegregation was the only major redistributive educational program that was terminated. Title I and other major grants remained largely intact due to bipartisan support (Wong 1999).

Congressional politics, however, took a sharp turn in 1995. The 1994 midterm elections produced the first Republican majority in Congress in forty years. The new congressional leadership claimed a public mandate to shrink the federal role in social programs and to shift programmatic authority to state and local governments. The new House Speaker Newt Gingrich tended to undermine long-term institutional practices in decision making. He depicted the government as the major cause of poverty, the bureaucracy as the major source of waste of taxpayers dollars, and the private sector as the only real solution to social inequality. Further, he circumscribed the seniority practice to make sure that his first-term allies gained greater representation in crucial committees. For example, he handpicked three "activist conservatives," sidestepping seniority consideration, to lead three major committees. Consequently, he was able to secure House approval on nine of the ten items in his "Contract with America."

The heightened political confrontation between Congress and the president became highly visible in education policy during 1995. The Republican leadership wanted to reduce Title I by 19 percent, to cut bilingual education by two-thirds, and special education by 7 percent (Wong 1999). To demonstrate its control over the government purse, the Republican leadership even shut down the federal government when the budget expired. In the end, the retrenchment tactics backfired. Within two years, education policy regained bipartisan support in the Republican Congress.

Although Title I seemed to have survived budgetary retrenchment, its effectiveness was increasingly called into question in the new climate of outcome-based accountability. From a broader perspective, there are three directions in charting the future of Title I. First, Title I schools are encouraged to adopt externally designed models (or CSRD models) that are proven to have been effective elsewhere. However, evaluation of the first phase of CSRD reform has been largely mixed. The most comprehensive study of CSRD reform models was conducted by the American Institutes for Research (AIR) in 1999. The AIR study examined the design, implementation, and performance outcomes of twenty-four whole school reform models. The study synthesized student achievement information, conducted a survey of the support provided by the model designers during the start up phase, costs to the schools, the duration of the project, and the number of schools using the whole school reform approach. Using these diverse sources of information, the AIR observed that few reform models have substantiated their claims with hard evidence. Approaches have been adopted by schools without taking into full consideration local circumstances and needs. In terms of student achievement, only three of the twenty-four whole school reform approaches showed strong evidence of positive effects. In contrast to the AIR study, several case studies have identified effective strategies (Bodilly 1998; Stringfield et al. 1997). In short, there is a need for an empirical research base to address whether the 1997 whole school reform legislative expectations are being realized at district, school, and classroom levels.

Second, Title I schools are shaped by the level of district-wide support and sanctions to raise academic standards, to make "adequate yearly progress," and to improve professional development. A multiyear evaluation of the New American Schools (NAS) conducted by Rand Corporation suggests several necessary functions that the district needs to perform in order to produce effective whole school reform. These district functions include supporting appropriate matches between design teams and schools; providing adequate funding for design-based assistance; providing a conductive regulatory system, and mobilizing school personnel toward supporting whole school improvement (Bodilly and Berends 1999). To a certain extent, Chicago has begun to perform some of these supportive functions since the mayor took over the school system in 1995. In this latest reform, Chicago has sharpened its focus on low-performing schools and their students (Wong 2000). Beginning in 1996, the chief executive officer and the school board launched an educational accountability agenda focused on raising standards and improving student achievement. Low performing schools were put on probation and, in some case, reconstituted. Failing students are required to attend summer programs and social promotion has been terminated. The combination of sanctions and support seems to have improved the overall conditions and lead to better student performance across the system. Since 1996, test scores have risen in many Title I elementary schools and in some of the more problematic high schools. The Chicago model of turning around low performing schools is now considered as a viable reform strategy. In short, Title I reform is closely linked to district capacity, which may facilitate new linkages between Title I and other children-oriented services in the larger community.

Third, Title I schools, particularly low-performing, inner-city schools, have been the target of experimental vouchers, as proposed by Governor Jeb Bush, congressional leaders, and think tanks. Seeing virtually no cost efficiency in the billions of Title I dollars spent, proponents of this approach look for consumer-parents to pressure schools to improve (Peterson and Noyes 1997; Walberg 1998; Ravitch and Viteritti 1997; Kanstoroom and Palmaffy 2002). Parents would decide whether their chosen schools meet their preferences and expectations. Dollars follow the students, even when they select nonpublic schools. In the longer run, the consumer-centered process may create competition among schools, which may lead to the closure of failing schools. Converting Title I grants into vouchers has been attempted in the course of Title I history. The Reagan administration tried three times to convert the federal program into a voucher arrangement. The most serious proposal was the Equity Choice Act (H.R. 3821) in November 1985, also known as "TEACH." This bill would have allowed Title I students, at their parents' request, to attend any school in the district. No funding increase was proposed for Title I's conversion. None of the Reagan proposals was seriously considered by the Democratic-controlled Congress. However, since 1995, when the Republicans gained control over Congress, voucher proposals have gained support. In the spring of 2000, for example, the Senate Republican majority pushed through major changes in the Health, Education, Labor and Pensions Committee. In the proposed Senate Bill 2, the GOP plan would allow ten states to turn Title I into a "portable" voucher program. In these states, Title I funds would follow the students even when they enroll in nonpublic schools. The GOP plan also identifies over 7,000 failing Title I schools where students would be allowed to transfer to other public schools if the schools' performance does not improve in four years (*CQ Weekly* March 11, 2000, 541–42). Regardless of which political party dominates the Congress and the White House in 2001, there is an increasing likelihood that an experimental program on Title I voucher may be implemented.

Conclusion: Making Better Use of Federal Title I Resources

The history of Title I implementation suggests a broadening agenda for school reform (see Table 3.1), thereby creating a paradox for the future of this major federal program. On the one hand, the original antipoverty goal of Title I has received long term, stable, bipartisan support, albeit interrupted by partisan contention in Congress during 1995. On the other hand, this federal commitment does not constitute "an entitlement" and is increasingly dependent on the program's track record of academic productivity. Although it is unlikely that Title I will significantly narrow the gap between disadvantaged students and their peers, it is important for the federal government to become more strategic in the use of resources to improve schooling opportunities.

A major challenge for Title I policy, then, is to decide where to allocate federal resources that would bring about better life chances for at-risk students. I suggest two areas for greater federal attention. First, major federal support is needed to deal with the concentration effects in inner-city schools. Clearly, the ecological context of urban schools has changed significantly since the 1965 enactment of the original ESEA. At that time, the nation had extensive rural poverty, its central cities were economically stable, and suburbs were emerging as viable communities. By the 1990s, we see a widening educational gap between the central city and its surrounding suburbs. This is especially evident in major metropolitan areas, where schools in outlying suburban communities are predominantly white and those in central cities serve primarily minority, low-income pupils. Clearly, to combat concentration effects in the classroom, schools in major urban centers need additional resources (federal and otherwise) to create incentives to attract highly qualified teachers, fill chronic staffing shortages in science and mathematics, and strengthen professional development in subject areas and new technologies.

The second area in which a federal role can make a difference is in helping Title I schools to build and sustain their organizational capacity. Regardless of whether Title I is converted to a voucher experiment or restructured after a CSRD model, what goes on inside the schoolhouse is critical to learning and teaching. To facilitate better conditions for learning, Title I policy can be less regulatory but more supportive in instructional and curriculum issues. Federal programs should focus less on auditing compliance and more on within-school coordination between Title I and regular instruction. Federal resources can provide incentives to schoolwide programs to monitor and address learning gaps among racial and ethnic groups. Technical training can also help teachers to conduct more effective assessment of progress and the needs of their students in meeting standards-based curriculum. To that end, disadvantaged children would be better served if they were taught the core academic curriculum in regular classrooms, placed in heterogeneous groups, and asked to live up to higher academic expectations. In short, federal policy can move away from the "compliance mentality" and become a supportive partner in making a difference in classroom learning.

References

Bodilly, S. and M. Berends. 1999. Necessary district support for comprehensive school reform. In *Hard Work for Good Schools: Facts Not Fads in Title I Reform*, ed. G. Orfield and E. DeBray. Cambridge, Mass.: Harvard University, Civil Rights Project.

Elmore, R. 1980. Backward mapping: Implementation research and policy decisions. *Political Science Quarterly* 94(4): 601–16.

Kanstoroom, M. and T. Palmaffy. Forthcoming. Using market forces to make Title I more effective. In *Accountability, Efficiency and Equity Issues in Title I Schoolwide Program Implementation*, ed. K. Wong and M. Wang. Greenwich, Conn.: Information Age Publishing.

Kirst, M. 1988. The federal role and Chapter 1: Rethinking some basic assumptions. In *Federal Aid to the Disadvantaged: What Future for Chapter 1?,* ed. D. Doyle and B. Cooper. London: Falmer Press.

Lowi, T. 1964. American business, public policy, case studies, and political theory. *World Politics* 16(4): 677–715.

Martin, R. and P. McClure. 1969. *Title I of ESEA: Is it helping poor children?* Washington, D.C.: Washington Research Project of the Southern Center for Studies in Public Policy and the NAACP Legal Defense of Education Fund.

McLaughlin, M. 1987. Learning from experience: Lessons form policy implementation. *Educational Evaluation and Policy Analysis* 9(2): 171–78.

———. 1990. The Rand change agent study revisited: Macro perspective and realities. *Educational Researcher* 19(9): 11–16.

McLaughlin, M. and P. Berman. *Federal Program Supporting Educational Change Vol. 8*, 1978, Washington, D.C.: U.S. Office of Education.

Millsap, M.A., B. Turnbull, M. Moss, N. Brigham, B. Gamse, and E. Marks. 1992. *The Chapter 1 implementation study: Interim report*. Washington, D.C.: U.S. Government Printing Office.

National Association of State Coordinators of Compensatory Education. 1996. *Distinguished schools report 1995–1996 school year: Title I schoolwide projects*. Washington, D.C.: Author.

Peterson, P. E. 1981. *City limits*. Chicago: University of Chicago Press.

Peterson, P. E. and C. Noyes. 1997. School choice in Milwaukee. In *New schools for a new century*, ed. D. Ravitch and J. Viteritti. New Haven, Conn.: Yale University Press.

Peterson, P. E., B. Rabe, and K. Wong. 1986. *When federalism works*. Washington, D.C.: Brookings Institution.

Ravitch, D. and J. Viteritti, eds. 1997. *New schools for a new century*. New Haven, Conn.: Yale University Press.

Schenck, E. A. and S. Beckstrom. 1993. *Chapter I schoolwide project study: Final report*. Hampton, N.H.: RMC Research.

Slavin, R. E., N. A. Madden, L. J. Dolan, B. A. Wasik, S. Ross, L. Smith, and M. Dianda. 1996. Success for all: A summary of research. *Journal of Education for Students Placed at Risk* I(1): 41–76.

Smith, M. S. 1988. Selecting students and services for Chapter 1. In *Federal aid to the disadvantaged: What future for Chapter 1?*, ed. D. Doyle and B. Cooper. London: Falmer Press.

Stringfield, S., M. A. Millsap, R. Herman, N. Yoder, N. Brigham, P. Nesselrodt, E. Schaffer, N. Karweit, M. Levin, and R. Stevens. 1997. *Urban and suburban/rural special strategies for educating disadvantaged children: Final report*. Washington, D.C.: U.S. Government Printing Office.

Stringfield, S., L. Winfield, M. A. Millsap, M. Puma, B. Gamse, and B. Randall. 1994. *Urban and suburban/rural special strategies for educating disadvantaged children: First year report*. Washington, D.C.: U.S. Government Printing Office.

Timar, T. 1992. Program design and assessment strategies in Chapter 1. In *Rethinking policy for at-risk students*, ed. K. K. Wong and M. C. Wang. Berkeley, Calif.: McCutchan.

Turnbull, B. J., S. Zeldin, and T. Cain. 1990. *State administration of the amended Chapter 1 program*. Washington, D.C.: Policy Studies Associates.

U.S. Congress. 1965. The Elementary and Secondary Education Act of 1965, Pub. L. 89–10, 89th Cong., 1st Sess., 11 April 1965, 779 Stat.27, Sec.201.

U.S. Department of Education. 1992. *National assessment of the Chapter 1 program: The interim report*. Washington, D.C.: U.S. Government Printing Office.

———. 1993. *Reinventing Chapter 1: The current Chapter 1 program and new directions, final report of the national assessment of the Chapter 1 program*. Washington, D.C.: U.S. Government Printing Office.

U.S. General Accounting Office. 1992. *Compensatory education: Most Chapter 1 funds in eight districts used for classroom services*. Washington D.C.: Author.

Walberg, H. 1998. Uncompetitive American schools: Causes and cures. In *Brookings Papers on Education Policy 1998*, ed. D. Ravitch. Washington, D.C.: Brookings Institution.

Wang, M., K. Wong, and J. R. Kim. 1999. The need for developing procedural accountability in Title I schoolwide programs. In *Hard work for good schools: Facts not fads in Title I reform*, ed. G. Orfield and E. DeBray. Cambridge, Mass.: Harvard University, Civil Rights Project.

Wilson, W. J. 1987. *The truly disadvantaged*. Chicago: University of Chicago Press.

Winfield, L. F. and R. Hawkins. 1993. *Longitudinal effects of Chapter 1 schoolwide projects on the achievement of disadvantaged students.* Baltimore, Md.: Johns Hopkins University Press.

Wong, K. K. 1990. *City choices: Education and housing.* Albany: State University of New York Press.

———. 1999. *Funding public schools: Politics and policy.* Lawrence: University Press of Kansas.

———. 2000. Chicago school reform: From decentralization to integrated governance. *Journal of Educational Change* 1(1): 97–105.

Wong, K. and S. Meyer. 1998. Title I schoolwide programs: A synthesis of findings from recent evaluation. *Educational Evaluation and Policy Analysis* 20(2): 115–36.

Wong, K., G. Sunderman, and J. Lee. 1997. Redesigning the federal compensatory education program: Lessons from the implementation of the Title I schoolwide projects. In *Implementing school reform: Practice and policy imperatives*, ed. M. Wang and K. Wong. Philadelphia: Temple University Press.

———. 1997. Redesigning the federal compensatory education program: Lessons from the implementation of the Title I schoolwide projects. In *Implementing school reform: Practic and policy imperatives*, ed. M. C. Wong and K. Wong. Philadelphia: Temple University Center for Research in Human Development and Education.

Chapter 4

Inclusive Education in High Stakes, High Poverty Environments: The Case of Students with Learning Disabilities in Indiana's Urban Schools and the Graduation Qualifying Examination

Genevieve Manset
and
Sandra Washburn

The inclusion movement, and the introduction of high stakes, minimum competency tests (MCT) as a requirement for graduation, are two school reforms that have particular implications for high poverty secondary schools. High-poverty schools generally have a higher percentage of students who are low-achieving, drop out, and fail MCTs. In addition, students from impoverished families are more at risk for developing a learning disability. The relatively high proportions of students at-risk for school failure in high-poverty schools render these schools more sensitive to reforms that target the lowest achieving students than schools that primarily serve students from households with middle and upper incomes. Both the inclusion movement, and MCT reforms are designed to address the instruction of low achieving students. These reforms involve both similar students and draw on the same limited resources. Success, therefore, is dependent on the degree to which the reforms share goals as well. In this chapter, the goals of the inclusion and use of minimum competency graduation exams are examined. Findings are discussed in light of implications for high-poverty schools.

A Study of Conflicting Goals

Goals of Inclusive Education for Students with Learning Disabilities

The movement towards inclusive education for students with learning disabilities began in the 1980s, not many years after students with learning disabilities were guaranteed the right to a free and appropriate education through the Education of All Handicapped Children Act (P.L. 94-142, now known as the Individuals with Disabilities Education Act, or IDEA). Advocates of inclusion, referred to early on as the Regular Education Initiative, proposed a system that would meet the individual needs of these students without resorting to pull-out instruction and the maintenance of a "second system" (Goetz and Sailor 1990; Reschly 1988; Reynolds, Wang, and Walberg 1987; Sigmon 1990; Wang, Reynolds, and Walberg 1986, 1988; Will 1984). The essential goals of inclusion can not adequately be discussed outside the context of special education for students with learning disabilities. Learning Disabilities (LD) is essentially a Western construct created to describe a neurologically based disorder that was first identified at the early part of this century. Educators and psychologists were puzzled by a phenomenon they witnessed a small percentage of students. These students appeared on all accounts to function normally, had adequate access to literacy instruction, tested within a normal range on intelligence tests, and yet failed to learn to read. Students were described as having minimum brain damage (Bender 1998). Later the term *dyslexia* was used to describe this inexplicable failure to learn to read. Currently, the legal diagnosis of Learning Disabled is used to describe those students with intelligence in the normal range, but have a severe difficulties with academics, generally reading or writing but also frequently math. Academic problems often stem from disorders in language processing, auditory perception, or deficiencies in visual or auditory short-term memory. Often there are related deficits in attention and inappropriate social and behavior skills. While their reading abilities vary greatly, on average, high school. On average, high school students with LD read at about a fifth grade level (Gajar, Goodman, and McAfee 1993). A small percentage of students with LD will attend college. Overall, secondary students with LD are at higher risk for dropping out of high school, incarceration, substance abuse, unemployment, and underemployment. There is no known cure for LD, although there are instructional approaches that can accelerate learning and provide strategic supports so that students can be successful. The goals for secondary special education were to provide remedial and compensatory instruction for these students, and to assist secondary students in their transition to adulthood. This assistance went beyond academics to address the often common social and behavioral skill deficits that these student exhibit. These services were provided in a variety of settings, ranging from special separate schools and classrooms to resource rooms students attended part time. These goals were naturally incorporated into those of inclusive education (see Table 4.1).

Criticism of special education grew as the identification of students as having a learning disability became increasingly common in public schools. Since the introduction of PL. 94-142, the number of students identified as Learning Disabled more than doubled by the 1988 school year when close to 2 million children were receiving services (U.S. Department of Education 1989). Advocates for inclusion questioned the reliability of identification of students as Learning Disabled, efficacy of pull-out programs, curriculum misalignment, and the cost-effectiveness of maintaining a dual system when students with LD often resembled their nondisabled, low achieving peers. Proponents advocated for consolidation of special and general education to create an educational system that addressed the individual differences of all children within the regular classroom.

To inclusion advocates, it was general education, rather than special education, that should be reformed. They argued that students with LD were created in part by failure of general education teachers to share responsibility for the lowest achieving children and federal policy that encouraged the perception that children at the extremes of academic ability were the responsibility of specialists. Advocates suggested alternatives to traditional special education that they felt were both preferable and feasible. School-wide model inclusion programs were designed with some success (see Manset and Semmel 1998 for a review), and many schools have moved toward inclusion models over the past two decades (McLesky, Henry, and Hodges 1988). The preponderance of research, however, was conducted on the elementary level, where the skill deficits of students with LD were not as great as those of students in secondary programs (Schumaker and Deshler 1988). The goals of the inclusion movement went beyond appropriate individualized instruction to access to mainstream curriculum through the elimination of pull-out programs, advocacy for students with LD, and the support of general educators through resources and collaboration.

TABLE 4.1

Goals of Inclusion and Graduation Qualifying Examinations in Secondary Programs

	Goals of Reform	
	Inclusion	*Graduation Qualifying Examinations*
Curriculum and Instruction	Provide appropriate, individualized instruction (remedial and compensatory)	Align Basic Skills Curriculum
	Support Transition to Adulthood	Improve Instruction in low performing schools
	Access to Mainstream Curriculum	Standardize Diploma
Resources and Staffing	External Support for General Educators	Increase instructional resources targeting minimum competency in basic skills
	Consolidate Instructional and Remedial Resources	
Climate	Advocacy for Students with LD	High, Common Standards
	Increased expectations for students with LD	Increased Expectations for Lowest Achieving Students and Schools
	Shared Responsibility for Students with LD	
Social/Behavioral	Social Integration	
	Self-advocacy, increased independence	
	Social/Behavioral Skills instruction	

Goals of Minimum Competency Tests

State and district assessment programs have been a central part of public school reform for the last fifty years. Accountability programs based primarily on standardized tests were instituted in an effort to affect the content and quality of education. Typically these exams are given on a regular basis to students, twice in elementary school, once in middle school, and once in high school. Educators and administrators can use test results to inform decisions about the direction of resources and instructional effort.

Increasingly, high stakes have been attached to these examinations. These high stakes may consist of the public posting of results (which indirectly can affect local property values), cash benefits, or the loss or revenue, accreditation, or local control. High stakes are imposed on schools by policymakers as a way to control curricular content and performance in schools. High-stakes accountability programs have also been used by politicians as a relatively simple and inexpensive way to demonstrate a commitment to education and high standards. However, there is little evidence that fifty years of this essentially "carrot-and-stick" approach to pedagogical reform has improved public education (Airasian 1988; Linn 2000). There is also evidence that the addition of high stakes corrupts and inflates test scores. For instance, simply having students practice with the testing format alone will increase test scores. Strong gains are usually documented within the first four years of a test, and then level off after that (Linn 2000). These initial gains after the introduction of new tests look particularly good for the politicians who support the high stakes examinations. Although policymakers may wish to take the credit for this increase, because of the possibility of test score inflation, gains may not necessarily reflect actual improvement in student skills.

In the late 1970s, minimum competency tests (MCT) were introduced as a requirement for graduation from high school. Graduation examinations, like other high-stakes tests, are associated with the application of high standards to education. They differ from other high-stakes examinations, however, in that the stakes are directed at the student rather than the school or district. The goals of MCTs, like other high-stakes examinations are to force an alignment of the curriculum, create common standards, and increase expectations for the lowest achieving students. In addition, the intent is to improve instruction in low performing schools, often times by increasing instructional resources towards basic skills instruction. Since their inception, MCT have been linked to higher drop-out rates and the narrowing of curriculum, particularly for those students at-risk for school failure (MacMillan et al. 1990; Manset and Washburn 2000). The impact of MCT are particularly felt by low-achieving students, students from ethnic minority groups, students in urban schools, and students with disabilities (Linn 2000; MacMillan et al. 1990; Manset and Washburn 1999). Despite the differential impact of mandating MCT, states have continued the practice and courts have upheld states' right to define the requirements for a diploma (Phillips 1993; Thurlow, Ysseldyke, and Anderson 1995).

Inclusive Education in High Stakes, High Poverty Environments

Indiana, like many states that have MCTs, requires students with LD to pass the graduation requirement in order to receive a diploma. The inclusion of students in this test is partially influenced by the fact that beginning this year, with the passing of the latest version of the federal Individuals with Disabilities Education Act (IDEA 1997), all students with disabilities must be included in state and district accountability programs. This requirement came about as a result of concerns that students with disabilities were being ignored by districts because they were not required to take high-stakes tests. There were also indications that students were being over-identified as having a learning disability. Once students were labeled, they would not be included in the testing pool and therefore would not lower school scores (McGill-Franzen and Allington 1993). These arguments were made primarily to include students with disabilities in high-stakes assessment programs in general, not necessarily in exit examinations. The justification for requiring all students, including students with disabilities, to pass the exit examination is one of fairness. That is, if there is going to high standards, the content of these standards must be the same for all students. It suggests a tough stance with high expectations.

The intent of inclusive education is to educate students with LD in mainstream settings. The success of inclusion is dependent on whether goals of inclusion are consistent with those of general education: in this case, whether the goals of inclusion can be met in secondary settings where there are MCTs required for graduation. The increase of resources and attention directed at basic skills instruction is evident in both reform efforts. However, the efforts to standardize the diploma contradicts efforts toward creating an appropriate, individualized curriculum for students with learning disabilities.

The Case of the Indiana's Graduation Qualifying Examination (GQE)

Beginning in 2000, all students, including students with LD, were required to pass the English/Language Arts and Mathematics portions of Indiana's ISTEP+ Graduation Qualifying Examination (GQE).[1] As a part of Project EXIT, the authors have examined the research to date on the new graduation requirement, as well as administrators perspectives on the impact of the examination on students with LD (Manset and Washburn 2000a; 2000b; 1999). Here we report on related outcomes for urban schools on the exam and administrators' perspectives on the alignment of the goals for students with LD and the content of the GQE. The purpose here is to determine whether administrators perceive the goals of inclusion for students with LD and mandatory exit exam as contradictory.

Methods

Data Collection

All data except passing rates for students with LD were made available by the state of Indiana (Indiana Department of Education). Because passing rates are currently not available in a disaggregate form for student with disabilities, we collected this information as a part of Project EXIT high school principal survey. In the survey, we requested a count of students with LD in their school who had attempted the ISTEP+ (language arts/English and Mathematics) and the number of students with LD who had passed the exam.

Survey Instrument

Two related surveys (Manset and Washburn 1998a, 1998b) were designed for this study based on an extensive review of the literature on minimum competency examinations (Manset and Washburn 2000). The survey consisted of five major parts with a total of sixty-five closed items. Questions pertained to the current and future impact of requiring the passing of the GQE for graduation, remediation efforts, and instructional practices and programming that predict success on the examination. In addition to these questions, administrators were asked whether requiring the GQE contributed

[1]GQE and ISTEP+ are often used interchangeably when referring to the exam.

to students' decisions to drop out of school as well as an open ended question pertaining to alignment of goals for students with learning disabilities and the content of the examination. The survey also contained three open-ended questions that are not addressed here.

Participants

Directors or assistant directors of special education responsible for secondary students with disabilities in all planning districts as well as all high school principals in Indiana received a survey. Of this initial sample, representatives from 60 percent of the planning districts and 57 percent of the public high schools were responded (N=262). Graduation rates and poverty rates for the high schools represented by principals as indicated by the percent of students receiving free or reduced lunch approximate the mean values for the state as a whole (See Table 4.2).

VARIABLES

Socioeconomic status (SES) was calculated using the percent of students not participating in the free lunch program at the school. *Graduation rate* is the percentage of students graduating with a diploma. *Attendance rate* is the mean percentage of enrolled students attending daily. *Students per teacher* is the mean number of students per teacher in core classes. *FTE non-core subjects* is the number of full-time equivalents of teachers per student teaching noncore courses. And, *Seniors taking SAT* is the percent of twelfth-graders taking SAT. *Percent Passing English / Language Arts* is a variable representing the percent of students passing the language arts portion of the ISTEP+ in 1998, while *Percent Passing Mathematics* is a variable representing the percent of students passing the mathematics portion of the ISTEP+ in 1998. *LD Passing English / Language Arts* is a variable representing the percent of students with LD passing the language arts portion of the ISTEP+ in 1998, whereas *LD Passing Mathematics* is a variable representing the percent of students with learning disabilities passing the mathematics portion of the ISTEP+ in 1998.

Data Analysis

Mean differences between outcomes for urban schools and schools in the sample as a whole were compared using a one-sample t test, with two-tailed significance determined at $p < 0.05$. The one

TABLE 4.2
Mean Values for School Level Factors and Outcome Variables of Schools

School Level Factor	*All Schools (n=148)*	*Urban Schools (N=25)*
Attendance Rate		
M	95.18	94.06*
SD	1.40	2.30
Graduation Rate		
M	87.83	82.24*
SD	7.20	.75
Enrollment		
M	898.45	1208.11*
SD	553.27	435.98
SES (Students Not Receiving Free Lunch)		
M	88.32	78.74*
SD	8.40	11.20
Seniors Taking SAT		
M	52.01	48.00*
SD	12.64	16.23
% Passing Graduation Exit Exam		
English/Language Arts		
M	72.03	65.26*
SD	9.70	12.63
Mathematics		
M	60.41	50.88*
SD	12.48	14.93
% Students with LD Passing Graduation Exam		
English/Language Arts		
M	20.93	14.00*
SD	17.70	17.60
Mathematics		
M	17.33	12.66*
SD	17.10	14.20
Students with LD Taking Graduation Exam[a]		
M	19.44	27.23*
SD	20.36	18.14
Rate of Students with LD Taking Graduation Exam		
M	2.21	2.23*
SD	1.45	1.56

(continued)

TABLE 4.2 (*cont.*)
Mean Values for School Level Factors and Outcome Variables of Schools

School Level Factor	*All Schools (n=148)*	*Large Urban Schools (N=25)*
FTE per student (Non Core Teachers)[a]		
M	0.02	0.03*
SD	0.01	0.01
Students per Teacher (Core Classes)[a]		
M	29.68	29.57
SD	3.86	4.21

Note. The values represent mean percentages unless noted otherwise.

[a]Values represent numbers or students.
*Statistically significantly different than sample as a whole at $p < 0.01$.

open ended question related to the goals for students with learning disabilities and the content of the ISTEP+ was analyzed qualitatively by coding for themes using a constant comparative method (Glaser and Strauss 1967).

Results

Means Comparisons of School-level Data

Means and standard deviations for both predictor and outcome variables are presented in Table 4.2. As anticipated, urban schools have a student population with a significantly lower socioeconomic status than schools as a whole. Urban schools also have a significantly lower rate of graduation and percentage of seniors taking the SAT exam. A greater number and rate of urban school students taking the exam are identified as having a learning disability.

For all schools in the sample, 71 percent of tenth grade students passed the English/language arts portion and 60 percent passed the mathematics portion of the ISTEP+ examination. In stark contrast, on average, only 21 percent of students with LD passed the English/language arts portion and only 17 percent of students with LD passed the mathematics portion of the examination. For all students, the passing rates are notably lower than the current mean graduation rate of 88 percent. Urban school students, and students with LD were also less likely to pass the examination than students in general. In urban schools, 65 percent of students passed the English/Language Arts examination, and 51 percent passed the mathematics portion of the examination. Only 14 percent of students with LD in urban schools passed the English/language arts examination and 13 percent passed the mathematics examination.

Summary of Open-Ended Question: "Is the content of the ISTEP+ (GQE) aligned with the goals of most students with learning disabilities?"

On the questionnaire, the final item read "Is the content of the ISTEP+ (GQE) aligned with the goals of most students with learning disabilities? Please comment." A total of 189 administrators responded to this question. Most respondents, in addition to explicitly stating either "yes" or "no," also elaborated or otherwise commented. Using a constant comparative method, the analysis generated six major themes or categories, each with several sub-themes. In order of prominence the major themes were: 1) Education goals are not aligned (49%); 2) education goals are aligned; 3) educational goals are aligned, but reservations exist; 4) schools are making progress in this direction; 5) goals are aligned for some students or with some parts of the GQE, and; 6) no stand, with or without explanation (see Table 4.3).

No, Content of ISTEP+ and Goals are Not Aligned. As stated above, close to half of the respondents denied that most student goals are aligned with the content of the exam; however, it is important to note that the comments that followed such a declaration mentioned little of postschool outcomes or terminal education goals. Administrator comments that denied the alignment between goals and test content primarily communicated one idea: *that the content of the state GQE requires skill levels that are not realistic aspirations or expectation for students with LD.* Most respondents stopped at that, simply stating something akin to "many students with learning disabilities cannot achieve at the level required" to meet the minimum standard required to pass the graduation exam. Several respondents specifically mentioned that the nature of the "disability itself involves processing problems" that prevent students with disabilities from demonstrating "true" competence given the nature of the assessment format. Likewise, many administrators specifically pointed to the frequency of "reading comprehension difficulties" among students with LD and given this, charged that the test

TABLE 4.3

Summary of Responses to the Question: "Is the content of the ISTEP+ (GQE) aligned with the goals of most students with learning disabilities?

No, Content Is Not Aligned With The Goals Of Most Students With Learning Disabilities	*Yes, Content Is Aligned With The Goals Of Most Students With Learning Disabilities*
Content of the state GQE requires skill levels that are not realistic aspirations or expectation for students with learning disabilities.	Support for the standards as reasonable expectations for earning a high school diploma and a belief that all students ought to meet these expectations for post-secondary success.
Students with learning disabilities had not experienced adequate exposure to a school curriculum that focused on the essential skills.	Participation in the general education curriculum assures that the educational goals of students with learning disabilities were aligned with the content of the GQE.
Lack of support for a standardized (i.e. non-individualized) demonstration of the essential skills.	Development of Individual Education Plans (IEP's) that considered the essentials skills included in the GQE.
Students with disabilities have post school aspirations that would be better served by content that is not adequately reflected by the ISTEP+.	Educational goals are aligned, but reservations exist, such as goals are aligned for some students or with some parts of the GQE.
Prohibition of any testing modifications and certain testing accommodations is unfair to students with learning disabilities.	**Schools are making progress in this direction [toward alignment].**

required too much reading and reading at a proficiency level incommensurate with their achievement levels. The following comment provides an apt summary of the majority of comments that comprised this theme: "We are testing students in their areas of disability with a testing format that is not conducive to their success."

Four subthemes emerged form the remainder of the comments. First was *consideration of postschool outcomes.* Many responses reflected the idea that students with disabilities might have postschool aspirations that would be better served by content that is not adequately reflected by the ISTEP+ (vocational skills, technological training, and practical mathematics were mentioned). Additionally, respondents acknowledged that students were not only more capable of demonstrating competence with more performance-oriented tasks, but that they actually preferred these (hands-on tasks).

Second, a number of administrators shared concerns that students with learning disabilities had not experienced *adequate exposure to a school curriculum that focused on the essential skills.* One respondent specifically mentioned "the content of special education program," another acknowledged, "we have not challenged the LD students" whereas others spoke more generally of timing within the school curriculum, or lack of curriculum alignment, and remediation needs that interfere with teaching more advanced topics.

A third idea can be characterized as *lack of support for a standardized demonstration of the essential skills.* Administrators acknowledged student diversity in achievement and learning styles and condemned the "one size fits all" approach of the ISTEP+. Many specifically mentioned lack of attention to individual needs in terms of educational goals being reflected within the content of the GQE.

Last, administrators declared that the *prohibition of any testing modifications and certain testing accommodations* was unfair to students with LD, specifically those for whom particular modifications and accommodations are specified in their IEPs and allowed during throughout the school year. One comment pointed to students' abilities to compensate for their disabilities in natural environments, compensation strategies that are disallowed during the test administration.

A few responses charged that the GQE is not aligned with anyone's educational goals, but that it is "a blatant misuse of funds, "a political pawn to 'finger point' blame. . . ." *Yes, GQE is aligned with goals of most students with LD.* Several subthemes emerged. The most prominent subtheme can be characterized as *support for the standards as reasonable expectations for earning a high school diploma and a belief that all students ought to meet these expectations for post-secondary success.* For example, one administrator stated,

"Yes, the proficiencies are well developed standards that reflect higher order thinking which should be required of all students."

Another prominent idea reflected a belief that *participation in the general education curriculum* assured that the educational goals of students with LD were aligned with the content of the GQE. A related set of comments specifically affirmed that school(s) had aligned the curriculum with the essential skills and that students with learning disabilities have access to this curriculum, either through general education or special education classes.

Responses that referenced the *development of Individual Education Plans (IEPs) that considered the essentials skills* included in the GQE generated a fourth subtheme. One respondent stated "yes" that the goals were aligned and added a comment that the majority of students with LD could pass the GQE if "our Special Ed program is working as it should" and another affirmed the same, adding "if they complete remediation sessions." Another principal supported the essential skills as goals for all students. "Yes, after all, it is a ninth grade proficiency tests. One hundred percent of all of our kids need [these essential] skills.

Discussion and Conclusions

These findings suggest considerations for current policy and questions for future research. In this sample, urban schools had a higher rate of economically disadvantaged students, students with learning disabilities, and students that fail to pass the GQE. It can be anticipated that the graduation rate, already relatively low in these areas, will be further depressed by these new graduation examinations. These qualities of urban schools render them particularly vulnerable to a misalignment of the goals of inclusion and mandatory graduation examinations.

Clearly, the passing rates for students with LD were extremely low relative to those for students in general. They were also, however, variable from school to school and it is that variability that is of interest to educators. Unfortunately, deriving meaning from relatively high passing rates is difficult, given that for any one school district, the ability level of students who are referred and identified as having a learning disability in itself varies. For a high school to have a high passing rate of students with LD on the exam can be interpreted several ways. At first thought, high passing rates may indicate that schools have exceptional practice, commitment, focus, and expectations for their students with LD. On the other hand, it may simply indicate that in those schools, the students with LD are relatively high achieving as compared to those students identified as having LD in another district. Or, in that school, students with LD with relatively low academic skills drop out before they reach the tenth grade. In any case, a higher rate of students with LD taking the examination again underscores the importance of examining the consistency in intent in both reforms, and the practices that stem from those goals. Of course, inclusive programming, curricular changes, and support will become irrelevant issues if students with LD leave school early on in their high school education.

In response to the question of whether the goals of the GQE are aligned with the content of the GQE examination, administrators were almost split in their perspectives. Close to half the respondents felt that there was a misalignment between the examination and goals for their students. Those who feel there is a misalignment between goals for students with LD and GQE content most often refer to the inappropriateness of a nonindividualized curriculum for their students, as well as the unrealistic minimum standard set by the test. In stark contrast, many respondents who felt there was alignment stated that the content and the standards of examination *were appropriate* for students with LD. It is as if there is either confusion or argument over both the characteristics of students with LD and the goals of inclusive education. Interesting enough, both respondents who agreed and disagreed with the alignment between goals and GQE content felt that access to the mainstream curriculum would contribute to success on the test. Those who felt there was misalignment, however, stated that students with LD had not been allowed access to the examination, whereas those who agreed there was alignment felt their students had adequate access and that their IEPs were consistent with the examination.

It is clear from the data that students in urban schools and students with learning disabilities are disproportionably affected by the mandatory graduation examination. The intent of inclusive education is to educate students with LD in the mainstream. The success of inclusion is dependent on whether goals of inclusion are consistent with those of general education. Specifically in this case, whether the goals of inclusive education can be met in secondary settings where minimum competency tests are required for graduation. Although the goal of improving instruction for the lowest achieving students is common to both practices, the creation of a standardized diploma precludes the ability to individualize a program for a student with LD. In urban centers, students from low income or minority populations in essence are held responsible not only for passing a test, but for reforming the poor public education system that contributed to their failure. Those students with LD are, in addition, held responsible for not finding a cure for their disability. It is also evident that administrators are not in agreement that the goals and content of the GQE are aligned, indicating confusion over the direction of a policy that will guarantee the success of secondary students with learning disabilities in high-poverty, high-stakes environments.

References

Baker, J. M. and N. Zigmond. 1995. The meaning and practice of inclusion for students with learning disabilities: Themes and implications from the five cases. *Journal of Special Education* 29: 163–180.

Bender, W. N. 1998. *Learning disabilities: Characteristics, identification, and teaching strategies.* 3rd edition. Needham Heights, Mass.: Allyn and Bacon.

Gajar, A., L. Goodman, and J. McAfee. 1993. *Secondary schools and beyond: Transition of individuals with mild disabilities*. New York: Macmillan.

Glaser, B., and A. Strauss. 1967. *The discovery of grounded theory*. Chicago: Aldine.

Goetz, L., and W. Sailor. 1990. Much ado about babies, murky bath water, and trickle down politics: A reply to Kauffman. *Journal of Special Education* 24: 334–39.

Herman, J. L., and S. Golan. 1990. *Effects of standardized testing on teachers and learning: Another look*. Los Angeles: Center for Research and Improvement.

MacMillan, D., I. Balow, K. Widaman, and R. Hemsley. 1990. *A study of minimum competency tests and their impact: Final report.* Washington, D.C.: U.S. Department of Education.

Manset, G., and S. Washburn. 2000a. Equity through accountability? Mandating minimum competency exit examinations for secondary students with learning disabilities. *Learning Disabilities Research and Practice* 15(3): 160–67.

———. 2000b. Administrators' perspectives of the impact of mandatory graduation qualifying examinations for secondary students with learning disabilities. Paper presented at the annual conference of the American Educational Research Association, New Orleans, LA.

———. 1998a. EXIT Survey for Directors of Special Education (DSE-EXIT). Unpublished survey, Indiana University.

———. 1998b. EXIT Survey for Principals (P-EXIT). Unpublished survey, Indiana University.

Mcleskey, J., D. Henry, and D. Hodges. 1998. Inclusion: Where is it happening? *Teaching Exceptional Children* 31(1): 4–10.

Reschly, D. J. 1988. Special education reform: School psychology revolution. *School Psychology Review* 17: 459–75.

Reynolds, M. C., M. C. Wang, and H. J. Walberg. 1987. The necessary restructuring of special and regular education. *Exceptional Children* 53: 391–98.

Schumaker, J. B., and D. D. Deshler. 1988. Implementing the regular education initiative in secondary schools: A different ball game. *Journal of Learning Disabilities* 21(1): 36–42.

Shepard, L. A., and K. C. Doughty. 1991. *Effects of high-stakes testing on instruction*. Paper presented at the Annual Meeting of the American Ecuational Research Association (Chicago, IL, April 1991). (ERIC Document Reproduction Services No. ED 337 468).

Sigmon, S. 1990. *Critical voices on special education*. Albany: State University of New York Press.

Smith, M. L. 1991. Put it to the test: The effects of external testing on teachers. *Educational Researcher* 20(5): 8–11.

Thurlow, M. L., J. E. Ysseldyke, and C. L. Anderson. 1995. *High school graduation requirements: What's happening for students with disabilities?* Report No. 20. Minnesota: National Center on Educational Outcomes. Available at http://www.coled.umn.edu/NCEO/OnlinePubs/Synthesis20.html.

U.S. Department of Education. 1989. *Eleventh annual report to Congress on the implementation of the education of the handicapped act*. Washington, D.C.: U.S. Government Printing Office.

Wang, M. C., M. C. Reynolds, and H. J. Walberg. 1988. Integrating the children of the second system. *Phi Delta Kappan* 70: 248–51.

———. 1986. Rethinking special education. *Educational Leadership* 44: 26–31.

Will, M. 1984. Let us pause and reflect—But not too long. *Exceptional Children* 51: 11–16.

Chapter 5

Race, Restructuring, and Educational Reform: The Mayoral Takeover of the Detroit Public Schools

Barry M. Franklin

On May 4, 2000, Detroit's reform school board selected Kenneth Burnely, the then superintendent of the Colorado Springs Public Schools, as its choice for the city schools' first permanent chief executive officer (CEO) (Miller 2000; Nichols and Harmon 2000; Walsh-Sarnecki and Schmitt 2000). His appointment marked the culmination of a year and a half struggle, modeled in large part after the 1995 mayoral takeover of the Chicago public schools, to replace the city's elected school board with one appointed by the mayor and to replace a traditional superintendent with the new position of CEO. It was a battle that pitted segments of the city's majority African-American population against each other, that brought Detroit's largely African-American Democratic legislative delegation into conflict with both the city's African-American Democratic Mayor, Dennis Archer, and the virtually all white Republican dominated state legislature, and created a working alliance around school reform between Mayor Archer and Michigan's Republican governor, John Engler. This battle over the governance of the Detroit public schools, then, provides a good case study of an effort to transfer a reform initiative, in this case a mayoral takeover, from one setting to another and the resulting pattern of conflicts and alliances over school reform that at least one city school system is currently experiencing. In this essay, I will examine the debates surrounding the takeover legislation from the end of 1998 through its passage in March 1999, explore the resulting pattern of discord and agreement, look at how issues of race played themselves out in these engagements, and consider what these battles tell us about the prospects of a mayoral takeover as a reform strategy.

The approach that I will take in this essay is that of the critical-empirical review. Developed by St. John and Hossler (1998), this method first seeks to place the reform, in this case mayoral takeovers, in a historical context. In doing so, the essay provides the reader some sense of how the reform came about. With that setting established, the review then considers the ideological claims of its supporters and opponents, the theoretical frameworks underlying those claims, and the research deployed by proponents and opponents to support their assertions about the reform in question. Finally, the review explores the Detroit reform in light of what existing research tells us about mayoral takeovers as a reform strategy.

Situating Mayoral Takeovers in a Historical Context

Despite our historic tradition of local control, the ultimate legal authority of the states for public education has made for a long history of state intervention. New York Governor William Seward's successful effort in 1842 to replace the New York City Public School Society with a truly public school system governed by a central board of education and a number of ward boards can be viewed as a state intervention. So, too, can the effort of the New York State Legislature some fifty years later in 1896 to abolish the ward boards in favor of a centralized system of public schooling in New York City (Ravitch 1974). Similarly, the attempt of the California legislature in 1870 to end San Francisco's exemption from the state's textbook adoption law constitutes another nineteenth century example of this practice (Tyack, James, and Benavot 1987).

There have been at least two twentieth century precedents that have lent support for such interventions. One has been the actions of the federal courts in the aftermath of the *Brown* decision to intervene in the operation of local school districts to implement desegregation. Although occurring at the federal level, an array of strategies including the appointment of special masters to administer public school systems, the establishment of intradistrict and interdistrict busing programs, the adjustment of attendance boundaries, and merging of urban and suburban schools, have bestowed a sense of reasonableness about the prospect of external takeovers (Armour 1995; Douglas 1995; Orfield et al. 1996). A second, and perhaps more direct precedent has been the actions of state governments to restructure school systems that have been identified as failing because of financial difficulties and/or the academic underperformance of their students

(Education Commission of the States 1999; Hunter and Swan 1999; Henig et al. 1999; Kirst 1992). In some instances, as was the case in 1996 in New York City, the state legislature gave the city school's chancellor new authority over the systems thirty-two local boards of education (Purday 1996). In other instances, such as in Newark, New Jersey, the state itself took over the administration and operation of the affected school system (Anyon 1997). And in still other takeovers, including Chicago and Cleveland, state legislation authorized the ceding of authority for operating public schools to the mayors of the cities in which these districts were located (Bryk, Kerbow, and Rollow 1997; Eisinger 2000; Harmon 1996; Mirel 1993; McWhirter and Kennedy 1999; Terry 1995).[1] Detroit represents the latest instance of such a mayoral takeover.

There have been a number of reasons offered to justify these state takeovers. First, this reform is seen as a reasonable response to popular dissatisfaction with the effectiveness of local school bureaucracies. Second, a state takeover is viewed as a mechanism for achieving financial and academic accountability in failing school systems. Third, a state intervention is often promoted as a response to current demands for the structural reform of public schools. Finally, mayoral takeovers fit nicely with an increasingly popular belief that a new group of mayors have come on the scene who possess both the will and ability to overcome the problems facing city schools (Henig et al. 1999; Kirst and Bulkley 2000).

There were in Michigan a number of events during the last ten or so years that had created a climate conducive to a state takeover of the Detroit public schools. In the late 1980s state officials had in fact threatened the Detroit Board of Education with a takeover if they could not resolve the district's financial problems. In 1989 Mayor Coleman Young had called for the abolition of the Board of Education and direct mayoral control as a solution to the school system's fiscal difficulties (Mirel 1998). Five years later, the passage of Proposition A, which shifted the support of public schooling from local property taxes to state appropriations, created conditions for a greater role for the state in the management of public education (Henig et al. 1999; Arsen, Plank, and Sykes 2000; Kearney 1994). In 1996, Governor Engler offered Mayor Archer the prospect of managing Detroit's schools, but Archer turned him down (Robles and Christoff 1997). And in his 1997 State of the State address, Michigan's governor had proposed the state takeover of school districts with high dropout rates or high failure rates on state proficiency tests. In that talk, he made specific reference to two low performing, largely African-American school systems, Benton Harbor and

Detroit. ("Text of State of the State Address" 1997; "Comment: Local Control Can't be Used" 1997).

Governor Engler's Mayoral Takeover Plan

In his State of the State address in January 1999, Governor Engler renewed the call that he made two years earlier for a state takeover of failing school districts. Citing the action of the Illinois legislature to give Chicago's Mayor, Richard Daley, the power to appoint the city's school board and the system's CEO, Engler proposed that the legislature give the state's mayors authority over their city's schools. In his words, they should have the authority to "break the bureaucracy, fix the schools, and put our children first." As Engler saw it, this reform in Chicago was the result of a bipartisan and multiracial coalition and it was leading to higher test scores, increased attendance, higher standards, better graduation rates, the end of social promotion, and the reduction of waste, fraud, and corruption in the management of the city schools (Engler 1999).

Hoping to counter Engler's plan even before it was officially presented, the Detroit Board of Education announced some three days before the State of the State address that they would soon be issuing a series of reforms that they labeled as "revolutionary" and "unprecedented." It was a series of reforms, according to one board member, Juan Jose Marinez, that would remind people of the things that were currently happening in the Chicago public schools. Board of Education President Darryl Redmond challenged the need for a state takeover noting that the district was currently enjoying a budget surplus and that scores on the state competency test were on the increase. As Redmond put it, "we're going to shake up the status quo and make sure that never again anyone will be able to point a finger and say, 'there's bad education in the city of Detroit.'" ("Board Calls Its Plan Revolutionary," 1999).

The following day, Redmond went on to criticize Engler on the grounds that his real motive for the proposed takeover was not student achievement but rather the money that he claimed the state would control from the city's 1994 $1.5 billion bond referendum ("Schools Resist State Takeover" 1999). Democratic State Senator Burton Leland, a white member of the Detroit delegation in the legislature, viewed Engler's proposal as having "troubling racial overtones." He likened the takeover to the successful effort of the governor in 1995 to merge Detroit's Recorders Court into the Wayne County Circuit Court. It was a move that many African-American

Detroiters viewed as an attempt to dilute African-American voting strength and the influence of the court's African-American judges as well as retribution for the conviction, in Recorders Court, of two white policemen for the beating death of an African-American Detroiter, Malice Green. As Leland stated, "the notion of a white legislature and white governor dictating to a city that is 80 percent African American and a school district that is 90 percent African American is . . . ridiculous and outrageous" ("Board Calls Its Plan Revolutionary" 1999; "Lessons of the Court Merger" 1999; "Who Will Fix the Schools" 1999).

Legislative Debates Surrounding the Takeover

The following month, Dan DeGrow, the Republican Majority Leader of the Michigan Senate along with three colleagues, two Republicans and a Democrat, introduced a bill, ostensibly to revise the state school code, but in fact written to apply only to Detroit. Key to this legislation was the provision to allow mayors in cities with school districts enrolling at least 100,000 students, the only one in Michigan being Detroit, to appoint a reform school board comprised of five members, each of whom would serve a four year term. It would be the board's responsibility to employ a CEO who would serve at their pleasure. Once this legislation was enacted, the duties and the powers of the elected school board and its officers would be suspended. The proposal was to be in effect for five years, after which time Detroit voters could petition for a referendum on the continuation of the mayoral appointed Board of Education (Michigan Senate 1999).

In Detroit, particularly, the rationale for a mayoral takeover was two-pronged. The city's schools were characterized as having failed academically with a pattern of persistent low achievement, poor state proficiency test scores, low graduation rates, and high drop out rates ("City Schools Must Reform" 1999; "Should State Require" 1999). And at the same time, the district was depicted as inept in its administration of the schools, particularly its management of fiscal affairs. The Board of Education, specifically, was thought to be more interested in offering "perks" to its members than on providing students with "enough textbooks, pencils, and other supplies." ("School Change" 1999; "Detroit's Costly School Board" 1999).

A week after the bill was introduced, Senator DeGrow and Darryl Redmond, the newly elected president of the Detroit Board of Education, presented their differing interpretations on the proposed takeover in an exchange in the *Detroit News*. Invoking the language of the 1983 "A Nation at Risk" report, DeGrow described Detroit's schools as the victim of an "act of war." In this vein, he noted that the city's schools had a graduation rate of 30 percent, that only 6 percent of Detroit's high school students met or exceeded state standards on the High School Proficiency Test, and that only 25 of the city's 245 elementary schools were fully accredited by the state. This was the case, he went on to say, despite the fact that the school system ranked in the top 10 percent in level of expenditures for Michigan school districts and had enjoyed an 18 percent increase in per pupil expenditures since 1967. In this context, DeGrow characterized the takeover bill as an opportunity to reverse this pattern of failure. The proposed legislation was not, he noted, "about process, power, or political agendas. It is about what is best for the children attending the Detroit Public Schools" (DeGrow 1999).

Redmond, painted a distinctly different picture of the condition of the city's schools. The key phrase in his description was "improved significantly." From his perspective, the schools were "a few years ago" in difficult straits both in terms of the academic performance of their students and the management of their finances. At present, however, the district under the leadership of the Board is addressing these problems. He noted that state proficiency test scores have increased, that the city outscored 146 districts in fourth grade mathematics, 231 districts in fifth grade science, and 100 districts in eighth grade writing on state proficiency tests, and that the budget deficit has been replaced by a $93 million surplus. Not surprisingly, Redmond offered a different twist on the issue of accreditation. Ignoring the distinction that DeGrow evidently had made between schools that had received only interim accreditation and those better performing schools that were fully accredited, he claimed that all of Detroit's schools were in fact accredited. Redmond also noted that Detroit did not have the academic and budgetary problems of the Chicago public schools, which seemed to be the model that supporters of the takeover used to justify their efforts.

In addition to challenging the actual assessment of takeover supporters, Redmond injected another issues into the debate, that of local control. Not only did the takeover legislation, in his estimation, fail to address the problems facing the city's schools, it did not "create the conducive collaborative atmosphere for all stakeholders." He went on to say that "this legislation seemingly was created in a vacuum by state bureaucrats in the executive branch without consultation by superintendents, parents or other public school stakeholders" (Redmond 1999).

A few days earlier, Detroit Superintendent Eddie Green had also voiced opposition to the takeover. Like Redmond, he noted that Detroit students need to perform better than they are doing but that that they have made significant progress during the last four years. He stated in that vein that Detroit children were currently outscoring such districts as Grand Rapids, Flint, Lansing, Pontiac, and Muskegon in some areas of the state proficiency tests. Green also wondered why there was such a rush on the part of the state to replace the city's Board of Education. He noted that the Board would soon reveal its own reform plan and that what was called for was a thorough discussion and debate on various proposals for improvement that involved all of the "stakeholders." Finally, Green questioned why Detroit was singled out for a takeover. The initial version of the legislation allowed for a state takeover of any school district that did not meet certain academic and fiscal conditions. He charged, however, that as a result of political pressure, the final version of the legislation was limited to Detroit (Green 1999).

In mid-February, the Board issued its four-part reform plan. First and foremost, parents would be asked to volunteer for forty hours during the year to help in their child's school either in the classroom or on the playground. To increase the likelihood of this happening, employers and unions would be asked to allow parents to take a half a day a month to work as a volunteer in their children's school, and clergy would be asked to promote such participation from the pulpit. As part of this provision, parents would be required to assist the school in managing any discipline problems exhibited by their children. Second, the Board of Education would resist efforts to micromanage the school system. The authority to approve bids and issue contracts would be shifted from the Board to the Superintendent. Third, the Board would use all of its current budget surplus to address the hundred or so lowest performing schools in the city. Finally, the Board agreed to implement an array of management reforms that had been recommended by New Detroit, a coalition of white corporate executives and black community leaders dedicated to civic improvement and improved racial relations (Ortiz 1999a; "Highlights" 1999).

The hearings before a joint meeting of the House and Senate Education Committees during February brought out an array of opponents and supporters of the takeover legislation. Some of the opponents echoed Senator Leland's charge that the motivation behind the proposal was racial. Democratic Representative Ed Vaughn, an African American from Detroit, challenged Senator DeGrow's assertion that the city was singled out for this legislation because of its size. He claimed that the takeover was primarily about race. "The only school district targeted," he charged, "is the biggest and the blackest." More common among the opponents, however, was the claim that the takeover legislation violated both the principles of local control and threatened the voting rights of Detroiters. Rev. Thomas Jackson, a Baptist minister whose six children had attended the city's schools, commented at a citizens roundtable organized by the *Detroit News* that "everybody that's voting on this thing to takeaway my right to vote are [legislators from] another area, and I don't have the right to vote them out of office." This interpretation of the takeover effort was not, however, devoid of racial overtones. Jackson went on to say that this initiative was both "wrong" and "racist" because those who were voting on the mayoral takeover were not "beholden" to him ("Is It Reform or Racism?" 1999).

Supporters of the takeover expressed a quite different view. Some, like Richard Blouse, President of Detroit's Regional Chamber of Commerce noted, that the legislation is supportive of local control by placing the power to appoint the Board of Education in the hands of Detroit's mayor. The Republican chair of the Senate Education Committee, Loren Bennett, went further and claimed that local control was beside the point. Local governments, he noted, derived their authority from the state, and the state could enact legislation to alter that authority ("Takeover Foes Turn to Threats" 1999; Hornbeck 1999).

Popular opinion more or less paralleled the divisions among those attending the hearings. A February 14 poll published in the *Detroit News* reported that a majority of Detroiters believed that the schools were in need of reform. When it came to the takeover legislation, however, about three-quarters of whites were in support of the proposal whereas over half of the African-Americans polled were opposed. Sterling Jones, an African-American carpenter who had a stepdaughter in the city's schools saw the takeover as "a racist move." The Republicans," he stated, are primarily a gang of white men trying to do whatever they can." Angela Williams, an African-American mother of four stepchildren in the city's schools, stated that she was aware of the problems facing Detroit's schools but was afraid of the prospect of losing her vote if the takeover proposal was successful. On the other side, Frances Irwin, a white parent who has adopted two sons, one African-American and one white, lauded what she saw as Engler's effort to do something about the condition of Detroit's schools (McWhirter 1999a). In another sampling of public opinion a few days earlier, Earl Chambliss, an African-American Detroiter who sent his son to a parochial school, commented to the

News that he has lost confidence in the city's schools ("What Detroit Residents are Saying" 1999).

Mayor Archer and the Takeover

Using Chicago as a model for his takeover proposal, Governor Engler looked to Detroit's Mayor, Dennis Archer, to play a key role in this effort. He wanted Archer to be ready to appoint a reform board as soon as the legislation passed and to have a new CEO selected by July ("Engler Puts Heat" 1999). The previous December, Archer, who was Detroit's second African-American mayor following Coleman Young into office in 1993, appeared to be a likely supporter of a takeover when he told the Detroit Board of Education to "shape up or else" ("Archer to DPS Board" 1998). Yet once the actual takeover legislation had been introduced and was being debated, his position was harder to pin down.

For several weeks, Archer claimed that he had not made up his mind regarding the takeover bill or his role in the effort ("Archer Still Undecided" 1999). In his State of the City Address on February 15, Archer urged caution about the takeover proposal and called for its careful scrutiny before any plan is enacted. He went on to say that the kind of legislation that he wanted would do more than just provide the mayor with power to appoint the Board of Education. He thought that there were a number of other initiatives that should be part of this legislation, including a cap on class size of seventeen in grades one to three and twenty in the remaining grades, mandatory summer school for underachieving children, the establishment of after school programs, and program for recruiting 1,200 new teachers for the city. What the city schools needed, he noted, was a "Marshall Plan." Finally, he urged Senate Majority Leader DeGrow not to report the takeover bill out of committee until Archer had the opportunity to share his views with the legislature (Archer 1999).

A week later at a speech to the Economic Club of Detroit, Archer took a more definitive stand in favor of the takeover and stated if the legislation passed, he would, in his words, "take the bull by the horns." He went on to say that he was currently working with the legislature to incorporate into the bill some of the provisions he called for in his State of the City Address (McWhirter and Harmon 1999; "Archer Ready for School Role" 1999). What seems to have brought Archer on board was a bipartisan deal negotiated by Senator Virgil Smith, the only African-American member of the Detroit legislative delegation in support of the takeover, to provide the city's schools with an additional

$15 million to help pay for the additional initiatives that Archer had requested (McConnell and Christoff 1999a).

Archer's slowness and sometimes equivocation on the takeover can be explained by a number of factors. He was in the midst of his own struggle to fend off a recall drive that began six months after his reelection to a second term at the behest of a coalition upset with his failure to back a proposal to give one the city's new casino licenses to a local black developer. Although the recall effort would ultimately fail, there were other doubts raised about his leadership ability as a result of a failed effort to deal with snow removal in the wake of a surprise blizzard in January 1999 that left many of the city's residential streets blocked and closed the schools for almost a week There was some speculation that the city's business leaders would seek an alternative candidate if he sought a third term (Pepper 1999; "Group Push Archer Recall Effort" 1999). And there were city residents who were less concerned that he reform the schools than that he act on an array of what they saw as neighborhood issues, including the modernization of the fire department, community policing, and the demolition of abandoned buildings to name but a few. In this vein the president of the Bewick Block Club, Leontine Person, told the *Free Press* that "I want to see him stick a shovel in the ground and say this is what we're going to do for the people of Detroit instead of what these big corporations are doing" (Dixon 1999).

Beyond these immediate issues, Archer leadership style seemed to frustrate some Detroiters. More of a conciliator and more willing to try to work with Detroit's corporate leaders and white suburban communities than his predecessor, Coleman Young, Archer's penchant for compromise and consensus, which was no doubt due to the fifteen years he spent as a state supreme court judge, was often interpreted as inaction and an inability to lead (Henig et al. 1999) Pete Waldmeir, a columnist for the *Detroit News* claimed that Archer did what he did best in his comments on the takeover in his State of the City address. In Waldmeir's words, "he talked about it." The columnist went on to question why the Mayor had asked Senator DeGrow to delay reporting the bill out of committee until "who knows when." As Waldmeir put, "maybe he thinks lightning will strike and fix everything" (Waldmeir 1999). The following day another *News* columnist, George Weeks, urged Archer to act with more speed. "Archer should," he noted, "seize the moment, not try to delay it" (Weeks 1999).

While Archer was deciding what role he would play in the takeover initiative, the legislature was continuing its deliberations. On February 25 as 100 or so protesters crowded the halls of the capitol in Lansing chanting, singing, and issuing threats of recall, the

Senate Education Committee, although interrupted briefly by two Detroit House members who voiced opposition to the bill as an "affront" to the voting rights of their constituents, voted 3–1 to report out the takeover proposal to the full Senate without amendments (Christoff 1999). At the same time, a number of Senate Democrats were contemplating attempts to amend the bill on the Senate floor. Gary Peters, a Democratic Senator from Bloomfield Township, had two such amendments in mind. One would require a referendum by Detroit voters to approve the takeover. He argued that the abolition of the elected board required by the legislation as well as the fact that the Mayor had not been elected to operate the schools had implications for the "voting rights" of Detroiters that could only be settled by popular vote. The other amendment that he wanted would require an election at the end of five years to determine if Detroiters wanted the takeover plan to continue. As Peters saw it, the Republican legislature had the votes to approve the takeover legislation for implementation the following year. What they lacked, however, was the two-thirds majority necessary to implement the bill immediately as Governor Engler wished. Under such circumstance, he believed that there was an opportunity for Democrats to play a role in shaping the final outcome ("Presidential Primary" 1999). As it turned out, neither amendment ended up in the final bill that the Senate passed at the beginning of March.

Rather than amending the Senate bill when they received it, the House with bipartisan support passed its own version of a takeover bill. Under the provisions of this plan, Governor Engler was to appoint a monitor who would run the schools while retaining the elected Board of Education in an advisory capacity. When the Monitor's term expires in 2003, Board members could run for re-election and their authority to manage the schools would be returned to them.

The six Detroit Democrats who supported the House takeover plan claimed that it, unlike the Senate bill, protected the voting rights of Detroiters and placed responsibility for reform clearly on the Governor. Equally important in their support of the House alternative was their distrust and dislike of Archer. They generally questioned the quality of his leadership of the city as well as being upset that they had not been consulted in the development of the original takeover plan. There was also some feeling among these legislators that Archer's apparent support of the takeover proposal was a betrayal of African-American interests. One of their number, Representative Lamar Lemmons, noted that if there had to be a takeover, it would be better to give the power to Engler than to Archer. "If you want a plantation analogy," he told the *Detroit Free Press*, it's

African Americans' experience that overseers are often worse than dealing directly with the master." (Bell 1999b; Hornbeck and Harmon 1999; Walsh-Sarnecki 1999). The House bill was not just, however, an attack on Archer. The minority Floor Leader of the House Democrats, Detroiter Kwame Kilpatrick, saw the effort as a "strategic move" to force Republicans to negotiate on the terms of the takeover (McConnell 1999b).

In response to the House action, the Senate did in fact introduce some changes into their takeover legislation. They altered the membership of the appointed board to seven members, six appointed by Mayor Archer with the seventh seat given to state school Superintendent Art Ellis or his designee. The board would, in turn, appoint a CEO. And they agreed to maintain the elected Board of Education in an advisory capacity (Bell and Christoff 1999; Gregg 1999b). A week later both the Senate and the House passed the bill with sufficient majorities to allow for its immediate implementation (McConnell and Christoff 1999b; Schulz 1999). Governor Engler quickly signed the bill into law and Mayor Archer designated Detroit's current general superintendent of schools, Eddie Green, as acting CEO until the new reform board selected a permanent CEO ("School Takeover Gets Rolling" 1999).

The Takeover as an Ideological Battleground

The dispute over the takeover legislation involved two distinct but related conflicts, one having to do with the governance of the Detroit public schools and the other dealing with political control of the city. The battle over the city school's governance pitted two lose groupings of individuals. On one side stood an African-American and white coalition in support of restructuring the schools including Governor Engler, Mayor Archer, a few key African-American community leaders, the Republican majority in the state legislature, a handful of Democratic legislatures, the city's two major newspapers and a number of their columnists, Detroit's principal black newspaper, and, according to one poll, about 40 percent of the city's African-American population. Arrayed against them was a largely but not exclusively African-American alliance comprising the vast majority of Detroit's Democratic legislative delegation, the Detroit City Council, several African-American community leaders, a number of politicians and school administrators and board of education members outside of Detroit, and, according to the poll cited above, about half of the city's African-American population (McWhirter 1999a; Ortiz 1999a).

At one level this was clearly an ideological conflict about how the city's schools should be run. Many of the supporters of the takeover legislation invoked the image of Chicago when they talked about the potential that a mayoral takeover held out for Detroit. What is less clear, however, is whether either the supporters or the opponents of the takeover understood where the reforms implemented in Chicago fitted into the larger process of school reform that had been underway in the nation since the early 1980s. When the takeover was first proposed by Governor Engler, Joe Stroud, a columnist for the *Detroit Free Press* pointed out that reforming the schools would require both "top down" district level reforms like the takeover to improve school accountability along with "bottom-up" initiatives involving parents, teachers, principals, and students to make changes within the classrooms (Stroud 1999a).

In a later column midway through the conflict, he pointed to the liabilities of relying wholly on either kind of initiative. As he saw it, a powerful state bureaucracy could interfere with the efforts of parents and teachers to improve the quality of education in the classroom. Local control, however, could undermine wider efforts to introduce higher standards. What had to be done if Detroit's schools were to improve, he argued, was for reformers to strike something of a balance between centralizing and decentralizing impulses so that the status quo would be challenged with "accountability imposed from above as well as from the empowerment of parents and students at the most intimate level." There were no simple solutions for addressing the problems facing public schools. "Working from both ends, though, from the top and the bottom, we just might get the education results we want for more nearly all the children of Michigan" (Stroud 199b). Stroud, then, seemed to be aware of the shifts between centralization and decentralization that had punctuated the various so-called "waves" of school reform that were then occurring as well as recognizing the strengths and limitations of the kind of restructuring that a mayoral takeover posed for school governance (Hess 1999; Murphy 1992).

The majority of the proponents of the takeover did not, however, frame their support in the language of educational reform or restructuring. Although both the *Detroit Free Press* and the *Detroit News* supported the takeover on their editorial pages, it was unclear what, if any, reform ideology drove either newspaper. Their advocacy of this initiative seemed to have little to do with their belief in any particular set of educational ideas but rather was motivated by more pragmatic concerns about the ability of the city's schools to operate effectively under its present administrative structure. A takeover was called for, according to both of these newspapers, because of the schools' seeming failure, despite numerous opportunities over a period of years, to educate Detroit's children and the Board of Education's ineptitude, if not outright corruption, when it came to managing the district's finances ("School Change" 1999; "Leadership" 1999; "Detroit's Costly School Board" 1999). The *Michigan Chronicle*, the state's African-American newspaper, saw the takeover as a means of wresting control of the schools from a politically oriented board of education whose major commitment was in maintaining its power. As the editors saw it, the existing board had placed a concern for the education of the city's children behind their concerns with "making a good impression at public meetings, controlling contracts, dispensing favors, and building a base to launch future political campaigns" ("The Michigan Chronicle" 1999).

Similarly the comments that ordinary Detroiters made to the press in support of the takeover do not seem to be driven by any specific educational ideology but rather by the belief that their schools were not well managed and not working to educate the city's children (McWhirter 1999a; "Would Takeover Help" 1999). As Yvette Anderson noted in a letter to the *Detroit News*, the takeover battle was not about race. "Black people," she went on to say "just want a proper education provided to their children so they can become productive citizens" ("Would Takeover Help" 1999).

The opponents of the takeover opposed this initiative on both pragmatic and ideological grounds. As a practical matter, those who were against the takeover thought that it was unnecessary because Detroit's schools were in fact improving on a number of fronts including student achievement. Beyond that, however, they did mount an ideological argument against mayoral control. Such an initiative, they argued, violated the principles of local control, denied Detroiters their voting rights, and was racist in intent. As Rev. Leonard Young, a Baptist minister from Detroit, made clear at the initial hearings before the House and Senate Education Committees, the takeover legislation was an effort to subvert a local election. He went on to say that "if you respect black people, you will respect our vote" ("Takeover Foes Turn to Threats" 1999).

Although the opponents to the takeover often expressed their descent in racialized terms, it is important to note that this dispute was not a monolithic black-white conflict. In fact, there were African-American and whites on both sides of the issue. The city's two major African-American organizations, the NAACP and the Urban League, took opposing positions on the takeover. The NAACP opposed the takeover on the grounds that removing an elected board of education in favor of an appointed one threatened the voting rights of Detroiters. The League, however, supported the takeover. The key issue, as they saw it, was not voting rights but the need to have quality schools that would prepare the city's children for jobs and other opportunities (Harmon 1999; Oritiz 1999b).

Supporters for the takeover in fact included African-American organizations such as the Detroit Association of Black Organizations, 100 Black Men, and the Ecumenical Ministers Alliance as well as such integrated groups as the Detroit Federation of Teachers, the Detroit Organization of School Administrators and Supervisors, New Detroit, and the Detroit Regional Chamber of Commerce (Oguntoyinbo 1999; Ortiz 1999kb; Pardo 1999; Van Moorlehem 1999; Van Moorlehem and Bell 1999). Rev. Horace Sheffield, pastor of Detroit's New Galilee Missionary Baptist Church and co-chair of the Ecumenical Alliance, reflected the frustration of many of these supporters over the emphasis that had been given to issues of race in this dispute. He challenged the claim of many of the opponents of the takeover that attributed racist motives to Engler and those whites that supported him. In his words, "the only race that matters is the race that succeeds in properly educating our children before another generation is lost" (Van Moorlehem 1999).

Similarly, opposition to the takeover did not just come from Detroit African Americans. A number of largely if not virtually all white school districts, including such suburban Detroit systems as West Bloomfield, Royal Oak, and Hazel Park as well as those in the rural out-state communities of Boyne and L'Anse, opposed the takeover as did a majority of the membership of the Michigan Association of School Boards. The issue for these opponents was not of course race but local control. From their vantage point, the takeover proposal if passed would provide a precedent that might threaten the future independence of their districts (Audi 1999).

The battle for political control of the city was a conflict within Detroit's African-American community involving Mayor Archer on one side and the city's legislative delegation, particularly State Representatives Ed Vaughn and Kwame Kilpatrick, on the other. This dispute was certainly connected to the takeover conflict in that educational reform was, as we have seen, a point of division for them. Yet the quarrel between Archer and these African-American Detroit Democrats predates the takeover debate. Ed Vaughn had run for mayor against Archer in 1997 and lost, whereas both Kilpatrick's parents, Congresswomen Carolyn Kilpatrick and Wayne County Commissioner Bernard Kilpatrick, had at times contemplated running for mayor. Kwame Kilpatrick and his father in fact were members of the

African-American Men's Organization, a group that was organized in 1997 to counter Archer's influence (Bell 1999a; Waldmeir 1999).

The takeover offered Archer's African-American rivals the perfect opportunity for expressing their antipathy toward him. Archer's ongoing problems, particularly the recall attempt, his botched effort to deal with snow removal, and the criticism of his conciliatory approach to addressing city problems had rendered him vulnerable to attacks from his opponents (Puls 1999; McWhirter 1999b). At the same time, the Mayor's African-American support for the takeover was weak. Bill Beckham, president of New Detroit and a proponent of the takeover, was rumored to be a possible challenger to Archer if the Mayor sought a third term. As it turned out, however, Beckham died suddenly the month following the passage of the takeover legislation. And Senator Virgil Smith's support was attributed to his desire to cooperate with Republicans in order to secure an appointment of some kind when term limit legislation forced him to leave the Senate in 2002 (Pepper 1999; "Takeover Makes Odd Allies" 1999). Under these circumstances, the support that African-American Detroiters gave to the passage of a House version of a takeover bill was their way of embarrassing Archer by telling him in effect that they preferred the leadership of a white Republican governor than their fellow African-American Democrat (McConnell 1999a; Bell 1999b; Johnson 1999).

The takeover dispute was, however, not just about conflict. It also was the vehicle for an alliance between an African-American, Democratic mayor and a white Republican governor. Although Archer and Engler voiced similar criticisms of the Detroit public schools, it is not clear to what extent they agreed on educational matters. In fact when the House passed its own takeover proposal that placed the governor in charge, Engler angered Archer by stating that he would be satisfied with either the Senate's mayoral takeover plan or the House legislation. He did, however, after a brief meeting with Archer following the House's action, reaffirm his support for the Senate plan (Bell 1999b).

In the end, Engler and Archer's alliance may have had more to do with the politics of the moment than with educational ideology. The success of the takeover proposal was the most recent indication of the fact that Detroit was losing the influence that it once had enjoyed in the state legislature. The city's declining population, Republican control of the state government, and recent term limit legislation were the culprits behind this change. Between 1950 and 1990 Detroit's population fell from about 1.8 million to just over 1 million. As a result, the city has lost membership in the state House of Representatives from thirty seats in 1950 to twenty in 1970, to thirteen in 1999. Declining population had also affected Detroit's voting power. In the 1958 gubernatorial election, about 25 percent of the votes came from Detroit. In 1978, the city accounted for 11.5 percent of the votes, and in the 1998 election for 7.5 percent of the votes. And recently passed term limit legislation would soon force the most senior members of the Detroit legislative delegation, whose tenure and experience provided them with the greatest influence, to leave office.

The result was that Republicans at the state level could act notwithstanding the opposition of Detroit Democrats. In the 1998 legislative session, they were able to pass a bill to mandate drug testing welfare recipients despite objections from Detroit lawmakers. And they were able to force the city to lower its income tax in exchange for a guaranteed share of state revenues. It was no doubt this shift in power relations that Representative Vaughn had in mind when he accused Governor Engler of practicing, in his words, "plantation politics" (Gregg 1999a).

Seen in this light, Engler may have viewed the takeover as a means of cementing an alliance with Archer that would divide state Democrats and as a result further diminish Democratic party power in Michigan. For Engler, the takeover, if it actually served to improve the schools, offered him the opportunity to enhance his reputation as a visionary and a leader without much risk. He could undertake the initiative without worrying about angering Detroit African Americans since he did not need their votes to get elected. And if the takeover failed to improve the schools, he could blame Archer. The mayor was also attracted to the takeover by the prospect of reforming the city's schools, which would further advance the leadership role that he was assuming in national Democratic Party politics. For Archer, however, the venture was riskier. If the schools did not improve, he would in all likelihood suffer increased opposition to his administration (Ryan 1999; "Archer Puts Political Future" 1999).

Theories Underlying the Takeover

The conflict over the takeover was not for the most part, as I have said, framed in theoretical terms. Only rarely did either the supporters or opponents of a mayoral takeover in Detroit mount an explicitly ideological argument to support their position. They made their case on the more or less pragmatic grounds of the efficacy of Detroit's schools in educating the city's children. Nonetheless, the nature of the conflict does become more understandable if we interpret it through a theoretical lens. Labaree (1997) offers such a framework in his discussion of the conflicting goals that Americans routinely invoke to talk about the purposes of U.S. education. As Labaree sees it debates about school restructuring, which is at the heart of the Detroit takeover conflict, are one of the myriad of issues about which educational reformers routinely argue. Such a conflict, he goes on to say, is not really about organizational issues but about political ones. That is, the dispute over the takeover is not so much a battle over differing conceptions of how to make schools better but rather about the goals to which we wish schools to be directed.

Labaree identifies three such conflicting goals, democratic equality, social efficiency, and social mobility, that have emerged out of the historic tensions and contradictions in U.S. society between the ideals of democracy and those of capitalism. Arrayed against each other for the loyalties of Americans, it is the ebb and flow of their influence as they come to the fore, retreat to the sidelines, and then emerge again that characterizes for him the history of American education. From the perspective of democratic equality, education is a public good that benefits all members of society by preparing youth with the knowledge, skills, and dispositions required for citizenship and political participation in American society. To ensure that all students have equal opportunity to acquire these educational opportunities, this goal requires that schooling be widely accessible to all segments of society. A second goal for Labaree is that of social efficiency. Here, too, education is a public good for promoting society's economic development and well-being. The purpose of education from this perspective is to prepare youth to fulfill the economic roles that are essential for a prosperous and productive economy. Meeting such a purpose requires a differentiated curriculum that channels students toward their appropriate occupational destiny, which in turn entails that schools will be highly stratified with selective access. A third goal that Labaree identifies is that of social mobility. From this vantage point, education is a private good that enables individuals to obtain an advantage over other members of society. The goal of education from this vantage point is to prepare youth for desirable social, economic, or political positions and in so doing to offer them a competitive advantage over others.

Labaree's framework does indicate a clear political conflict between the supporters and opponents of the takeover. In defending a mayoral takeover its proponents talked at times about the potential of this reform for enhancing standards, improving test scores and graduation rates, and eliminating waste in the administration of the schools. Such results were important for these reformers because they would enhance the efficiency of Detroit's schools in preparing its students for their occupational roles in adult society. In promoting the takeover on these grounds, its supporters were in effect extolling the goal of social efficiency. The opponents of the takeover, on the other hand, challenged this proposal on egalitarian grounds. As they saw it, the takeover threatened the voting rights of Detroiters thereby undermining their ability to act as participating citizens in a democratic society. Such voting rights were of particular salience for African Americans, they went on to say, because they were the hard fought fruits of their victory over the forces of discrimination and racism. In making this argument, the opponents of the takeover were in effect justifying their position in terms of the goal of democratic equality.

Lest we assume, however, that the positions of the supporters and opponents of the takeover were that unified and monolithic and the battle lines between them were that clear, we should also note a commonality in their arguments to which Labaree's framework points. In defending their positions both supporters and opponents argued about the relative success of Detroit's schools in educating children in general and their children in particular. That is when the supporters of the takeover talked about the failure of the city's schools to educate children, they were in effect noting the fact that the schools did not offer children, particularly African-American children, the knowledge and skills that they need to compete effectively in adult society. And when the opponents of the takeover noted the fact that Detroit's schools were improving they were claiming that these schools were making progress in offering the city's children the competitive advantage that they required to succeed in the larger society. To the degree that both the proponents and opponents defended their position in these terms, they were invoking the goal of social mobility.

Labaree (1997) alerts us to the fact that it is not unusual for both the supporters and the opponents of the takeover to share a commitment to the goal of social mobility. Proponents of democratic equality have often invoked the doctrine of social mobility to bolster their opposition to the goal of social efficiency. Both democratic equality and social mobility, he notes, can be invoked to justify increasing student access to educational opportunity over and against the tendency of advocates of social efficiency to favor differential and restricted access to schooling. Similarly, supporters of social efficiency have often supported the goal of social mobility to strengthen their opposition to democratic equality. Labaree points out in this vein that both goals can support the commitment to increased stratification through tracking and curriculum differentiation as opposed to the challenge that a belief in democratic equality poses to these two practices. Labaree's framework, then, makes theoretical sense of the diversity of rationales offered in defense and in opposition to the takeover proposal.

Assessing the Research on Mayoral Takeovers

The supporters of the takeover, I noted earlier in this chapter, claimed to be motivated by two goals. First, they wanted to address what they believed to be the academic failure of the district to secure high levels of learning and achievement on the part of their students. Second, they wanted to deal with an array of administrative problems that had to do with the management, particularly the fiscal management, of the city's schools. Some nine months into this reform initiative, it is clearly premature to assess these outcomes in Detroit. There is, however, some research data from Chicago, whose restructuring initiative was directed toward similar goals to those of Detroit, that can offer us something in the way of a tentative assessment of this reform strategy.

Chicago, it is important to note, approached its restructuring effort in a very different way than did Detroit. Chicago's initiative began in 1988 with the passage by the Illinois state legislature of a school reform act to provide for greater site-based control by shifting authority and resources from the central administration to the local schools. An important feature of this proposal was the establishment of local school councils (LSC) at each of the city's school as a means of providing greater power to parents in the management of their local schools. Composed of parents, community members, teachers, and the principal, the LSC was given authority to hire and fire the principal, to approve the school budget, and to approve the School Improvement Plan that guided the school's reform effort. The other key components of this proposal included the removal of principal tenure in favor of making principals accountable to the LSC while at the same time giving them greater control over school budgets, the physical plan, and the recruitment and hiring of new teachers. All in all, the 1988 reforms were designed to decentralize control of the city's schools while empowering parents, teachers, and principals as the agents of change (Bryk et al. 1998).

The 1995 mayoral takeover in Chicago, on which the Detroit reforms were modeled, only occurred when it became clear that the local efforts called for in the earlier reform plan had accomplished all that they could without reform of the central administration. Despite the new authority granted to LSCs and principals, it had turned out that the discretionary funds that principals were granted in the 1988 reform package were slow in being released by the Board of Education, that principals had difficulty getting the staff that they now had authority to hire on the payroll, that it was difficult for local schools to obtain needed supplies, and that capital improvement projects including building construction and renovation were slow in coming. To remedy these problems, the 1995 reform act introduced a centralizing element into the initiative by replacing a fifteen-member Board of Education appointed by the mayor from a list of nominees with a five-member Board of Trustees appointed directly by the mayor; by establishing the position of a CEO and a management team to administer the system; by giving the CEO authority to privatize a number of auxiliary school functions; and by giving the CEO authority to take action against failing schools, including the ability to reorganize and restaff them. These centralizing initiatives at the top ultimately came to be seen by Chicago reformers as the preconditions necessary if the academic problems affecting the school system were to be addressed.

There is some evidence in Detroit that the new CEO is beginning to address the inadequacies in the district's fiscal management. A financial audit of the school system that was ordered by the interim CEO, David Adamany, before Burnley was hired, uncovered what appeared to be a longstanding practice on the part of school employees of misappropriating school funds. The first such audit in twelve years, it revealed numerous instances of shoddy bookkeeping, charges of embezzlement against three former school bookkeepers, and the citing of fifteen high school principals for missing funds, unrecorded ticket sales, and the use of school funds for personal expenses. The most egregious of these cases was that of the principal of Henry Ford High School who claimed reimbursement for numerous personal expenses including alcohol, home improvement expenses, and his son's vacation in Italy. All in all, the auditors recommended that he repay the district over $76,000 for unallowable expenditures. The audit not only identified problems that existed prior to the takeover, it pointed to what appears to be continuing administrative inadequacies. Among the principals criticized for their misappropriations were four who had been appointed by Burnley to a newly established position, that of Executive Director of Accountability. Burnley's creation of this new position, which was designed to provide assistance to principals in remedying the district's low graduation rate and poor performance on standardized tests, was itself criticized on several grounds. First, it was felt that the district was already administratively top-heavy. Second, seven of his appointees, it turned out, were former principals of schools with low test scores that had declined even further under their leadership. Finally, Burnley was accused of cronyism because these appointees included his high school track coach and the wife of a school board member (Harmon 2000a, 2000c, 2000d). As of the writing of this essay, the three former bookkeepers have been or are being prosecuted, two of the high school principals accused of misappropriating funds have been fired, and three of the principals who were promoted to Executive Director of Accountability have been reassigned to their former or to other positions (Harmon 2000b, 2000e; Ross, 2000; Walsh-Sarnecki, Schaefer, and Ross 2000).

The fact that the audit was initiated and completed by CEOs appointed by the reform board does suggest that the mayoral takeover could, given sufficient time, address the management problems that have historically plagued Detroit's schools. Chicago's reformers in fact have identified that kind of success as a result of their 1995 mayoral takeover (Bryk et al. 1998). Yet there are some early warning signs that the changes mandated in Detroit by the takeover, specifically a mayoral appointed board and the creation of the CEO might not be sufficient. Not only has Burnley been criticized for appointment practices, the *Detroit News* accused the district's administration of withholding the results of the financial audit for four months. They went on to claim that he, in fact, knew about the result of the audit before he promoted the four principals cited in the report for financial irregularities (Harmon 2000c, 2000d).

Research data from Chicago about student achievement as a result of both the 1988 and 1995 reforms have been inconclusive. Early assessments that relied on the Illinois Goals Assessment Program tests pointed to some modest improvements in mathematics and writing and declines in reading. More recent assessments that employed the Iowa Tests of Basic Skills have indicated gains in mathematics and reading. Notwithstanding these differences, however, questions have been raised about the meaning of these academic gains and declines as well as the potential role of Chicago's restructuring efforts in enhancing student learning. Because an array of externally and internally funded programs designed to improve mathematics and writing achievement were in place independent of the reform initiative, it is not clear that any of these academic gains hinged on restructuring. It is also not clear whether standardized tests represent a good vehicle for capturing the kind of improvements in student learning that have been predicated as the outcome of restructuring. And finally, it is not clear if restructuring has been in place long enough for there to be any indication of improvements in student learning (Bryk, Kerbow, and Rollow 1997; Bryk 1999; Mirel 1993).

From what we know thus far about Chicago, it is uncertain whether the Detroit takeover can by itself enhance academic achievement in the city's schools. The kind of mayoral takeover that occurred in Chicago was in fact the second phase of a larger reform effort that began in 1988. Such an initiative may turn out, then, to be an insufficient reform strategy or perhaps even the wrong tactic for ensuring the kind of academic improvements for which its supporters in Detroit are hoping. Thus far the results of Detroit's mayoral takeover point to a mixed record in addressing the management problems of the city's public schools. If Chicago is a good guide, and it is the only guide we now have, it would appear that by itself, such a reform may not address the academic problems of Detroit's schools. There is some evidence, again from Chicago, to suggest that such an outcome would require changes in the organization and operation of local schools that a mayoral takeover may render more effective. And these "bottom-up" reforms are no where to be found in Detroit takeover proposal. Joe Stroud, the *Detroit Free Press* columnist who alone among supporters of the takeover seemed to understand its ideological roots, said as much when Engler announced his proposal. One wonders if anyone in Detroit was listening?

Conclusions

In this chapter, I have examined the debates surrounding the mayoral takeover of the Detroit public schools, explored the resulting patterns of conflict and agreement, looked at the role that race has played in that dispute, and considered what this conflict tells us about the efficacy of mayoral takeovers as a reform strategy. Promoted by Michigan's Governor John Engler in his 1999 State of the State Address, a mayoral takeover was presented as a solution to the academic and management problems of the Detroit public schools. The takeover soon became the vehicle to address both the persistent academic underperformance of Detroit's students as well as continuing pattern of administrative mismanagement bordering at times on corruption.

The introduction of a mayoral takeover bill into the Michigan Legislature in February 1999 both precipitated a conflict over educational reform as well as fuelled an ongoing dispute over the political control of the city. This battle over educational reform produced two loosely formed groups. On one side stood a black-white coalition that supported the takeover as a means of restructuring the city's schools. And on the other side was a more decidedly African-American group, which included whites, that opposed the takeover because they saw it as threatening the principles of local control and the voting rights of African-American Detroiters. Despite, however, these clear ideological differences, it is important to note that much of the support and opposition to this reform was not ideological but rather came from individuals on both sides who defended their position on the pragmatic grounds of the efficacy of Detroit's schools in educating city children, particularly their children. Labaree's conceptual framework in fact points to the diversity of views held by both the supporters and opponents of the takeover. The proponents of the takeover did at times invoke what Labaree called the goal of social efficiency. And the opponents frequently challenged the takeover in accordance, again using Labaree's language, with the goal of democratic equality. Yet, the principal argument advanced by both the supporters and opponents of this proposal was made in terms of what Labaree defines as the goal of social mobility.

The combination of the pragmatic quality of the debates surrounding the takeover proposal coupled with the fact that African Americans and whites were on both sides of the conflict might lead one to assume that race did not play a large role in this dispute. Certainly the supporters of the takeover made that claim at every opportunity. In fact, however, race played a major role. Opponents of the takeover labeled the proposal as a racist attack on African-American Detroiters from whites outside of Detroit, particularly Republicans. Detroit's African-American House Democrats labeled Archer, who himself was African-American, a traitor to African-American interests for his support of the takeover. Even when opponents did not talk explicitly about race but instead criticized the takeover on the grounds that it violated local control and threatened the voting rights of Detroiters, race was on their mind. Local control in this context meant African-American control and that along with the right to vote were seen by those opposed to the takeover as the fruits of the nation's civil rights revolution. Detroit's transformation from the mid-1970s onward to an African-American led city no doubt has changed racial dynamics within the life of the city. Yet, it is clear from the takeover conflict that the salience of race in conflicts over urban educational reform must not be ignored.

The conflict between Mayor Archer and Detroit's Democratic legislative delegation does alert us to two factors that we should consider when investigating urban education reform. First, their dispute should remind us of the fact that battles over urban schooling cannot be separated from larger political disputes within cities. As Labaree suggests, conflicts over school organization as well as any of a number of educational issues are at their core political conflicts. As our study of Detroit suggests, educational reform for Archer, for the city's Democratic legislatures, and for Engler may have been a side issue to what was a larger dispute over political power in the wake of the changing city-state and urban-nonurban relationships. Of particular importance here may be the kind of diminishing power and influence of cities like Detroit in state politics. Second, we should not ignore the fact that this was largely a black-black conflict. As I previously noted, racial conflict in African-American led cities with African-American majority populations may take a different form than was the case when city populations included substantial numbers of white residents. All and all, if we are to understand the promise and limitations of a mayoral takeover as an urban educational reform strategy, we must pay attention to its interplay with larger political conflicts within the city and between the city and the state and the impact that changes in those relationships have had on issues of race.

Finally, this study of Detroit's mayoral takeover may point to the strengths and limitations of this reform strategy. One of the arguments advanced by the proponents of this reform was that it could address the management shortcomings of Detroit's schools. To some degree, the persistent financial misappropriations that the district's financial audit revealed point to the ability of this administrative structure to uncover management problems. Yet, at the same time the appointment practices of CEO Burnely suggest that there is nothing magic about a mayoral takeover. Faulty appointments and perhaps other management failings evidently are equally likely in a traditional bureaucracy as it is in a restructured school administration.

Proponents of the takeover also argued that it could help to remedy the academic failings of Detroit's schools. In looking to Chicago as their guide, it seems that these supporters did not realize that Chicago's mayoral takeover was the second phase of a restructuring initiative that employed school level decentralizing strategies to secure improvements in academic achievement and a mayoral takeover to create the structural conditions for the realization of that reform. As a consequence, they seem to be embracing the centralizing force of a mayoral takeover to accomplish what it by itself is not capable of attaining. Ultimately a mayoral takeover may or may not be the reform of the moment for curing the ills of urban schools like Detroit. Whatever its efficacy, however, the structural and demographic transformation of U.S. cities like Detroit since World War II, particularly the shift to African-American control of schools, has altered the terrain in which such initiatives must be developed. Detroit's mayoral takeover conflict represents a case in point.

Note

1. Two other but similar forms of state takeovers are worth mentioning. In Maryland, the state legislature removed much of the authority that the mayor had historically for the operation of the schools and created in its place a city-state partnership with both the mayor and governor appointing a school board from a list of candidates submitted by the Maryland State Board of Education (see El Boghdady 1999b). And in Washington, D.C., it was a financial control board created by Congress that removed most of the powers of the city's elected board of education in favor of their appointed board of trustees (see Janofsky 1996; El Boghdady 1999a).

References

Anyon, J. 1997. *Ghetto schools: A political economy of urban educational reform.* New York: Teachers College Press.

Archer, D. 1999, February 15. *The road to excellence: State of the city address.* (City of Detroit, Executive Office, 1126 City County Building, Detroit, MI 48226)

Armour, D. J. 1995. *Forced justice: School desegregation and the law.* New York: Oxford University Press.

Arsen, D., D. Plank, and G. Sykes. 1999. *School choice politics in Michigan: The rules matter.* East Lansing: College of Education, University of Michigan.

Audi, T. 1999, March 11. Opposition mounts over takeover plan. *Detroit Free Press,* 1A, 2A.

Bell, D. 1999a, March 16. Detroit awaits today's vote on school takeover. *Detroit Free Press,* 1A, 3A.

———. 1999b, March 18. 2 competing proposals display divided loyalties and capitol confusion. *Detroit Free Press,* 1A, 12A.

Bell, D., and C. Christoff. 1999, March 19. Senate puts schools on Archer's chalkboard. *Detroit Free Press,* 1A, 2A.

Bryk, A. S. 1999. Policy lessons from Chicago's experience with decentralization. In D. Ravitch (Ed.) *Brookings papers on educational policy 1999* (pp. 67–127). Washington, D.C.: Brookings Institution Press.

Bryk, A. S., D. Kerbow, and S. Rollow. 1997. Chicago school reform. In D. Ravitch and J. P. Viteritti (Eds.), *New schools for a new century: The redesign of urban education* (pp. 164–200). New Haven: Yale University Press.

Bryk, A. S., P. B. Sebring, D. Kerbow, S. Rollow, and J. O. Easton. 1998. *Charting Chicago school reform: Democratic localism as a lever for change*. Boulder: Westview Press.

Christoff, C. 1999, February 25. School bill ok'd in capitol chaos. *Detroit Free Press*, 1A, 8A.

DeGrow, D. 1999, February 14. Reversing failure remains goal of changing structure of board. *Detroit News*, 7B.

Detroit Free Press. 1999, January 1. Board calls its plan revolutionary, 1A, 6A.

———. 1999, January 27. School change: Detroit board talks a good game, but it's too late, 10A.

———. 1999, January 30. Engler puts heat on over schools, 1A, 5A.

———. 1999, February 13. Highlights of school board plan, 8A.

———. 1999, February 15. Leadership: Only Archer can fill the most crucial school need, 6A.

———. 1999, February 26. Takeover makes odd allies, 1A, 7A.

———. 1999, March 26. School takeover gets rolling.

Detroit News. 1999, January 27. Schools resist state takeover.

———. 1999, January 29. Text of state of the state address.

———. 1999, February 2. Comment: Local control can't be asked to justify school failure.

———. 1999, February 10. What Detroit residents are saying, 8A.

———. 1999, February 11a. Archer still undecided on school takeover plan, 2A.

———. 1999, February 11b. Takeover foes turn to threats, 1A.

———. 1999, February 14a. Detroit's costly school board, 6B.

———. 1999, February 14b. Should state require Detroit to change its school governance, 7B.

———. 1999, February 21a. Is it reform or racism? Either way there's heat, 15A.

———. 1999, February 21b. Who will fix the schools, 1A, 12A.

———. 1999, February 23. Lessons of the court merger.

———. 1999, February 24. Groups push Archer recall effort.

———. 1999, February 25a. Archer puts political future at risk by leading school takeover, 1A, 2A.

———. 1999, February 25b. Would takeover help Detroit students, 8A.

Dixon, J. 1999, February 15. Focus on small things, Archer is told. *Detroit Free Press,* 3B.

Douglas, D.M. 1995. *Reading, writing, and race: The desegregation of the Charlotte schools.* Chapel Hill: University of North Carolina Press.

Education Commission of the States. 1999. *Governing America's schools: Changing the rules.* Denver: Education Commission of the States.

Eisinger, P. 2000, April. *Mayoral takeover in Detroit.* Paper presented at the meeting of the American Educational Research Association, New Orleans, LA.

El Boghdady, D. 1999a, March 21. D.C. school chief's vision, bold moves pay off. *Detroit News*, 12A.

———. 1999b, March 21. Overhaul is demanding and rewarding. *Detroit News*, 12A.

Engler, J. 1999, January. Michigan the 'smart state': First in the 21st century. 1999 State of the State Address (www.migov.state.mi.us/speeches/sos1999.html).

Flint Journal. 1999, February 22. Presidential primary, schools top senate agenda, A3.

———. 1999, February 23. Archer ready for school role, 1A.

Green, E. L. 1999, February 11. Why the urgency to take over Detroit Schools? *Detroit News*, 15A.

Gregg, B. G. 1999a, February 22. Detroit loses clout. *Detroit News*, 1A, 10A.

———. 1999b, March 19. Senate plan lets Archer lead schools. *Detroit News*, 1A, 3A.

Harmon, B. 1999, March 21. Detroit district's plight echoes in Cleveland. *Detroit News*, 12A.

———. 2000a, October 1. Detroit school hirings questioned. *Detroit News*, 1A, 9A.

———. 2000b, November 20. Detroit school funds misused. *Detroit News.*

———. 2000c, November 21. Burnley elevated 4 tied to lost cash. *Detroit News*, 1A, 2A.

———. 2000d, November 22. Burnley reviews promotions. *Detroit News*, 1A, 2A.

———. 2000e, December 4. School funds bought booze. *Detroit News*, 1C, 2C.

Henig, J. R., R. C. Hula, M. Orr, and D. S. Pedescleauz. 1999. *The color of school reform: Race, politics, and the challenge of urban education*. Princeton: Princeton University Press.

Hess, F. M. 1999. *Spinning wheels: The politics of urban school reform*. Washington, D.C.: Brookings Institution Press.

Hornbeck, M. 1999, February 18. Takeover foes jam hearing. *Detroit News*, 1D, 6D.

Hornbeck, M., and B. Harmon. 1999, March 18. Schools out for Archer. *Detroit News*, 1A, 11A.

Hunter, R. C., and J. Swann. 1999. School takeover and enhanced answerability. *Education Urban Society, 31,* 238–254.

Janofsky, M. 1996, November 16. School board in Washington is stripped of all its Authority. *New York Times*.

Johnson, B. 1999, March 19. Lansing intrigue ensures Detroit education will never be the same. *Detroit News*.

Kearney, C. P. A primer on Michigan school finance (3rd ed.). Ann Arbor: School of Education, University of Michigan.

Kirst, M. W. 1992. The state role in school restructuring. In C. E. Finn and T. Rebarber (Eds.), *Education reform in the '90s* (23–35). New York: Macmillan Publishing Company.

Kirst, M., and K. Bulkley. 2000. 'New, improved' mayors take over city schools. *Phi Delta Kappan* 81: 538–546.

Labaree, D. 1997. *How to succeed in school without really learning: The credentials race in American education*. New Haven: Yale University Press.

McConnell, D. 1999a, March 18. Insiders say the mayor shot himself in the foot with Arrogant demeanor. *Detroit Free Press,* 1A, 13A.

———. 1999b, March 20. Kilpatrick suggests school plan he'd back. *Detroit Free Press*, 10A

McConnell, D., and C. Christoff. 1999a, February 24. School deal add $15 million. *Detroit Free Press*, 1A, 3A.

McConnell, D., and C. Christoff. 1999b, March 26. School reform now needs names. *Detroit Free Press*, 1A, 11A.

McWhirter, C. 1999a, February 14. Blacks oppose Engler plan. *Detroit News*, 12A.

———. 1999b, March 28. Archer focused as enemies stay on attack. *Detroit News*, 1A, 10A.

McWhirter, C., and B. Harmon. 1999, February 23. Archer back takeover. *Detroit News*, 1A, 6A.

McWhirter, C., and S. Kennedy. 1999, March 21. Windy city shines as school reform success. *Detroit News*, 10A.

Michigan Chronicle. 1998, December 23–29. Archer to DPS board: "Shape up or else," A1, A4.

———. 1999, January 27–February 4. City schools must reform, A1, A4.

———. 1999, March 10–16. The Michigan Chronicle endorses school reform, A1.

Michigan Senate. 1999, February 10. *Senate bill no. 297.*

Miller, G. 2000, May 4. Detroit school board votes for new CEO. *Detroit News.*

Mirel, J. 1993. School reform Chicago style: Educational innovation in a changing urban context, 1976–1991. *Urban Education, 28,* 116–149.

Mirel, J. 1998. After the fall: Continuity and change in Detroit, 1981–1995. *History of Education Quarterly, 38,* 237–267.

Murphy, J. 1992. Restructuring America's schools: An overview. In C. E. Finn and T. Rebarber (Eds.), *Education reform in the '90s* (pp. 3–20). New York: Macmillan.

Nichols, D. A., and B. Harmon. 2000, May 5. Detroit schools pick CEO. *Detroit News.*

Oguntoyinbo, L. 1999, February 2. NAACP opposed to school takeover. *Detroit Free Press*, 1B, 2B.

Orfield, G., S. E. Eaton, et al. 1996. *Dismantling desegregation: The quiet reversal of Brown v. Board of Education*. New York: The New Press.

Ortiz, M. G. 1999a, February 13. District school board has its own plan for reform. *Detroit Free Press*, 8A.

———. 1999b, February 16. Urban League supports takeover of Detroit schools. *Detroit Free Press.*

Pardo, S. 1999, March 9. 100 black men favor Archer-led reform. *Detroit Free Press*, 1A.

Pepper, J. 1999, February 17. Beckham has school reform on his mind, not a mayoral bid. *Detroit News.*

Puls, M. 1999, February 14. Groups push Archer recall effort. *Detroit News.*

Purdy, M. 1996, December 23. How an alliance altered New York City's schools. *New York Times*, A1, B12.

Ravitch, D. 1974. *The great school wars: New York City, 1805–1973*. New York: Basic Books.

Redmond, D. L. 1999, February 14. Plan fails to address challenges facing Detroit, all urban education. *Detroit News*, 7B.

Robles, J. J., and C. Christoff. 1997, January 25. School control uncertain. *Detroit Free Press, 1A, 6A.*

Ross, J. 2000, December 15. Schools take action after audit. *Detroit Free Press,* 1B, 6B.

Ryan, R. 1999, March 19. Archer poised for national role. *Detroit News.*

Schulz, K. 1999, March 26. Battle begins for school reformers. *Flint Journal*, A3.

St. John, E. P., and D. Hossler. 1998. Higher education desegregation in the post-Fordice Legal environment: A critical-empirical perspective. In R. Fossey (Ed.), *Race, the courts, and equal education: The limits of law* (pp. 123–156). New York: AMS Press.

Stroud, J. H. 1999a, January 27. Schools need help from top and bottom. *Detroit Free Press*, 11A.

———. 1999b, February 17. State, city and local participation for school balancing act. *Detroit Free Press.*

Terry, D. 1995, June 29. Chicago's mayor gains school control that New York's mayor would envy. *New York Times.*

Tyack, D., T. James, and A. Benavot. 1987. *Law and the shaping of public education.* Madison: University of Wisconsin Press.

Van Moorlehem, T. 1999, February 27. School takeover bid gets endorsement. *Detroit Free Press*, 8A.

Van Moorlehem, T., and D. Bell. 1999, February 18. Takeover gains favor of 2 more city groups. *Detroit Free Press*, 1B, 8B.

Waldmeir, P. 1999, February 17. Archer doesn't understand the urgency of school reform. *Detroit News*, 1C.

Walsh-Sarnecki, P. 1999, March 18. Board would retain titles but no power under plan. *Detroit Free Press*, 13A.

Walsh-Sarnecki, P., J. Schaefer, and J. Ross. 2000, November 11. Detroit school audits bring embezzlement charges. *Detroit News*, 1A, 9A.

Walsh-Sarnecki, P., and B. Schmitt. 2000, May 5. Schools CEO is ready, realistic. *Detroit Free Press.*

Weeks, G. 1999, February 18. It's time for Archer to act on schools. *Detroit News.*

Part III

Independently Adopted Research-Based Reforms

Chapter 6

Research-Based Reading Reform: The Impact of State-Funded Interventions on Educational Outcomes in Urban Elementary Schools

*Edward P. St. John, Genevieve Manset, Choong-Geun Chung, Ada B. Simmons, Glenda Droogsma Musoba, Kim Manoil, and Kim Worthington**

With passage of the Reading Excellence Act, many states now have the opportunity to develop programs that support local efforts to improve early reading. It has long been known that young children who attend urban schools are at greater risk of not learning to read compared to students attending other types of schools (Slavin 1991; Snow, Burns, and Griffith 1998). However, there is little agreement about what types of reading interventions work best in urban schools. Much of the research receiving attention from policymakers has emphasized explicit approaches to instruction (e.g., Foorman et al. 1998) and has been criticized because it promotes political agendas (Allington and Woodside-Jiron 1999) or uses biased research methods (Taylor et al. 2000). Although the researchers whose research, funded by the National Institute of Child and Human Development, is at the center of the storm have defended their methods and arguments (Foorman et al. 2000; Mathes and Torgesen 2000), the whole controversy creates ambiguity and uncertainty for reformers in states and urban districts. Specifically, the following questions merit consideration in states and urban school districts:

- Should urban schools follow the path toward adopting explicit approaches that emphasize phonological awareness, an approach that is widely advocated by the conservative politicians who are advocates for fundamental reform?

- Should urban schools adopt research-based interventions with comprehensive designs and an established research base (e.g., Success for All or Reading Recovery)?
- Should states provide funds to urban schools, as a means of encouraging them to research the options that they think will work best in their setting?

Such questions must be considered when states design interventions aimed at improving early reading opportunities for urban school children. In this chapter, we use a database on early reading programs in urban schools in Indiana to examine the impact of state-funded interventions on rates of special education referrals and retention in early primary grades. These outcomes are closely linked to the success of schools in teaching early reading skills. First, we review the claims about early reading interventions made by various education reformers in early reading. Then we describe the research method we used in this analysis and present the results. We conclude by examining the claims of various reformers.

A Critical Review

Although the idea of research-based reform sounds compelling, it can be difficult in an area like early reading to discern the types of reforms that merit consideration by local schools. A first step in untangling this knot involves examining the specific claims made by various types of reforms. Three types of claims are used in the research and policy literatures:

- Claims made by researchers about methods or combinations of methods that can improve early reading opportunity.
- Claims made by advocates of specific reforms that argue for a particular combination of program features, organized in cohesive programs, that are intended to improve early reading opportunity.
- Claims by policymakers for specific program approaches (e.g., requiring a particular method [e.g., phonics] for all schools versus categorical grant funding).

Researchers' Claims

The debates about early reading instruction are situated along a continuum with two poles: one that emphasizes meaning and context and another that emphasizes letter-sound relationships, or phonics (Chall 1967). In the current context, much of the controversy centers around two arguments.

Perhaps the most widely cited research on phonological awareness and the alphabetic principle is by Barbara Foorman and her colleagues (Foorman et al. 1998). Recently, in response to critics, Foorman and her colleagues summarized their argument:

> However, we do maintain that there are some instruction principles that teachers and schools can use to enhance the reading achievement of at-risk children, and that it makes sense to demonstrate effective implementation of these instructional principles before investing in more complex solutions. (Foorman et al. 2000, 27)

Thus, while Foorman and her colleagues do not explicitly oppose comprehensive approaches to early reading improvement, they do argue for a specific method as a first priority. They base this argument on research that found:

> Controlling for differences in age, ethnicity, and verbal IQ, we found that children in the direct code (DC) approach improved in word reading at a faster rate and had higher word recognition skills in April than children receiving the implicit code (IC) approach (either research-based IC or district's standard IC). More importantly, children in *all* instructional groups with higher phonological processing scores in the beginning of the year demonstrated improvement across the year. (29)

Thus, this argument rests on research that shows students who have instruction in direct coding learn to read words faster and that students who have skills in phonological processes learned to read faster. Based on these findings, Foorman and her colleagues conclude that schools should first emphasize direct instructional approaches.

There is a large array of counter arguments on early reading. One researcher who has recently received wide attention, Barbara Taylor and her colleagues (Taylor et al. 2000) argue that the Foorman research overlooked the context of education in the schools in which Foorman's research was situated. Specifically, they argue:

> Literacy research documents an array of practices important for struggling beginning readers. . . . These practices influence systematic instruction in word recognition, carefully selected texts, repeated reading, guided writing, regular assessment of pupil progress, extra time in reading, one-on-one tutoring, strong home connections, and ongoing staff development. (24)

This argument has two specific components. One component is that the specific practices that are emphasized are closely aligned with a holistic approach emphasizing a literature-rich approach to early reading instruction. A second component of their argument is that comprehensive intervention is needed rather than an approach that emphasizes a single method first, such as direct instruction.

There is a clear contrast between these two positions. One argument is that direct instruction is of primary importance and should be implemented before other approaches are tried (e.g., Foorman et al. 1998, 2000). The counter argument is that comprehensive approaches to intervention are appropriate (Taylor et al. 2000). Thus the claims of the two camps have clear and direct policy implications.

The Claims of Reform Advocates

Much of the research on early reading interventions has been conducted by advocates of specific reforms or by evaluators of these reforms. This complicates the situation facing urban educators who are interested in choosing a research-based intervention that works for their school. It is important that school leaders understand the features included in specific reforms and the confirmatory research base underlying each one. The implicit claim of most reading reforms is that implementation of the reform can improve early reading, as well as reduce the number of students who are retained or referred for special education services. Therefore, it is important that schools consider the features of reforms, to see if they complement the instructional methods they use. Five of the reforms that have well-defined, comprehensive approaches to early reading intervention are outlined below, along with descriptions of the types of services available to schools in Indiana.

Reading Recovery is a comprehensive approach to early reading that emphasizes one-on-one tutoring. In Indiana, Purdue University provides training for teachers interested in Reading Recovery. The state-funded training for teachers interested in Reading Recovery through the Early Literacy Intervention Grant Program (ELIGP) and Title I paid the direct operational costs in some of the schools that chose this option. It emphasizes:

- Ongoing professional development for reading specialists; uses a Vygotskian developmental philosophy;
- Involvement of parents in reading with their children;
- Using meaning in context to teach phonemes (rather than direct decoding), along with aligned drills and creative method; and
- A sequence of literature books to promote the development of reading skills by students who are at risk of not learning to read (Bardzell 1999b).

A confirmatory research base indicates that children who complete the program make normal process in their education (Askew and Frasier 1994; Lyons 1994; Pinnell et al. 1994; Pinnell, DeFord, and Lyons 1988). However, one set of researchers found that including more direct instruction within Reading Recovery improves the speed at which students complete the program (Iverson and Tunmer 1993), a finding that has created controversy for the proponents of this intervention method.

First Steps is a comprehensive classroom-wide intervention that was chosen by some schools applying for school-wide grants through Indiana's ELIGP. An intervention method developed originally in Australia, First Steps:

- Has options for ongoing support and networking available in the United States;
- Emphasizes a developmental approach and student empowerment;
- Provides training for parents in literacy instruction;
- Uses holistic and literature-rich approaches, but includes phonics in some versions of the intervention;
- Uses systematic diagnostic procedures and formative evaluation, along with a literature-rich environment (Manoil 1999).

Thus First Steps is an approach that is situated in the literature-rich tradition but that includes a number of systematic features that involve teachers in assessing the progress children make in learning to read. Although indicating that First Steps has an impact on students, teachers, and schools (e.g., Australian Council for Education Research 1993a, 1993b; Deschamp 1995), the research is largely descriptive.

Four Blocks is a classroom-wide intervention developed by Cunningham (1991) that strikes a balance between holistic and direct methods. This method includes:

- A philosophical approach that emphasizes both phonological awareness and student empowerment;
- Both literature-rich and direct approaches to early literacy instruction; and
- Basal readers and a literature-rich environment. (Manoil and Bardzell, 1999)

In the form originally proposed by Cunningham, Four Blocks did not include professional development or parental involvement. This program does have modest confirmatory research (Cunningham, Hall, and Defee, 1991, 1998). The Indiana Department of Education has offered workshops on Four Blocks. In addition, some schools have received grants through ELIGP to implement the program.

Literacy Collaborative is a new classroom-wide reading intervention designed to complement Reading Recovery. In Indiana, Purdue University provides ongoing professional development in support of the Literacy Collaborative and a few schools have received funding for this intervention through ELIGP. The program includes the following features:

- University training for both pullout (through Reading Recovery) and ongoing professional development in support of Literacy Collaborative;
- A philosophy that is developmental and emphasizes student empowerment and creating learning communities;
- A comprehensive approach to instruction that includes diverse writing, oral, and decoding methods; and
- A comprehensive, literature-based and systematic curriculum for all students in grades 1–3 (Bardzell 1999a).

Literacy Collaborative has only recently been developed by the Reading Recovery Project (1998) at Ohio State University and lacks any confirmatory research base. However, initial studies of implementation in Indiana indicate that the method promotes improvement in student outcomes (St. John et al. 2000).

Success for All is a comprehensive school-wide intervention approach (Slavin 1991) that has a well-developed early literacy component. This well-documented method includes the following features:

- Systemic ongoing professional development and support;
- A developmental approach that emphasizes phonological awareness and whole language;
- An emphasis on building parent awareness and skills development;
- A systematic approach to instruction that emphasizes cooperative learning as a means of teaching decoding in both explicit and meaning-oriented ways; and
- A balanced approach that emphasizes classroom-wide activities, small groups, and pullout. (Bardzell 1999c)

The research on the effects of Success for All is extensive. Most of the research uses specially selected comparison schools and word recognition tests (e.g., Madden et al. 1991; Madden et al. 1989), although there is also some confirmatory research by independent researchers (Ross and Smith 1994).

The outline of reforms above illustrates the array of comprehensive approaches to early reading reform available to urban schools, if they have funding. Some emphasize pullout, others classroom-wide interventions, and still others combine approaches. The reforms take different approaches to instruction in decoding, the topic that underlies the debate among researchers outlined above. Reading Recovery, Literacy Collaborative, and First Steps emphasize a meaning-oriented approach to teaching decoding, an approach Foorman and colleagues (Foorman et al. 2000) strongly criticized. In contrast, Success for All and Four Blocks take a balanced approach, emphasizing context-free decoding, the approach Foorman and colleagues (Foorman et al. 2000) favor.

Political Claims

Two policy paths are evident in the latest round of policy conversations that consider the research base on reading. One approach, adopted by Texas, Washington, California, New York, and Wisconsin, has been to require the teaching of phonics (Allington and Woodson-Jiron 1999; Taylor et al. 2000). This approach to policy takes the claim of Foorman and her colleagues (Foorman et al. 1998) literally. That is, these researchers essentially claim that direct phonics instruction is a necessary first step and legislators in these states have taken action, requiring this instructional approach. The implicit claim taken in this approach is that requiring all schools to use an explicit approach to phonics instruction will increase the number of students who learn to read and make normal educational progress.

An alternative approach is also now available to states to provide funding to schools for comprehensive reading interventions. This approach is being used in Kentucky, for example, as part of the state-funded program using federal funds from the Reading Excellence Act. In Indiana, the Early Literacy Intervention Grant Program (ELIGP) has used annual categorical grants to fund reading interventions in schools since 1997. One component of the program funds teachers seeking training for Reading Recovery. The other component includes a wide variety of interventions categorized as Other Early Literacy Interventions (OELI). The implicit claim of categorical grant programs is that comprehensive interventions can promote educational progress.

Research Approach

This paper presents an empirical study of the impact of ELIGP in urban schools, adapting a method developed from a statewide study of the intervention program (St. John et al. 2000). Our purpose in conducting this study is to untangle evidence related to the three types of claims outlined above.

We used three years of survey data on schools in Indiana, collected as part of a comprehensive evaluation of the Early Literacy Intervention Grant Program in Indiana. Below we describe the survey we used, the logical model used in the study, and the instruction and related factors developed from the longitudinal study.

Survey and Response

The Early Literacy Intervention Survey[1] included questions about the types of reading programs that were implemented, amount of time per day spent on reading, features of the early reading program, number of students referred and retained, and enrollment data that could be used to impute special education referral and retention rates. In addition, we had access to a state-level database with information on test scores.

The survey assessed the frequency of use of nine organizational and structural features (ability grouping, basal readers, child-initiated learning centers, independent reading, one-on-one tutorial, pullout instruction, small groups, systematic evaluation, and trade books). It also assessed the frequency of use of ten classroom instructional methods (Big Books, cooperative learning, creative writing and/or essays, drama, emergent spelling, paired reading, phonics, reading aloud, reading drills, and worksheets/workbooks). For these frequency-of-use questions, survey participants were asked to respond using a five-point scale from 1 for "never" to 5 for "everyday" for both the current year and the prior year by grade level (K, 1, 2, 3). The survey also asked whether five types of professional development processes (certified training, certified specialist, in-service workshops, networking, and opportunity for collaboration) and five features related to parent involvement (book distribution, family literacy, paired reading, parent conference, and parent volunteers) were used in kindergarten through grade three.

This study reports analyses for three years of surveys of funded and comparison schools. The overall response rate across the three years was 61 percent. Comparison schools were half as likely to be surveyed as funded schools. Therefore, comparison schools were weighted by 2 to adjust for the probability of being surveyed. The study uses a subpopulation of schools located in urban school districts.

Statistical Methods

The study used descriptive statistics, factor analysis, and multiple regression. Descriptive statistics were used to describe the population characteristics.

A factor analysis (principal components analysis with varimax rotation) was performed using SPSS (version 10.0) for nineteen variables related to instructional and classroom program features for the entire population. Specifically, the average Likert score for each of the three grades (1–3) was imputed for the nineteen program features on the survey related to instruction and structure/organization. Missing items were replaced with mean values. A factor-loading minimum of 0.40 was used for inclusion of a variable in interpretation of a factor, and only factors with eigenvalues greater than 1.0 were interpreted.

Ordinary least squares (OLS) regression was used to examine the influence of predictor variables on two outcomes. We present R^2, plus three levels of significance (0.01, 0.05, and 0.10) for each predictor variable. Because 0.1 is only a moderately significant association, we make note of this moderate association in the text, so the reader will not place undue emphasis on this statistical relationship.

Model Specifications

We have two versions of the multiple regression models, one assessing type of funding and the other assessing type of intervention. In addition, we consider two distinct outcomes with each mode: rate of special education referral and rate of retention in grade level. Initially, we used sequential regressions, adding blocks of related variables for each outcome. The blocks of variables included:

- *School Characteristics*: The average ISTEP+ score, the percentage of students receiving free or reduced lunch, the percentage of minority students, and school locale: urban or rural.

- *Funding Type or Intervention Type*: In the analyses of funding types, we considered Reading Recovery (RR), OELI-1-3 (an OELI intervention in grades 1 through 3), OELI-K (OELI in kindergarten), OELI-FDK (an OELI intervention for full-day kindergarten), and OELI-preK (an OELI intervention for pre-kindergarten). In the analysis of intervention types, we considered Reading Recovery,[2] Success for All, Literacy Collaborative, Full-Day Kindergarten, First Steps, Even Start, Accelerated Schools,[3] and Four Blocks Method. The two Type variables (funding or intervention) are not mutually exclusive.

- *Professional Development*: Variables designate whether each of the following is included in professional development: requiring reading teachers to be certified, bringing in certified specialists for training sessions, in-service workshops, opportunities for teachers to network with teachers in other schools, and opportunities for teachers to collaborate within the school on reading instruction.

- *Instruction and Related Factors*: For this factor, we included the scores on each of the nine structural/organizational features and ten classroom instructional methods.

Instructional and Related Factors

In order to reduce the large number of program features related to instruction and the organization of reading programs at the grade level, we performed a principal components factor analysis of the instructional and structural/organizational features. (The factor analysis is presented in St. John et al. 2000.)

The *Connected-Text Approaches* factor includes independent reading, cooperative learning, creative writing, emergent spelling, paired reading (student-to-student), and reading aloud. Schools that make use of these methods combine techniques that engage students in the learning process.

The *Explicit/Direct Approaches* factor combines basal readers, phonics instruction, reading drills, and worksheets/workbooks. Schools that emphasize explicit approaches utilize systematic approaches to teaching the components of language and reading.

The *Child-Centered/Expressive Approaches* factor combines child-initiated learning centers, Big Books, cooperative learning, and drama. These instructional approaches place an emphasis on the development of the whole child and peer engagement among children.

The *Ability Group/Pullout Approaches* factor combines ability grouping, one-to-one tutoring, pullout instruction, and small groups. Schools that use these techniques place more emphasis on classifying children and accelerating the learning of some while addressing developmental needs of others.

The *Trade Books Approaches* factor combines trade books and Big Books, but deemphasizes basal readers. Schools that use this approach emphasize using texts that are literature-based and engaging for students, rather than emphasizing the structured elements of reading programs organized around increasing levels of difficulty.

Of these factors, the variables included in the Explicit/Direct Approaches factor are closely aligned with the direct approaches advocated by Foorman and colleagues (Foorman et al. 1998, 2000). The other factors would seem more closely aligned with the more comprehensive approaches advocated by Taylor and other reform advocates.

Limitations

This study has a few limitations that merit consideration by readers. First, our analyses consider school-related outcomes rather than individual outcomes. Although most reading research focuses on individual students, we felt it was important for the funding agency to understand whether their funding influenced school-related outcomes. This approach, although unusual, is consistent with the ways school outcomes are frequently reported and appears appropriate for a policy study of this type.

Second, the survey queried respondents about program features of each grade level, rather than asking teachers to answer questions about their classrooms. We considered this approach appropriate for an initial test of the study methodology. In the future we plan to extend the method to include a survey of teachers, which would mean we could examine both school-level and classroom-level outcomes.

Third, we assumed that all schools in the funded and comparison groups had an equal probability of returning a survey. This assumption was necessary because of the statistical methods used here. This assumption is typical when researchers use survey responses in regression models.

Fourth, for consistency across studies, we used factor scores generated from an analysis of the entire population of schools in all locales. Because one of our aims is to compare this urban-schools analysis to a similar analysis of the entire population (i.e., St. John et al. 2000), we decided it was most appropriate to use a consistent set of factors. However, the reader is cautioned that new factor scores were not calculated for this population.

Findings

Sample Characteristics

The characteristics for the 150 urban schools in the sample are presented in Table 6.1. The average special education referral rate for the schools surveyed was 0.05, with a standard deviation of 0.03. The average retention rate was 0.03 with a standard deviation of 0.03. In the average school in the sample, 44 percent of the students qualified for free or reduced lunch and 31 percent were minority.

A larger percentage of the sample was funded through Reading Recovery (26%) than through OELI-1-3 (17%) or the other types of programs. Further, a substantially larger percentage of the sample had Reading Recovery in their schools (40%) than were funded through ELIGP, indicating that many schools continued the program after the initial training year funded by the state program. In addition, Success for All (4%) and Literacy Collaborative (7%) were

TABLE 6.1
Descriptive Statistics of the Sample

	Mean (%)[4]	*S.D.*
Outcome Variables		
Special education grade 1–3	0.05	0.03
Grade retention grade 1–3	0.03	0.03
% Passing ISTEP English/Language Arts Scale Score	0.56	0.17
School Characteristics		
ISTEP Reading Raw Score	32.63	2.84
% Free or Reduced Lunch	0.44	0.21
% Minority	0.31	0.28
ELIGP Funding Type[5]		
RR	26.0%	
OELI	17.0%	
OELI-K	1.3%	
PREK	1.3%	
Intervention Type[6]		
RR	40.0%	
Success for All	4.0%	
Literacy Collaborative	6.7%	
Full-Day Kindergarten	25.3%	
Even Start	1.3%	
Accelerated Schools	2.0%	
Four Blocks	12.7%	
Professional Development		
Certified Training	34.0%	
Certified Specialist Grade	37.3%	
In-Service Workshops	73.3%	
Networking	63.3%	
Opportunity for Collaboration	70.7%	
Parent Involvement		
Book Distribution	50.7%	
Family Literacy	28.7%	
Paired Reading (Parent-to-Child)	71.3%	
Parent Conferences	97.3%	
Parent Volunteers	55.3%	

Note: $n = 150$; double weight was given to comparison schools.

[4]Percentages only are reported for dichotomous variables. Averages and standard deviations are reported when percentages are used as continuous variables.

[5]Schools not receiving ELIGP funding were the reference group.

[6]Schools having no or other interventions were the reference group.

not widely used, whereas Full-Day Kindergarten (25%) and Four Blocks Method (13%) were moderately used. Because a relatively large percentage of schools had ongoing programs related to Full-Day Kindergarten and Four Blocks Method, it is apparent that schools found funding sources other than ELIGP to develop and maintain these programs. This illustrates why it was necessary to consider the impact of the types of programs, as well as the types of funding, in this analysis.

In-service workshops, networking, and collaboration were used in most Indiana schools, a pattern that is consistent with the state's commitment to support ongoing professional development (Bull and Buechler 1996). In addition, most schools had multiple types of parent involvement.

The Impact of Funding Type

The analyses of the impact of funding types considered both referral rates and retention rates (Table 6.2). The two models are separately examined.

Referral Rates. Only one variable related to school characteristics was associated with referral rates. ISTEP+ scores in reading scores were significant and positively associated with referral rates, indicating schools with higher scores had more referral. In fact, it is possible that the pressure to raise test scores influences schools to refer more students have trouble learning to read.

None of the funding types were significant when we considered the impact of the four funding types. However, before we conclude funding made no difference, we also need to consider the impact of intervention type because teachers were in training during the funding year.

One variable related to professional development was significant. Having a certified specialist was negatively associated with referral. This suggests that having a specialist who is already certified in Reading Recovery or some other type of reading method reduces special education referral.

Two variables related to parent involvement were significant. Having a family literacy program (i.e., teaching parents to read) and paired parent-child reading were both negatively associated with referral, indicating these methods increase the likelihood children would learn to read sufficiently well to remain in the regular classroom.

Finally, three of the instruction and related factors were significant. Connected-Text Approaches, Explicit/Direct Approaches,

TABLE 6.2
The Effects of State-Funded Reading Interventions on Educational Progress in Urban Schools: Standardized Coefficients of Predictors on Special Education Referral Rate and Retention Rate

	Referral Rate		*Retention Rate*	
Variables	*Beta*	*Sig.*	*Beta*	*Sig*
School Characteristics				
ISTEP Reading Raw Score	.195	*	.159	
% Free or Reduced Lunch	.121		.277	***
% Minority	.033		.273	**
ELIGP Funding Type[7]				
RR	.005		−.178	**
OELI-1-3	.061		−.175	**
OELI-K	.001		−.071	
PREK	.088		−.031	
Professional Development				
Certified Training	.136		−.050	
Certified Specialist Grade	−.318	***	−.118	
In-Service Workshops	−.042		.028	
Networking	.058		−.115	
Opportunity for Collaboration	.064		.096	
Parent Involvement				
Book Distribution	−.022		.004	
Family Literacy	−.213	***	.154	*
Paired Reading	−.265	***	.086	
Parent Conferences	.056		.083	
Parent Volunteers	−.056		.115	
Program Feature Factors				
Connected-Text Approaches	.184	**	−.174	**
Explicit/Direct Approaches	.205	**	−.061	
Child-Centered/Expressive Approaches	.057		.277	***
Ability Group/Pullout Approaches	−.131		.050	
Trade Books Approaches	.199	**	−.022	
Adjusted R^2	.240		.271	

Note: $n = 150$; * $p \leqslant 0.1$, ** $p \leqslant 0.05$, *** $p \leqslant 0.01$.

[7]Schools not receiving ELIGP funding were the reference group.

and Trade Books Approaches were associated with higher referral rates. This means that none of the combinations of program features that emerged in the analysis actually reduced referral rates in urban schools.

Retention Rates. Two variables related to school characteristics were significant. The percentages of minority students and of students on free and reduced lunch were significant and positively associated with retention rates. Although prior research clearly indicates that poverty and urban locales are associated with failure (Snow, Burns, and Griffin, 1998), it is also important to note that this pattern also holds for schools within urban districts.

Two funding type variables were significant. Having a teacher funded through Reading Recovery and having an OELI-1-3 intervention was associated with lower retention rates. This is an important finding because it indicates that the interventions funded through ELIGP improved educational opportunity in urban school districts.

One of the variables related to parent involvement was significant. Family literacy was positively associated with retention. Because family literacy programs are more frequently offered in schools with more undereducated, language minority families, it is possible that other forces explain this association.

Two of the instruction and related factors were significant. Connected-Text Approaches were negatively associated with retention, indicating they help lower retention rates by enabling more students to learn to read. However, Child-Centered/Expressive Approaches were positively associated with higher persistence rates, indicating these methods were not as likely to help children make educational progress. This certainly merits further inquiry, given that there was a similar finding in the analysis of the entire population (St. John et al. 2000).

The Effects of Program Types

Because the amount of variance explained in the regression analyses of program types is higher than for funding type (compare Tables 6.2 and 6.3), it is possible to conclude that it is more appropriate to examine the impact of program type rather than funding source. However, several new insights emerge from comparing the two approaches.

Referral Rates. First, none of the variables related to school characteristics were significant (Table 6.3). The fact that test scores were no longer significant is intriguing and merits consideration because it indicates a confounding relationship with variables related to program types.

TABLE 6.3
The Effects of Reading Interventions on Educational Progress in Urban Schools: Standardized Coefficients of Predictors on Special Education Referral Rate and Retention Rate

	Referral Rate		*Retention Rate*	
Variables	*Beta*	*Sig.*	*Beta*	*Sig*
School Characteristics				
ISTEP Reading Raw Score	.120		.048	
% Free or Reduced Lunch	.163		.244	*
% Minority	−.055		.223	*
Intervention Type[8]				
RR	−.137	*	−.094	
Success for All	−.060		−.036	
Literacy Collaborative	−.009		−.146	*
Full-Day Kindergarten	.330	***	.001	
Even Start	−.002		.029	
Accelerated Schools	.024		.194	**
Four Blocks	−.065		−.132	
Professional Development				
Certified Training	.142	*	−.052	
Certified Specialist Grade	−.385	***	−.208	**
In-Service Workshops	−.007		.044	
Networking	.026		−.151	
Opportunity for Collaboration	.103		.051	
Parent Involvement				
Book Distribution	−.062		.049	
Family Literacy	−.173	**	.167	**
Paired Reading	−.216	**	.102	
Parent Conferences	.060		.094	
Parent Volunteers	−.078		.126	
Program Feature Factors				
Connected-Text Approaches	.152	*	−.123	
Explicit/Direct Approaches	.082		−.091	
Child-Centered/Expressive Approaches	.038		.302	***
Ability Group/Pullout Approaches	−.104		.025	
Trade Books Approaches	.230	***	−.008	
Adjusted R^2	.317		.418	

Note: $n = 150$; * $p \leqslant 0.1$, ** $p = \leqslant 0.05$, *** $p \leqslant 0.01$.

[8]Schools having no or other interventions were the reference group.

Second, two of the program types were significant and associated with referral rates. Interestingly, Reading Recovery was associated with lower referral rates. Given that more programs with ongoing and fully implemented Reading Recovery projects were included in this analysis, it is apparent that once these programs have matured, they have a more substantial influence on reducing special education referral.

Full-Day Kindergarten was associated with higher referral rates. Again, this analysis picks up more schools with ongoing and fully implemented programs. This relationship is difficult to explain from the evidence here, but could be attributable to a confounding relationship with test scores. This possibility merits further exploration, as to other possible explanations.

Third, two variables related to professional development were significant. Having a certified specialist continued to be significant and negatively associated with referral, indicating that the presence of trained reading specialists—a development more likely in schools with mature Reading Recovery Programs—reduced the need to referral. Having certified training was associated with higher referral rates. Since Reading Recovery was the primary certified training opportunity, it seems likely that this variable indicates a teacher in training (i.e., a funded Reading Recovery project). This further suggests that more mature Reading Recovery projects have more substantial effects in urban schools.

Fourth, two variables related to parent involvement were also significant. Family literacy and paired reading continued to be significant and negatively associated with special education referral.

Finally, only two variables related to instructional factors were statistically significant. Connected-Text Approaches and Trade Books Approaches continued to be statistically significant and positively associated with referral.

However, Explicit/Direct Approaches were no longer significant, indicating a confounding relationship between intervention type and this factor. This is important because it indicates that the ways various types of instructional programs interact within a comprehensive approach to early reading may be more important than any single instructional approach, supporting the argument of Taylor and colleagues (Taylor et al. 2000).

Retention Rates. First, the percentages of minority students and of students on free and reduced lunch continued to be positively associated with retention rates, indicating that program types had little interaction with these variables. This pattern was also evident in the analysis of the entire population (St. John et al. 2000).

Second, two program types were significant. Literacy Collaborative was significant and negatively associated with retention. This is important for a couple of reasons. First, the category Literacy Collaborative was reserved for schools that were working with the Purdue Reading Recovery project. It is apparent that a combination of Reading Recovery and a comprehensive and closely aligned schoolwide process represent a powerful force for change. In addition, we think it is important that these schools have ongoing support with a partnering university.

Accelerated Schools was significant and positively associated with retention. No Accelerated Schools received funding through ELIGP. Further, the few Accelerated Schools included in this study were not affiliated with either the national service center or the regional center. Only one school in Indiana now has state funding through Comprehensive School Reform and it was not included in the study. Therefore, the finding in this study that Accelerated Schools was associated with higher retention rates could be an artifact of inadequate funding or other factors.

Interestingly, Success for All was not significant in urban schools. In the analysis of the effects of program types of retention rates for all schools, we found that Success for All was associated with lower retention (St. John et al. 2000). This finding is important because the effects of interventions may depend on context. Success for All was originally created as an intervention for urban schools, but in this analysis it was not significant in urban schools. This may be an artifact of the different sources of funding, or it could be attributable to partial implementation or insufficient funding. More probing of this question is needed.

Third, consistent with the analysis of funding types, one variable related to parent involvement was significant. Having a family literacy program was associated with higher retention rates.

Finally, one instruction and related factor was significant. Child-Centered/Expressive Approaches continued to be significant and positively associated with retention rates.

It is also important to note that Connected-Text Approaches were no longer significant and associated with lower retention rates. It appears that the effects of this variable are confounded by using program types rather than funding types to predict retention rates in urban schools. In the analysis of all schools, Connected-Text Approaches were significant in the program types analysis (St. John et al. 2000). Thus, it appears that there is a relationship between having a comprehensive intervention, possibly Literacy Collaborative, and lower retention rates in urban schools. Literacy Collaborative seems possible, both because of the emphasis on program features related to the holistic approach in this model (Ohio State University 1998) and because this variable was significant and negative in the analysis above.

Conclusions

These analyses provide new insights into the impact of reading interventions. Below, we examine the empirical evidence in relation to the three sets of claims, then return to the policy questions in the introduction.

Reconsidering the Claims

Reseachers' Claims. These findings offer compelling evidence relative to the arguments advanced in the two schools of thought about early reading interventions. The Explicit Approaches factor did not influence reductions in either special education referral or retention rates. It is not clear that placing more emphasis on explicit instruction would help reduce the learning difficulties of school children in early grades.

There is, however, compelling evidence to suggest that comprehensive approaches to early reading improvement make a difference in the learning opportunities for urban school children. Specifically, having funded projects for both Reading Recovery and other literacy interventions (OELI-1-3) improved educational progress related to early reading. Funding comprehensive programs aimed at improving early reading appears to make a difference for urban school children.

Program Advocates' Claims. This study provides important evidence relative to the claims made by the advocates of reading reforms. Specifically, the holistic approaches used by Reading Recovery and the Literacy Collaborative seemed related to improvement in educational progress by urban school children. More generally, having funding through ELIGP for school-wide and classroom-wide reforms apparently helped schools improve student outcomes in urban schools.

The study also indicates that both funding and program maturity are important forces. In the case of Reading Recovery, there is evidence that mature programs had more substantial effects. In the case of Accelerated Schools, the lack of funding may have helped explain why this project was associated with higher retention rates.

Political Claims. These analyses suggest that requiring schools to implement any specific instructional approach would be shortsighted. There is certainly no evidence to suggest that requiring explicit instruction in phonics would improve student outcomes in urban schools.

However, there is strong evidence to support the idea that categorical funding for early reading interventions can improve educational outcomes in urban schools. Providing schools a chance to secure training and then implement Reading Recovery seems to make a difference. Further, providing funding for direct comprehensive reforms apparently made a difference, consistent with arguments by Taylor and colleagues (Taylor et al. 2000).

Making Informed Decisions about Early Interventions

These findings also help inform policy decisions about strategies for improving early reading in urban schools. Below we reconsider the questions noted in the introduction.

- *Should urban schools follow the path toward emphasizing explicit approaches that focus on phonological awareness, an approach that is widely advocated by the conservative politicians who are advocates for fundamental reform?*

This provides further insight into the debates about the merits of following the path toward explicit instructional approaches in urban schools. At the very least, this study suggests extreme caution is needed in following this path and, indeed, suggests an alternative approach may have merit.

- *Should urban schools adopt research-based interventions with comprehensive designs and an established research base (e.g., Success for All or Reading Recovery)?*

This study supports arguments advanced by Reading Recovery and by advocates of comprehensive research-based reforms. However, it does not confirm that Success for All is the most appropriate intervention method for urban schools. Indeed, the evidence here is more compelling for the new program, Literacy Collaborative, than for the more systematically studied Success for All. Apparently, the process of intervening to improve early literacy instruction in urban schools is more complex than is implied in the notion of adopting any single intervention method, or any combination of intervention methods, as *the* answer. These findings suggest that there are complex forces that influence the success of early literacy interventions in urban schools. We expect that the close collaboration between Purdue University and schools with Literacy Collaborative projects was a factor in the relative success of this program. We also expect that the lack of support for the early Accelerated Schools in Indiana may have inhibited their success. Thus, there is reason to expect that university partnerships can help urban schools. There is also compelling evidence to suggest that well-designed categorical programs can have a substantial influence in urban schools.

- *Should states provide funds to urban schools, as a means of encouraging them to research the options that they think will work best in their setting?*

This study provides compelling evidence that the provision of categorical grants that encourage schools to develop well-defined proposals, which is the case with ELIGP in Indiana, is a workable approach to early literacy intervention. With the passage of the *Reading Excellence Act*, states now have the opportunity to develop comprehensive programs that encourage schools to research possible solutions and develop well reasoned proposals.

Such an approach can be a great deal of work for state officials. It requires developing rubrics that can be used to communicate with schools about possible intervention strategies and that encourage educators in schools to develop proposals. However, the evidence in this study at least suggests that encouraging this type of thoughtful activity in schools offers greater hope for improving schools than do the alternative approaches currently being used by policymakers.

Notes

*We gratefully acknowledge the financial support of the Indiana Department of Education. The opinions expressed in this chapter represent the views of the authors and do not represent official policies or positions of the Indiana Department of Education.

1. Copies of the Survey can be obtained on request from the Indiana Education Policy Center. A simplified version of the instrument that can be used to survey teachers is available on-line (St. John, Manset, and Michael 1999).

2. This variable coding included schools with Reading Recovery whether or not they were funded through ELIGP.

3. The ELIGP did not fund any Accelerated Schools, although this intervention type was discussed in documents disseminated through the

program (St. John and Bardzell 1999) and there were a few Accelerated Schools in the State.

References

Allington, R. L., and H. Woodside-Jiron. 1999. The politics of literacy teaching: How 'research' shaped policy. *Educational Researcher* 28(8): 4–12.

Askew, B. J., and D. F. Frazier. 1994. Substantial effects of reading of Reading Recovery interventions on the cognitive behaviors of second grade children and the perceptions of their teachers. *Literacy, Teaching, and Learning* 1(1): 240–63.

Australian Council for Education Research. 1993a. *The impact of First Steps on the reading and writing ability of Western Australian year 5 school students*. An Interim Report to the Curriculum Development Branch Western Australia Ministry of Education.

———. 1993b. *The impact of First Steps on schools and teachers.* An Interim Report to the Curriculum Development Branch Western Australia Ministry of Education.

Bardzell, J. 1999a. Literacy Collaborative. In *Improving early reading and literacy: A guide for developing research-based programs*, edited by E. P. St. John, J. S. Bardzell, and associates. Bloomington: Indiana Education Policy Center.

———. 1999b. Reading Recovery. In *Improving early reading and literacy: A guide for developing research-based programs*, edited by E. P. St. John, J. S. Bardzell, and associates. Bloomington: Indiana Education Policy Center.

———. 1999c. Success for All. In *Improving early reading and literacy: A guide for developing research-based programs*, edited by E. P. St. John, J. S. Bardzell, and associates. Bloomington: Indiana Education Policy Center.

Bull, B., and M. Buechler. 1996. *Learning together: Professional development for better schools.* Bloomington: Indiana Education Policy Center.

Chall, J. S. 1967. *Learning to read: The great debate.* New York: McGraw-Hill.

Cunningham, P. M. 1991. Research directions: Multi-method, multilevel, literacy instruction in first grade. *Language Arts* 68: 578–84.

Cunningham, P. M., D. P. Hall, and M. Defee. 1991. Non-ability grouped, multilevel instruction: A year in a first grade classroom. *Reading Teacher* 44(8): 566–71.

———. 1998. Non-ability grouped, multilevel instruction: Eight years later. *Reading Teacher* 51(8): 652–64.

Deschamp, P. 1995. *Case studies of the implementation of the First Steps Project in twelve schools.* Western Australia, Education Department. (ERIC Document Reproduction Service No. ED 419 425).

Foorman, B. R., J. M. Fletcher, D. J. Francis, and C. Schatschneider. 2000. Response: Misrepresentation of research by other researchers. *Educational Researcher* 29(6): 27–37.

Foorman, B. R., D. J. Francis, J. M. Fletcher, C. Schatschneider, and P. Mehta. 1998. The role of instruction in learning to read: Preventing reading failure in at-risk children. *Journal of Educational Psychology* 90(1): 37–55.

Iverson, S., and W. E. Tunmer. 1993. Phonological processing skills and the Reading Recovery program. *Journal of Educational Psychology* 85(1): 112–26.

Lyons, C. A. 1994. Reading Recovery and learning disability: Issues, challenges, and implications. *Literacy, Teaching, and Learning* 1(1): 109–19.

Madden, N. A., R. E. Slavin, N. L. Karweit, L. Dolan, and B. A. Wasik. 1991. *Success for All: Multi-year effects of a school-wide elementary restructuring program.* Report no. 18. Baltimore, Md.: Center for Research on Effective Schools.

Madden, N. A., R. E. Slavin, N. L. Karweit, B. J. Livermon, and L. Donlan. 1989. *Success for All: First-year effects of a comprehensive plan for reforming urban education.* Report no. 30. Baltimore, Md.: Center for Research on Elementary and Middle Schools.

Manoil, K. 1999. First steps. In *Improving early reading and literacy: A guide for developing research-based programs*, edited by E. P. St. John, J. S. Bardzell, and associates. Bloomington: Indiana Education Policy Center.

Manoil, K., and J. Bardzell. 1999. Four Blocks. In *Improving early reading and literacy: A guide for developing research-based programs*, ed. E. P. St. John, J. S. Bardzell, and associates. Bloomington: Indiana Education Policy Center.

Mathes, P. B., and J. K. Torgesen. 2000. A call for equity in reading instruction for all students: A response to Allington and Woodside. *Educational Researcher* 29(6): 4–14.

Pinnell, G., C. A. Lyons, D. DeFord, A. Bryk, and M. Seltzer. 1994. Comparing instructional models for literacy education of high-risk first graders. *Reading Research Quarterly* 29(1): 9–39.

Pinnell, G. S., D. E. DeFord, and C. A. Lyons. 1998. *Reading Recovery: Early intervention for at-risk first graders.* Arlington, PA: Educators Research Service.

Reading Recovery Project. 1998. Literacy Collaborative. Columbus, OH: Author.

Ross, P. M., and L. J. Smith. 1994. Effects of the success for all model on kindergarten through second-grade reading achievement, teachers' adjustment, and classroom-school climate at an inner-city school. *Elementary School Journal* 95(2): 121–38.

St. John, E. P., J. S. Bardzell, and associates. 1999. *Improving early reading and literacy: A guide for developing research-based programs.* Bloomington: Indiana Education Policy Center.

St. John, E. P., J. S. Bardzell, R. Michael, G. Hall, K. Manoil, E. Asker, and M. Clements. 1998. *Indiana's Early Literacy Intervention Grant Program implementation study.* Bloomington: Indiana Education Policy Center.

St. John, E. P., G. Manset, C. G. Chung, A. B. Simmons, and G. D. Musoba. 2000. *Research-based reading interventions: The impact of Indiana's early literacy intervention grant program.* Policy Research Report 00-07. Bloomington: Indiana Education Policy Center.

St. John, E. P., G. Manset, and R. Michael. 1999. Early reading and literacy classroom survey. In *Improving early reading and literacy: A guide for developing research-based programs*, edited by E. P. St. John, J. S. Bardzell, and associates. Bloomington: Indiana Education Policy Center.

St. John, E. P., G. Manset, S. Hu, A. Simmons, and R. Michael. 2000. *Assessing the impact of reading interventions: Indiana's Early Literacy Intervention Grant Program.* Policy Research Report #00-01. Bloomington: Indiana Education Policy Center.

Slavin, R. 1991. *Education for all: Contexts of learning*. Lisse, Netherlands: Swets and Zeitlinger.

Slavin, R., N. Madden, L. Dolan, B. Wasik, S. Ross, and L. Smith. 1994. Whenever and wherever we choose: The replication of "Success for All." *Phi Delta Kappan* 75(8): 639–47.

Snow, C., M. Burns, and P. Griffin. 1998. *Preventing reading difficulties in young children.* Washington, D.C.: National Academy Press.

Taylor, B. M., R. C. Anderson, K. H. Au, and E. R. Taffy. 2000. Discretion in translation of research to policy: A case from beginning reading. *Educational Researcher* 29(6): 16–26.

Chapter 7

Comprehensive School Reform: An Exploratory Study

*Edward P. St. John, Genevieve Manset, Choong-Geun Chung, Glenda Droogsma Musoba, Siri Loescher, Ada B. Simmons, David Gordon, and Carol Anne Hossler**

Comprehensive school reform (CSR) models were originally developed and tested by independent reformers, but are now widely available for school adoption through Title I. Accelerated Schools (developed by Henry Levin), Success for All (developed by Robert Slavin), and School Development Program (developed by James Comer) were the early models that were targeted for high-risk students in urban schools. In 1994, Congress enabled high-poverty schools to adopt CSR models, as part of the school-wide option under Title I. Then in 1997, Congress passed the Comprehensive School Reform Demonstration Project Act, which provided funding for multiyear, school-improvement efforts. As of July 2000, over 1,800 schools received large, multiyear grants for implementing these reforms (Datnow 2000).

Although these independent CSR models are generally characterized as "research based" and schools applying for funding are required to rationalize their choice based on the research literature, there is very little research that compares these reform models. Much of the research to date on CSR models has been conducted by reform advocates. The most widely acknowledged method has been experimental studies that compared schools engaged in reform to "control" schools with similar characteristics (e.g., Knight and Stallings 1995; Madden et al. 1991). Initial studies that compare reforms have examined the implementation process of these reforms and reveal that local politics often influence the choice of reform models (Datnow 2000). Therefore, research that looks critically at the claims of reformers and examines the impact of reforms, controlling for the characteristics of schools, can potentially inform school decisions, as well as add to a general understanding of the efficacy of the comprehensive reform strategy, a form of policy intervention.

This chapter presents an exploratory study of CSR models in Wisconsin that tests some claims made by reformers. First, we review some of the literature on comprehensive reform models and suggest a preliminary conceptual framework for assessing the impact of comprehensive reforms. Then we describe the research approach used in this exploratory study, discuss the findings, and consider the implications for educators in urban schools who are considering CSR models. We analyze surveys of classroom teachers in specially selected high poverty/high performing schools and CSR schools in Wisconsin. Given that Wisconsin does not allow social promotion, it was especially appropriate to assess the impact of these reforms on reductions in grade retention as an equity-related educational outcome. Reduction in special education referral was also examined as an outcome.

Assessing Comprehensive Reforms

The advocates of the early comprehensive school reform models—Slavin, Comer, and Levin—focused on improving urban schools. Over time, these initial models have been generalized beyond urban settings, and additional models have been added to the catalog of CSR models included in federal and state lists (e.g., Northwest Regional Educational Laboratory 1998). This evolution, from models targeted at the needs of urban schools to models that are generalized for all schools, complicates efforts to understand which reform approaches will be of greatest help in urban schools. As a way of illustrating how CSR models have evolved, we briefly review two of the models below—Accelerated Schools and America's Choice—then present the conceptual framework we used to assess the effects of these reforms in the Wisconsin study described below. These two models offer contrasting approaches to reform.

Accelerated Schools

The Accelerated Schools Project (ASP) is a process-oriented CSR model that involves the whole school staff and the entire school community in school-wide reform process (Finnan et al. 1996; Hopfenberg, Levin, and associates 1993). During the first stage of the process, school communities take stock of their current status, develop a vision for the future of the school, and identify challenges—the gaps between the schools' current state and the vision—that they need to address to reach the vision. In the second stage, the schools organize cadres that use an inquiry process to address the challenge. Initiated as an elementary school reform model, the ASP has been extended to middle schools, but has not been widely adopted in high schools. The ASP remains a process-oriented reform but is now placing more emphasis on curriculum. Recent estimates suggest that 1,600 schools use the ASP.

The ASP provides a set of philosophies to guide the school improvement process. A core belief in the early ASP movement was the notion that the techniques that were used for gifted children could also be used for at-risk children. The core learning philosophy that has evolved in accelerated schools is constructivist. Referred to as "powerful learning," the model's philosophy is rooted in cognitive psychology. It has five central instructional components that are based on the research literature: authentic, interactive, inclusive, learner-centered, and continuous (Accelerated Schools 1997).

Professional development is central to the ASP. Teams from the schools (usually comprised of teachers, the principal, a parent, and an external coach) attend a training session where they learn the first-year process. They return to the school and provide training for others. As the reform process continues, the teams receive more advanced training in inquiry, powerful learning, and other topics. The model emphasizes collaboration among teachers and parents and advocates building learning communities within schools (Finnan et al. 1996).

Early in the accelerated schools movement, the goal was to enable every child to achieve on grade level by the end of the third grade. Conceptually this relates to the two equity-related outcomes used in this study, reduction in retention in grade level and reduction in special education referral. However, since the program lacks a specific curriculum, the linkages to standardized tests are weak compared to Success for All (reviewed in chapter 6).

In the past few years, with the advent of statewide learning standards in most states, the ASP has been adapted to integrate an emphasis on meeting state standards. Schools are encouraged to consider how well they meet state standards when they take stock and to consider ways to meeting standards when they identify challenges. If this process is used, then it is possible that the ASP will evolve a more explicit emphasis on curriculum innovations that could enable schools to meet learning standards. However, ASP remains a school-wide reform method that focuses on the entire school community.

America's Choice

The America's Choice reform model, previously known as the National Alliance for Restructuring Education, is associated with the National Center on Education and the Economy and its New Standards Program. The America's Choice design grew out of the New Standards Project, which had developed internationally benchmarked content and performance standards and related performance-based exams. The America's Choice model built on this work to create school programs that offer rigorous, standards-based courses of study. America's Choice combines a process-oriented model with a defined curriculum. This is a K–12 reform model with curriculum for elementary, middle, and high schools (National Center for Education and the Economy 2000b, 2000c, 2000d).

The America's Choice model requires a one-year buy-in process during which a reform team is formed that studies the model. Once they decide to use this model, they initiate the reform process by taking stock, a study process in which they collect base-line information. They form a study team that compares student performance to the New Standards's performance standards. The standards provide the basis for the instructional model and methods.

America's Choice provides curricula in language arts and math that are closely aligned with the New Standards (National Center for Education and the Economy 2000). The learning system includes ongoing written observations and frequent assessments. However, the model also encourages teachers to reflect on their instructional practices and to experiment with alternative instructional approaches. Thus, America's Choice offers more freedom in instructional processes than do some of the other prescriptive reform methods, such as Success for All.

With the heavy emphasis on standards and curriculum alignment, the America's Choice model emphasizes tests as the primary outcome. However, since the model provides a "double dose" of math and reading for students who have trouble learning, the model could also improve equity outcomes (e.g., reduce retention and special education referral). Research on this model has been more limited than for some of the other CSR reform models, but they are developing a research base (New America Schools 1999).

A Preliminary Framework

These models illustrate the contrast in approaches that are being used for comprehensive reform, from process-oriented models that emphasize building community, to standards-oriented models that emphasize test and curriculum alignment. Given this diversity, it is important that urban schools have the opportunity to compare CSR models to discern which ones best meet their needs. Based on a recent review of CSR models (St. John et al. 2000), we suggest that two levels of analysis and review are needed.

First, it is important that schools compare the process features: school-wide processes, parent involvement, philosophies, and professional development processes. These school-wide processes create a culture for the school. Along with the specific instruction and organizational processes implemented, they provide a basis for improving student outcomes. Two types of outcomes are important:

- *Attainment/Equity*. Increasing graduation rates for all students. Intermediate measures include reduction in grade retention rates and reduction in special education referral rates.
- *Achievement*. Scores and passing rates on standardized tests in reading (and language arts), math, and science.

Focusing on both types of outcomes brings more balance to school reforms than is currently evident. Interventions that emphasize standardized tests can reduce equity in education attainment (see chapter 6).

Second, we consider the ways that the curriculum components of reforms link to student learning outcomes. It is important to consider the types of learning outcomes that are emphasized and how the curriculum links to these outcomes. For example, some reading reforms take a meaning-oriented approach and emphasize embedded sound-letter relationships, whereas others focus explicitly on phonemic relationships between letters and sounds. These differences have implications for the ways students learn to read (see chapter 6) and merit consideration when reform methods are chosen. There are also substantial differences in the approaches that reforms take to math. In this chapter we consider how general patterns of curriculum and instruction on the one hand and specific learning outcomes on the other provide the scaffolding for student learning and merit specific consideration when schools choose reforms.

Based on these two levels of consideration, it is possible to develop an empirical model for assessing the impact of reforms on educational outcomes. In this study, we examined the effects of reform on reducing retention from one year to the next at the classroom level. Our model considers the influence of school characteristics (ethnicity, poverty, and locale), reform type, professional development, parent involvement, and classroom practices on reductions in retention and in special education referral. Improvements in these outcomes are likely to increase the percentage of children who graduate and are academically prepared to attend college.

Research Approach

A total of 667 teachers received the survey and 365 teachers responded, for a response rate of 54.3 percent. Some surveys were missing data and were also removed from the final analysis. This analysis includes teachers in seven High Poverty/High Performing (HP/HP) schools, chosen by the Wisconsin Department of Education because their percentage of economically disadvantaged students was double the state average at grade and their students scored at 90 percent of or above the state average on three of the four sections of the Wisconsin Knowledge and Concept Exam across the most recent two years. It also included six CSR schools, chosen to provide a match with the HP/HP schools. This section describes the survey instrument, statistical methods, model specifications, and study limitations.

Survey Instrument

The survey was developed in a two-step process. First, based on our research on early literacy in Indiana, we developed a survey instrument that asked about classroom practices that were closely aligned with the description of program features of reading reforms (St. John, Bardzell, and associates 1999; St. John, Manset, and Michael 1999). This instrument identified specific features related to professional development, parent involvement, and classroom practices (instruction and organization/structure) and asked about the extent of implementation.

At the outset of the Wisconsin study, we adapted the survey instrument to examine comprehensive reforms and to consider middle and high schools as well as elementary schools. The major adaptations were generalizing the curriculum features and adding features related to general classroom practices in K–12 schools. The revised instrument represents a general survey of classroom practice, but includes some questions related to comprehensive reform. Based on this preliminary study, as well as refinements to our review methods (St. John et al., forthcoming), it is possible to make further refinements in the instrument in the future that would align more directly with the features of comprehensive school reform models. The basic components of the survey are summarized briefly below.

First, the questionnaire included questions about reform models. Fifteen CSR models were identified and teachers were given an opportunity to indicate if they used these methods. These questions provide an indication of the classroom teachers' perceptions of the reform method they were using. These were simple yes/no responses.

Second, we had five questions about whether teachers had opportunities for five types of professional development (certified specialists, in-service workshops, networking, peer review/observation, and opportunities for collaboration). These questions were analyzed as a dichotomous outcome, yes or no "this feature was available to me."

Third, a set of questions was asked about parent involvement, which were analyzed with yes or no outcomes. Teachers were asked if there were parent-teacher conferences, material distribution, parents in the classroom, shared homework, family education, parents in the schools, and family communication.

Fourth, questions about structure/organization and instruction features used a Likert scale. Teachers were asked about frequency of use ("never" to "every day") using a Likert scale about structural/organizational features in their classrooms. Questions were asked about fifteen features. Similarly, teachers were asked about instructional practices using a Likert scale to indicate frequency of use. Questions were asked about twenty-one instructional practices representing a range of teaching methods.

In addition questions were asked about implemented philosophies, special education referral ("last year" and "this year"), and retention rates ("last year" and "this year"). As an outcome, this study focuses on whether there was a reduction in retention rates (for the current year in comparison to the prior year).

Statistical Methods

Three types of statistical analyses are presented in this exploratory study. First, we present a factor analysis of the program features related to instruction and structure organization. This ten-factor solution identifies patterns of classroom practice that were included in the statistical model. Second, we present the descriptive statistics for the variables included in the statistical model. Third, because we used dichotomous outcomes (whether there were reductions in retention and special education referral), we present a logistic regression analysis. Logistic regression is generally regarded as an appropriate statistical method for analyses that consider qualitative, dichotomous outcomes (Aldrich and Nelson 1986; Cabrera 1994).

Model Specification

This model represents a preliminary analysis of the influence of school reform methods on reduction in retention rates and a reduction in special education referrals. Specific variables related to school characteristics, reform models, professional development, parent involvement, and classroom practices are outlined below.

First, three variables related to school characteristics were examined. The school's percentages of minority students and economically disadvantaged students are entered as continuous variables. Schools in cities were compared to schools in other locales.

Second, the model included eight dichotomous variables related to the types of CSR models used in classrooms: Accelerated Schools, America's Choice, Co-NECT Schools, Core Knowledge, Direct Instruction, School Development Process, Success for All, and Other. Only slightly more than half of the respondents indicated that they used any reform type. These variables represent teachers' perceptions of the methods they were using in their classroom compared to all other cases in the sample.

Third, four variables related to professional development were examined. Certified specialists, networking, peer review/observations, and opportunities for collaboration were treated as independent dichotomous variables. These variables indicate whether teachers used these practices. Although teachers were also asked about in-service workshops, there was little variation in access to this form of professional development, so this variable was not included in the analysis.

Fourth, four variables related to parent involvement were examined: materials distribution, parents in the classroom, shared homework, and family education. They were also entered as independent dichotomous variables.

Finally, ten variables related to classroom practices were considered. These variables are continuous variables and represent the factor scores for each of these variables. The factors are described in the findings below.

Limitations

The analyses presented in this paper represent an exploratory analysis of the effects of CSRs on classroom outcomes. It represents a step forward in the research on comprehensive school reform, but it is a preliminary study. The analysis has some limitations.

First, the classrooms represented by the teacher surveys represent the practices in the schools surveyed, but the schools are not representative of the universe of schools in Wisconsin. The schools were selected for the study either because they were HP/HP schools or because they were CSR schools. School leaders had the opportunity to participate in the study. We consider this limitation in our discussion of findings. However, the study still has meaning as an exploratory study on the impact of comprehensive reform.

Second, the statistical model we use in this study could be further refined. Two specific refinements merit consideration in future studies. First, the reforms themselves could be classified into groups and compared to classrooms that did not use a reform model. If an appropriate typology were developed, it might be possible to assess how different types (i.e. process-based models, curriculum-based models, and so forth) of reforms influenced student outcomes. Second, the measures we use for classroom practices could be further refined, possibly developing sets of design variables related to classroom practices, an approach that might be better for logistic regression modeling.

Third, there was a relatively large number of missing values. Although there was an N of 365 in our descriptive analysis, fewer than half of these responses were included in the logistic models, due to missing cases. Consistent with the requirements of the statistical methods, we assumed that missing responses were randomly distributed. The low rate of response was probably related to asking questions about special education referral and retention for the current year, a calculation that some teachers could find hard to make. In the future better efforts should be made to adjust for missing responses.

In spite of these limitations, the current analyses provide insight into the effects of comprehensive reforms on student outcomes. Specifically, we examine reductions in retention and special education referral as equity-related outcomes. In the remainder of this chapter we summarize the findings and consider the implications for future research and practices.

Findings

Patterns of Classroom Practices

The factor analysis of the structural/organizational features and classroom/instructional features (Table 7.1) provided a ten-factor solution. These factors were:

- *Grouping Approaches.* Individualized instruction, ability grouping, small groups, and "pull-out" instruction.
- *Remedial Approaches.* One-on-one tutorials, preventive methodologies, and remedial methodologies.
- *Practical / Vocational Approaches.* Hands-on learning, computers, practical applications, and vocational studies.
- *Creative / Thematic Approaches.* Thematic units, portfolios, creative arts, and communication.
- *Special-Needs Approaches.* Adequate resources for at-risk students, students with disabilities, and students with limited English proficiency (LEP).
- *Cooperative Approaches.* Cooperative learning and assessment of performance tasks.
- *Basal Approaches.* Basal readers or textbooks and worksheets/workbooks.
- *Direct / Lecture Approaches.* Whole classroom instruction, teacher lecturing, and direct instruction.
- *Collaboration.* Teachers collaboratively teach and teachers collaboratively plan.
- *Independent-Reading Approaches.* Uses independent reading, but negatively associated with multi-age classrooms.

These combinations of variables represented common patterns of practice among teachers in the thirteen schools included in this study, a combination of CSR and HP/HP schools. In the logistic model, summarized below, we consider whether these patterns of practice were associated with reductions in retention rates and special education referral in these schools.

TABLE 7.1
Loading for Factors

	Factor 1	*Factor 2*	*Factor 3*	*Factor 4*	*Factor 5*	*Factor 6*	*Factor 7*	*Factor 8*	*Factor 9*	*Factor 10*
Structural / Organizational Features										
Individualized Instruction	0.53									
Ability Grouping	0.71									
Whole Classroom Instruction								0.63		
Small Group	0.65									
"Pullout" Instruction	0.64									
Cooperative Learning						0.64				
One-to-One Tutorial		0.56								
Performance Assessment						0.68				
Thematic Units				0.60						
Teachers Collaboratively Teach									0.70	
Teachers Collaboratively Plan									0.81	
Multiage Classrooms										−0.69
Classroom / Instructional Features										
Basal Readers or Textbooks							0.53			
Independent Reading										0.61
Portfolios				0.55						
Teacher Lecturing								0.59		
Direct Instruction								0.67		
Hands-On Learning Instruction			0.51							
Creative Arts				0.62						
Communication				0.60						
Resources for Students At-Risk					0.70					
Resources for Students with Disabilities					0.83					
Resources for Students with LEP					0.70					
Computers			0.62							
Practical Application			0.55							
Worksheets/Workbooks							0.68			
Vocational Studies			0.66							
Preventive Methodologies		0.74								
Remedial Methodologies		0.72								

Characteristics of the Populations

The population characteristics are summarized in Table 7.2. About 9 percent of the classrooms had a reduction in retention rates between 1998–99 and 1999–2000. The logistic analyses below examined the variables significantly associated with this outcome and with a reduction in special education referrals.

Most of these schools and classrooms were urban (68%), and there was some economic diversity. About 30 percent of the average school was economically disadvantaged (on free or reduced lunch) with a modest standard deviation (16%). However, the percentage of minorities was only 22 percent, with a standard deviation of 17 percent. This illustrates a wide variation in ethnicity, with some schools with very few minority students and a few with a high percentage of minority students. In five of the thirteen schools, over 90 percent of the students were white. In an additional five schools, at least 75 percent of the students were white. Three of the schools (two CSR and one HP/HP) would be considered diverse schools. In these schools, the percentage of white students ranged from 28 percent to 55 percent with African-American students being the other main group.

In this analysis Accelerated Schools was most often selected by teachers as a method they were using (7.1%). Other nationally known methods that were cited by more than two teachers included Direct Instruction (4.7%) or Co-NECT (4.4%), School Development Program (1.6%), America's Choice (1.4%), and Success for All (1.1%). In addition, other reforms were selected by about a third of the teachers. The "other" category included a few one- or two-person responses to other national reforms and a large number of teachers who indicated "other" (meaning their own locally developed reform method). The "other" category was about one-third (36%) of the population.

Professional development activities were evident. A majority of teachers indicated access to certified specialists. About half indicated use of networking and collaboration. Nearly one-third indicated a use of peer review/observation.

In addition, parent involvement was widespread in these classrooms. Virtually all of the teachers indicated a use of parent-teacher conferences and planned efforts to communicate with students' families. Shared homework, family education, and parents in schools were evident in most of these schools. Materials distribution was used in about 40 percent of the classrooms and parents were involved in about 30 percent of these classrooms.

TABLE 7.2
Descriptive Statistics of the Sample

	Mean (%)[1]	*S.D.*
Outcome Variables		
Having less retention	8.9%	
Having less referral	14.0%	
School Characteristics		
% Economically Disadvantaged	.30	.16
% Minority	.22	.17
City	68.2%	
Reform Model / Program		
Accelerated Schools	7.1%	
America's Choice School Design	1.4%	
Co-NECT Schools	4.4%	
Direct Instruction	4.7%	
School Development Program	1.6%	
Success For All	1.1%	
Other	36.4%	
Professional Development		
Certified Specialist	59.9%	
Networking	44.6%	
Peer Review/Observation	28.5%	
Opportunities for Collaboration	49.3%	
Parent Involvement		
Materials Distribution	39.9%	
Parents in the Classroom	28.2%	
Shared Homework	67.7%	
Family Education	61.8%	

Note: n = 365.

[1]Percentages only are reported for dichotomous variables. Averages and standard deviations are reported when percentages are used as continuous variables.

Reduction in Retention

The analysis of reductions in grade retention is an especially noteworthy outcome for schools in Wisconsin because the state has rules that prohibit social promotion. Therefore, we can assume that reduction in retention is related to gains in education. Below we consider the influence of five sets of variables on the outcome.

First, two variables related to school characteristics were associated with reductions in retention. The percentage of minority students was negatively associated with reductions in retention, whereas the percentage of economically disadvantaged students was positively associated with reductions in retention (0.1, a modest association). At first glance this might seem contradictory, but we need to consider that half of the schools were selected because they were high-poverty and high-performing. The state had a difficult time identifying urban schools that met the criteria of being high-performing and high-poverty, which complicated the findings. Apparently the high-performing schools, which had fewer minority students (because they were less urban), had a positive association with this outcome, controlling for other variables in the model.

Second, one of the school reform models, Accelerated Schools, was positively associated with reduction in retention. This finding is certainly consonant with the philosophy of Accelerated Schools, which emphasizes enabling every student to achieve on grade level (Hopfenberg, Levin, and associates 1993). Therefore this is a noteworthy finding for Accelerated Schools. However, the fact that other reforms were not significant is not necessarily problematic, given that the reference group for this set of design variables is classrooms in high-performing schools.

Third, none of the professional development variables were significant. This finding reaffirms the notion that professional development influences educational outcomes by influencing change in classroom practices (St. John, Ward, and Laine 1999). This hypothesis merits further examination in future studies.

Fourth, three variables related to parent involvement were significant. Distribution of material (books and so forth) to families was positively associated with reductions in retention (0.1, a modest association). This is reasonable, given that these interventions generally intend to involve parents directly in the education of their children. However, parents volunteering in classrooms and family education were negatively associated with reductions in retention. The reasons for these associations merit further exploration.

Finally, three of the instructional/structural factors were also significantly associated with reductions in retention. *Individualized/Small Groups Approaches* and *Basal Approaches* were both positively associated with reductions in retention. In contrast, *Collaborative Approaches* were negatively associated with reductions in referral. The factors represent combinations of classroom practices that usually fall together in day-to-day practice. Apparently, high-structured approaches (Basal) that can be individualized or adapted to work with small groups enabled more students in these schools to make academic progress. Further investigation would be needed to explain the negative association between collaborative approaches and retention.

TABLE 7.3
Coefficients of Predictors on Retention and Referral Changes in Binary Logistic Regressions

	Having Less Retention		*Having Less Referral*	
Variables	*Beta*	*Sig.*	*Beta*	*Sig*
School Characteristics				
City	29.25		3.96	*
% Minorities	−30.19	**	2.03	
% Economically Disadvantaged	47.92	*	−7.09	
Reform Model				
Accelerated Schools	12.74	**	−1.58	
America's Choice School Design	3.40		−8.72	
Co-NECT Schools	28.17		−6.24	
Direct Instruction	−12.78		−11.22	
Success For All	−2.98		−9.60	
Other	0.47		0.42	
Professional Development				
Certified Specialist	0.88		0.00	
Networking	0.51		1.65	
Peer Review/Observation	0.21		1.80	
Opportunities for Collaboration	−0.19		−1.80	*
Parent Involvement				
Materials Distribution	2.00	*	1.40	*
Parents in the Classroom	−4.10	**	−0.23	
Shared Homework	0.10		−0.15	
Family Education	−3.70	**	−0.87	
Factors				
Factor 1 Individualized/Small Group	1.50	*	0.25	
Factor 2 Preventive/Remedial	−0.55		−0.11	
Factor 3 Vocational	0.90		−0.25	
Factor 4 Creative/Thematic	−0.15		−0.01	
Factor 5 Special Needs	0.26		−0.93	*
Factor 6 Cooperative	0.33		0.28	
Factor 7 Basal	1.45	**	0.21	
Factor 8 Direct/Lecture	−0.31		0.11	
Factor 9 Collaborative	−1.32	**	0.28	
Factor 10 Independent Reading	−0.22		1.75	***
N	145		134	
−2logL	49.651		67.859	
Cox & Snell R^2	0.254		0.225	
% Correctly Predicted	90.3		88.8	

Note: * $p \leqslant 0.1$, ** $p \leqslant 0.05$, *** $p \leqslant 0.01$

Special Education Referral

Special education referral is another learning outcome that is occasionally used as an indicator of success in early reading interventions. In this study, we focused on reductions in referral because this measure is a reasonable indicator of whether equity is being realized in the opportunity to attain educationally.

First, only one of the school characteristics had a significant association with reduction in referral. Being an urban school was positively associated with reductions in referral (0.1, a modest association), but poverty and ethnicity per se were not significant. This suggests that the CSR schools, which were more likely to be urban schools, were successful. This is potentially good news for urban educators. It suggests that getting involved in a comprehensive reform can help more students achieve on grade level in urban schools. However, since this is a modest association and a preliminary study, we are cautious in reaching a firm conclusion.

Second, none of the specific reform models were statistically significant. This means that that teachers using these CSR models had about the same probability of reducing referrals as did teachers in high-performing, high-poverty schools.

Third, one variable related to professional development was associated with special education referral. Teachers who collaborated on planning and instruction were less likely to report reductions in special education referral (0.1, a modest association). Because classrooms that use mainstreaming for special education and Title I require more collaboration, it is possible that this finding is an artifact of this arrangement, a possibility that merits further exploration.

Fourth, materials distribution was positively associated with reductions in special education referral (0.1, modest association). The fact that this strategy for involving parents in the education of their children is once again significant and positive is a noteworthy finding. It reinforces the idea that involving parents in the education of their children is a workable approach.

Fifth, two of the factors related to classroom practices were significantly associated with reductions in special education referral. Using *Special-Needs Approaches* was negatively associated with reduction in special education referral (0.1, modest association). This finding is an artifact of sorts, in the sense that classrooms with *Special-Needs Approaches* have more referral. However, this finding also merits reflection, especially if the methods influence more referral. Finally, *Independent-Reading Approaches* were positively associated with reductions in special education referral, a finding that supports arguments for the use of gifted techniques in school reform.

Discussion

Although this study does not focus exclusively on urban communities, it does deal primarily with urban schools. However, the findings can help inform an understanding of the role of CSRs within the broader picture of urban school reform.

First, urban schools with high percentages of minority students face especially difficult challenges in efforts to improve educational outcome. Urban schools were significantly different than other schools in one analysis when the analysis controlled for both poverty and ethnicity. This finding suggests that comprehensive approaches to reform may help urban schools. However, schools with high percentages of minority students were less likely to reduce retention rates whereas schools with higher poverty rates were more likely to reduce retention rates. These findings on retention were troubling because they indicate that schools with high percentages of minority student were more resistant to improvement in this study.

Second, not all reforms are equal. In this study of Wisconsin schools, classrooms that used Accelerated Schools methods were more likely to reduce grade-level retention. However, the other reforms examined in this study were not significantly different than the nonreform classrooms. Because the reference group in this study was classrooms in high-performing/high-poverty schools, the finding that these other reforms were not statistically significant does not mean these methods were ineffectual. Rather using these methods was not significantly different than the reference group, classrooms in high performing schools.

Third, the professional development processes generally were not significantly associated with educational outcomes. Only the opportunity to collaborate was modestly significant and it was negatively associated with reductions in special education referral. However, the finding of nonsignificance does not preclude the possibility that professional development has an influence indirectly, by influencing changes in parental involvement and classroom practice. Indeed, the substance of professional development—the content of training and the methods they emphasize—may be more important than the type of training provided.

Fourth, classroom practices also have an influence on educational practice. Classrooms that used *Individualized/Small Group Approaches* and *Basal Approaches* were significant and associated with reductions in retention. Given that *Individualized / Small Group Approaches* and *Remedial Approaches* are distinct features, it is clear this former was associated with instructional practices. In contrast, the fact that *Basal Approaches* were associated with reduction in retention means that a systematic curriculum helps with reading and comprehension.

Interestingly, *Collaborative Approaches* were significant and negatively associated with less grade retention. It was unexpected that classrooms with collaborative planning and teaching were less likely to reduce retention, especially given the emphasis on collaborative methods in the professional development literature (Bull and Buechler 1996). This finding could be an artifact of mainstreaming, in the sense that these classrooms generally have more collaboration built in. If this is a plausible explanation, then these findings merit further examination.

Further, classrooms that used *Independent-Reading Approaches* were associated with reductions in special education referral, a finding that reinforces arguments for individualizing curriculum. Indeed, this finding on special education referral complements the finding on materials distribution. Strategies that encourage reading—through material distribution or independent reading—help keep more students in the educational mainstream.

Implications

First, these findings suggest that many factors influence improvements in learning outcomes. In this study one reform model—Accelerated Schools—was associated with improvement in student outcomes. The Accelerated Schools Project (ASP) differs from other types of reforms in the sense that it encourages schools to experiment with new approaches, rather than emphasizing a packaged approach. The ASP model is a school-wide reform process that welcomes the participation of the entire school staff and school community. The process is structured so that school community members reflect upon the current status, define a future vision of the school, and identify challenges that must be addressed in order to become what school community members have envisioned. This form of collaboration among teachers and building administrators is frequently mentioned as an effective strategy for changing and improving schools (Barth 1991; Fullan 1999; Joyce, Wolf, and Calhoun 1993; Wald 2000).

Several of the patterns of classroom practices were associated with reduction in retention. *Individualized / Small Group Approaches* and *Basal Approaches* were both associated with increasing the percentage of children who progress to the next grade. The latter of these is a systematic approach, whereas the former involves adapting the system to meet diverse learning needs. This suggests that a comprehensive and balanced approach may be important. The fact that *Independent Reading Approaches* were positively associated with reduction in special education referral further reinforces this line of reasoning.

Second, these findings support arguments that schools need to carefully study the features of reform and select reforms that complement their patterns of practice. In making decisions about reform methods, the specific method that is chosen may be less important than the ways the reform process influences classroom practice. Specifically, these findings suggest new directions in the focus of research on comprehensive schools reform. It is crucial that research move beyond the stage of comparing models and comparing different types of reforms, to focusing on the ways educational practices change in schools as a result of implementing CSR models. It is also important to examine the cultures in schools, along with the political forces, that influence the selection and implementation of CSR models. If classroom practices do impact student outcomes, then it is crucial to develop better ways of assessing how reforms change these practices.

Third, it is important to also consider more explicitly reforms in schools that serve mostly minority students. We found that schools with high percentages of minority students were more resistant to reduction in retention, a troubling finding. This means that in the efforts to find better reform models, researchers and policymakers need to focus on what works for schools that serve minority children. Although the comprehensive reforms are a step in the right direction, they do not appear to be a universal solution to the problems facing urban schools.

Fourth, because education reform is a complex process that involves changing classroom practices, policymakers should avoid simple solutions to school improvement. How and why schools change their classroom practices may be more important than the selection of any particular reform type. Reform methods that allow educators to adapt their methods appear more successful than reforms with more fixed curricular approaches. Thus, there is strong evidence from this study that it is important to encourage educators to focus on classroom practices when they choose and implement a reform model. This means that the process of studying, choosing, and implementing reforms may be more important than which reforms they choose.

Finally, this study has implications for future research on comprehensive school reform. Little systematic research has been conducted on comprehensive school reform efforts. Much of the published literature can be characterized as propositional in nature. In other words these publications advocate the benefits of CSR models based on extant research, but there are, in fact, few empirical studies that test the assertions made by advocates of various CSR models. Research on CSR models requires more systematic survey research, qualitative case studies, and analysis of available learning outcomes data that can be linked to CSR efforts. This is no easy task.

Notes

*We thank the North Central Regional Educational Laboratory (NCREL) for funding the survey analyzed in this chapter. The views are the authors' and do not represent official policies or positions of the funding agency.

1. Percentages only are reported for dichotomous variables. Averages and standard deviations are reported when percentages are used as continuous variables.

References

Accelerated Schools Project 1997. *Powerful learning: Conceptual foundation*. Stanford, Calif.: National Center for the Accelerated School Project.

Aldrich, J. H., and F. D. Nelson. 1986. *Linear probability, logit and probit models*. 3d ed. Beverly Hills, Calif.: Sage.

Barth, R. 1991. *Improving schools from within*. San Francisco: Jossey-Bass.

Bull, B., and M. Buechler. 1996. *Learning together: Professional development for better schools*. Bloomington: Indiana Education Policy Center.

Cabrera, A. F. 1994. Applied logistic regression. In *Higher education: Handbook of theory and research*, edited by J. C. Smart. New York: Agathon.

Datnow, A. 2000. Power and politics in the adoption of school reform models. *Education Evaluation and Policy Analysis* 22: 357–74.

Finnan, C., E. P. St. John, S. P. Slovacek, and J. McCarthy, eds. 1996. *Accelerated schools in action: Lessons from the field*. Thousand Oaks, Calif.: Corwin.

Fullan, M. 1999. *Change forces: The sequel*. Philadelphia: Falmer Press.

Hargreaves, A., A. Lieberman, M. Fullan, and D. Hopkins. 1998. *International Handbook of Educational Change*. Dordrecht, The Netherlands: Kluwer Academic.

Hopfenberg, W. S., H. M. Levin, and associates. 1993. *Accelerated Schools resource guide*. San Francisco: Jossey-Bass.

Joyce, B., J. Wolf, and E. Calhoun. 1993. *The self-renewing school.* Alexandria, Va.: Association for Supervision and Curriculum Development.

Knight, S. L., and J. A. Stallings. 1995. The implementation of the Accelerated School model in an urban elementary school. In *No quick fix: Rethinking literacy programs in America's schools*, edited by R. L. Allington and S. A. Walmsley. New York: Teachers College Press.

Madden, N. A., R. E. Slavin, N. L. Karweit, L. Dolan, and B. A. Wasik. 1991. *Success for all: Multi-year effects of a school-wide elementary restructuring program*. Report No. 18. Baltimore, Md.: Center for Research on Effective School for Disadvantaged Students.

McCarthy, J., and S. Still. 1993. Hollibrook Accelerated Elementary School. In *Restructuring schools: Learning from ongoing efforts*, edited by J. Murphy and P. Hallinger. Newbury Park, Calif.: Corwin.

National Center on Education and the Economy. 2000a. *America's choice comprehensive reform designs*. Washington, D.C.: Author.

———. 2000b. *Elementary School.* Vol. 1 of *New standards performance standards: English language arts, mathematics, sciences applied learning*. Washington, D.C.: Author.

———. 2000d. *High School*. Vol. 3 of *New standards performance standards: English language arts, mathematics, sciences applied learning.* Washington, D.C.: Author.

———. 2000c. *Middle School*. Vol. 2 of *New standards performance standards: English language arts, mathematics, sciences applied learning.* Washington, D.C.: Author.

New America Schools. 1999. *Working toward excellence: Examining the effectiveness of new American school designs*. Washington, D.C.: Author.

Newmann, F., and G. Wehlage. 1995. *Successful school restructuring*. Madison, Wisc.: Center on Organization and Restructuring of Schools.

Northwest Regional Educational Laboratory. 1998. *Catalog of school reform models*. Portland, Ore.: Author.

St. John, E. P., S. Loescher, S. Jacob, O. Cekic, and L. Kupersmith. (in preparation). *Comprehensive school reform models: A guide for comparing research-based models*. Bloomington: Indiana Education Policy Center.

St. John, E. P., J. G. Ward, and S. W. M. Laine. 1999. *State policy on professional development: Rethinking the linkages to student outcomes*. Oak Brook, Ill.: North Central Regional Educational Laboratory.

Wald, P., and M. Castleberry. 2000. *Creating a professional learning community in your school: Educators as learners*. Alexandria, Va.: Association for Supervision and Curriculum Development.

Chapter 8

Private Scholarships and School Choice: Innovation or Class Reproduction?

Carolyn S. Ridenour and Edward P. St. John

During the 1990s private donors in several urban communities organized private scholarship programs that partially subsidize the costs of attending private schools for children with financial need. Two major, publicly funded voucher programs—in Milwaukee (Witte 1998) and Cleveland (Metcalf et al. 1998)—have received a great deal of public attention. From the research on these experiments, it appears that students who use vouchers to attend public schools have modest improvement in achievement and substantial influence on parent satisfaction (Peterson 1998; Metcalf et al. 1998; Witte 1998). More recently, several cities have initiated privately funded scholarship programs (PFSPs) that provide need-based scholarships to low-income students to attend private schools. Some of these new programs even have included experimental designs with control groups of students who received and did not received private scholarships. These urban experiments may provide further information about the differences in achievement in public and private schools, but most of these new studies will not address questions related to the impact of these new market forces on what schools do to improve.

To understand why it is important to consider the impact of PFSPs on educational improvement, it is necessary only to reconsider the crisis in urban education. For decades urban schools have been confronted by severe poverty (Jencks and Peterson 1991). At the start of the twenty-first century, a larger percentage of students in urban settings are minorities than at any point in the prior century. Urban public schools have become predominantly minority. A larger percentage of African-American children, heavily concentrated in cities, attended predominantly or exclusively minority schools in the middle 1990s than in 1954, at the time of the *Brown* decision (Fossey 1998). In this context, it is important to recall that Chubb and Moe (1990, 1991) originally argued that vouchers should be used because they felt that the introduction of market forces would stimulate educational improvement in urban schools.

This chapter examines the results of a two-year study of the effects of a PFSP on educational improvement in an urban community in the Midwest (hereafter referred to as The City). We analyze interviews with teachers and parents conducted the year the PFSP was announced, base year (1997–98), and interviews in selected schools during the base year and the first year of the scholarship program (1998–99). The study also included interviews with senior administrators in public and private school systems (St. John and Ridenour 2000) and these results are summarized below. First, we provide an overview of the context (The City and the PFSP), summarize findings from analyses of the PFSP on strategic behavior of senior and site administrators, and critically examine arguments about the potential influence of market forces on schools. Next, we summarize the research methods used in the study. Then we examine perceptions of teachers and parents who have been involved in these schools. Finally, the conclusions are presented.

Background

The Context

The PSFP program was a local intervention initiated by a noted advocate of school reform and a strong market advocate. The City Public Schools, like many urban districts in the United States, had a history of declining achievement test scores and was subject to intense scrutiny by the state. It had a long history of court-mandated desegregation remedies and gained approval for a new choice-based approach to desegregation in 1998, the same year the PFSP was introduced. There was a strongly committed donor community in The City and they formed a Board to oversee the new PFSP. The members of the board were not only the major contributors to the program, but they had a long history of commitment to educational improvement efforts in both the public and private schools.

The public schools in The City had initiated a number of reforms in the years immediately preceding the introduction of the PFSP. They had initiated a restructuring process in 1997 that focused on schools with the lowest test schools. This process included collaboration with representatives of one of the nationally recognized comprehensive reforms as well a team of faculty from a local university. In addition, The City had a long history of using magnet schools as an integral part of its desegregation strategy. The City Public Schools (CPS) had implemented several distinctive schools that were intended to induce student choice, including Montessori schools, values based schools, and direct instruction schools. Thus the urban system was reasonably well positioned to respond to the introduction of private scholarships by emphasizing its own internal choices for families and competitive niches in several of its schools.

In addition, The City was located in a state with a history of providing direct financial support for private schools. This included support for busing, textbooks, and supplemental services (i.e., Title I and Special Education). In an interview conducted as part of this study, the Superintendent of the Catholic school system indicated that Catholic schools attracted about $600 of state support for each new urban student, which meant that there was a financial incentive to expand enrollment of poor students. Senior administrators in The City Public Schools interviewed as part of this study viewed these subsidies of private schools as a "drain" of resources from public schools. In addition, there was pending litigation over the adequacy and equity of funding within the state system. Thus, there were a number of concerns about public and private school funding among public educators in The City even before the PFSP was introduced.

The private schools had also undergone substantial adaptation during the two years immediately preceding introduction of the PFSP. The Catholic schools had used two innovative methods to induce market forces into their system. This included a "fill every desk" campaign that had involved teachers in recruiting local students into their schools. This was accompanied by an "average cost funding" strategy that facilitated the sharing of resources across wealthy and poorer parishes. This combination of strategies had enabled several of the Catholic schools to attract large numbers of new students who were paying a reduced cost through the fill-every-desk initiative. A few of the Catholic schools in The City had become entirely African-American as a result of these initiatives. In addition there was a large Christian school system in The City that had some school buildings with about half African-American students. The Christian schools did not accept any state support, but they were willing to participate in the PFSP. Thus there was a large, proactive set of urban schools that was already oriented toward competing with CPS for students.

The experimental design for The City's PFSP included a "student-effects study" that was intended to have a treatment group of at least

675 students and a control group of equal size. However, the donor board had committed enough funds to the program to award more than 1,000 scholarships. Thus, eligibility to the program was opened to students who were already attending private schools, along with public school students. Indeed, the private schools in The City, especially the Lutheran and Catholic schools, had already made extensive use of student aid for students from poor inner-city families.

The original experimental design for the PFSP also included scholarships for students in public schools within the metropolitan area to attend public schools in other public districts in the area. Most of the districts already had a tuition scheme that allowed out-of-district students to pay the equivalent of local taxes per student. The public schools received the state portion of funding in addition to the tuition, which meant that there had long been an opportunity for urban students with money to pay to attend suburban schools. When the PFSP program was introduced, proponents encouraged the public districts in the metropolitan area to participate, thus approaching a more open market. Some donors even offered to pay the differential between the advertised scholarship amount ($1,000 to $1,500 depending on the level of school) and the out-of-district tuition charge. However, all of the public districts in the metropolitan area refused to participate in this part of the program.

Given this contested context, it is perhaps not surprising that the PFSP ended up giving out many more scholarships than were intended, but induced less transfer than expected. Thus, a large number of the scholarships went to students who were already enrolled in private schools. Given that the number of students who changed their enrollment was smaller than expected, the experimental aspect of the study may not have been as critical as originally envisioned. However, as the review above indicates, there were substantial adaptations in the strategies used by both public and private educational systems, as a result of the PFSP.

Framing the Analysis

These developments raise three questions that were the original focus of our studies of the PFSP. What caused the extensive strategic adaptations by senior education officials in The City? How did the strategic adaptations by senior administrators in public and private systems influence the strategies used by building site administrators in public and private schools? And, how did educators and parents in public and private school buildings respond to the changes in policy and choice opportunities? These questions focus on the ways educators and families adapted to rapid change in local finance and educational strategies. Our analyses of interviews consider three possible ways of understanding local adaptations: a structural explanation, a market explanation, and a choice explanation.

The dominant model used for enrollment planning in schools and school systems is a structural model driven by historic enrollments and anticipated enrollment changes. Enrollment projections are typically adjusted for changes in the size of age cohorts and migration patterns across school districts (e.g., Hussar and Gerald 1996). Within this structural way of conceiving of school choice, tax dollars are thought to follow students. Because state and local tax dollars follow students in public schools, planners can use enrollment as a basis for annual financial planning. When this model is used, it is possible that the threat of a large enrollment loss will stimulate school systems to adapt to the introduction of a scholarship program.

When this structural frame is used to critique vouchers and other choice schemes that enable students to choose public as well as private schools, then the focus shifts to assessing the consequences of losing students. The concept of "skimming" has frequently been used to describe these consequences, including: increased average cost per student remaining in the system due to the fact that families with children in higher cost programs (e.g., special education) are less likely to choose to take advantage of vouchers; and a reduction of average scores in public schools due to the fact that higher achieving children are more likely to take advantage of private school choice opportunities (Kozol 1992). Those who hold structural beliefs would have a rationale for resisting choice proposals, especially proposals that include private schools.

Second, a market model has emerged in the school literature. This model argues both that parents deserve to have choices about schools and that school innovation will be influenced by the introduction of market forces (Chubb and Moe 1990; Glen 1991). School choice has gained substantial public support (Rose, Gallup, and Elam 1997), but recent evidence suggests that support might have "peaked," with only 22 percent favoring vouchers, and more than half (59%) favoring continuing the current system of schools (Rose and Gallup 2000). Nevertheless, many public school advocates have adapted to the market argument by advocating school choice within public school systems. However, the limited choice model advocated by public school proponents puts more constraints on family school choice and competition for students, forces that could influence market adaptations. The more limited model constrains choice to public schools, or at least to schools chartered by public authorities. It also limits market adaptations to schools that are eligible to receive students. Regardless of whether the full-market model or more limited, public-school-market model is advocated, the underlying logic of this approach is that family choice is a force that can influence change in schools.

When market assumptions are used in critiques of school choice proposals, the counter arguments are more likely to focus on whether all students can really afford to take advantage of scholarship subsidies. There also may be concerns when scholarships only cover a portion of the costs of attending private schools. Further, even if scholarships cover full tuition, there are other costs associated with attendance and, thus, the poorest students would not be able to take advantage of choice schemes; they would be left in inner-city schools of deteriorating quality. Thus, the market critique is similar to the structural, skimming critique.

A third explanation could be used to examine the adaptation of school administrators to respond to market incentives based on their predisposition. This perspective is based on research on financial and academic adaptations in higher education (e.g., St. John 1994, 1995; St. John and Elliott 1994; St. John and Hossler 1998) and of changes in schools that implemented comprehensive reforms (Finnan et al. 1996; St. John, Griffith, and Allen-Haynes 1997). This frame focuses on how individuals in different "situated" circumstances respond to incentives. It focuses on discerning how: students and their families respond to prices and price subsidies; administrators and educators respond to new competitive forces; and schools respond to financial incentives, based on their missions and shared values. Thus, the choice perspective incorporates the salient arguments of the structural and market claims, but it also incorporates a way of considering how and why individuals' circumstances, including their values and beliefs, can influence their response to new incentives.

Thus, the third perspective also provided a way of integrating our analysis of changes in planning and managerial processes with an interpretive analysis of the professional behavior by educators and the choice preferences of families. By focusing on the ways administrators responded to the new program, it was possible to discern better the influence the new program has on educational improvement processes. And, at the same time, by focusing on the circumstances that influence choices and actions, we had a way of discerning patterns of beliefs—in other words, the attitudes towards the innovation held by the various participants—and how these beliefs influenced the ways participants respond to the introduction of the program.

Findings on Strategic Behavior

In an earlier analysis we examined the influence of the PFSP on strategic behavior by system and site administrators (St. John and Ridenour 2000). Our main conclusion was that public and private school systems adapted to the new market conditions. This conclusion was evident from the review of interviews with central administrators and reform advocates, and site administrators. Below we briefly summarize the major conclusions reached from this review, then examine these finding through the three analytic lenses.

Complex Patterns of Adaptation. Examining the strategic adaptations at two levels within urban educational systems has provided insight into the complexity of system adaptation to the new market forces in education.

First, the most rapid changes were evident at the system level. Once briefed on the new privately funded scholarship program, senior administrators began to adapt both the educational and financial strategies used in their systems. The public schools hastened movement toward an emphasis on choice within the public school system. Pressure was placed on schools to develop distinctive missions that offered choices for parents. Retaining both students and public funding that followed students was the primary incentive for hastening the adaptation process. However, this did not represent a departure from past practices, but rather the PFSP provided an incentive to speed up this change process.

In the four private schools there were efforts to attract new students, as well as efforts to influence program donors to include poor students they had already recruited into the new program. This early adaptation in the design of the program substantially reduced the research controls for the student effects study. This compromise in the design of the program increased the local impact of the program, as it had a more direct and substantial influence on the financial well being of the private schools that had already begun to recruit inner-city poor students. The introduction of the PFSP did not have the intended impact; and it did not influence suburban schools to open their doors to urban students, nor did it substantially expand the range of private schools that marketed to poor urban children.

Second, the program also hastened changes in the marketing and educational strategies that urban schools used. Building level administrators in the urban private schools that actively participated in the program not only became more active in recruiting students, they also reflected on the need to provide a more complete range of services to the new children in their schools. However, this pattern of change was hastened by the fact that PFSP increased the number of high-need students these schools attracted, but in three of four private schools we studied, the majority of PFSP recipients were already enrolled in the schools. Administrators in these schools were reflecting on the need for change as a result of a historic pattern of change.

Third, in contrast, public schools were already confronted by the need to respond to the full range of needs of urban children. The two schools we studied that lost moderate numbers of students to PFSP were both schools with social workers who were an integral part of the educational program. These schools were also confronted by the challenge to develop a more distinctive mission. One of these schools was attempting to strengthen the emphasis it placed on direct instruction; the other was wrestling with the prospect of becoming a charter school. The other two schools we studied had well-developed and distinctive missions. They were all influenced by the introduction of the new scholarship program.

Understanding the Influence of Scholarships. The earlier study also examined the three different perspectives on scholarships in urban schools (St. John and Ridenour 2000). Each of the perspectives provides insight into the change process.

The first perspective, the structural view, focuses on the loses in enrollment and revenues that accrue to the public schools as a result of implementing choice schemes that involved private schools choice. The PFSP scholarships moved students from public to private schools and private schools did sort through applications as part of their admissions processes, in ways that kept some students with the greatest needs out of their schools. Thus, there was confirmatory evidence here that scholarships "skim" more able, low-income students and leave a higher percentage of high-need, high-cost students in urban public schools.

However, this view misses some important information about the nature of change in schools. Private schools did take some low-income children with more diverse learning needs. As a result of making these choices the private schools were confronted by a need to consider adding counselors and other personnel who might provide a fuller range of services. Thus, the structural view does not fully capture the fact that the scholarship can hasten change in both private and public schools. Further, there was evidence that the introduction of scholarships also influenced change within the public education system.

The second perspective, the market view, argues that introducing market forces will stimulate change in urban education. This study of leadership behavior provided substantial evidence that the introduction of scholarships hastened the change process in both public and private schools. The public schools hastened their efforts to move toward a public system of choice. They made efforts to influence schools to develop distinctive missions and initiated centralized efforts to market their choice scheme, expanding the educational options available to urban families. The market argument also explained why urban private schools might adapt their marketing and missions to address the needs of the more diverse students they attract.

However, the market view did not explain why there was so much resistance to change in the market. In particular, all of the metropolitan public school districts in the area refused to participate in the PFSP. The market model did not explain why these school systems would not respond to the incentive to attract more students. Nor did it explain why some private schools did not openly market to PSFP students. The market model also tends to overlook the fact that class differences separate urban and suburban schools (Jencks and Peterson 1991), which complicates the analysis of the impact of this PFSP because of the initial focus on free choice within the metropolitan area.

The third frame, the choice view, argues that individuals respond to incentives based on their situated circumstances. This alternative perspective helps explain both why some changes occurred and why others did not. Indeed, both system and building administrators used the opportunities provided by the PFSP to move further and faster to goals they already held. For urban public schools, the program hastened movement toward a more open choice scheme within the public system. For suburban public schools, the decision to resist the new program was predicated on the legal boundaries that separated the social classes, continuing to constrain the urban poor within the city limits. For private schools that were already oriented toward serving urban poor families, the PFSP provided an opportunity for continuing this new form of service. Finally, for the other private schools that provided havens for those opting out of public systems, the incentive to respond to the new clients was mitigated by the prospect of losing wealthier students who could pay the full price.

The limitation of the choice frame is that it does not fully deal with the political context. For example, it stops short of arguing that political power and social class differences determine the ways educational systems respond to new initiatives. It also stops short of uncritically extolling the virtues of the market frame. Thus, the implicit political neutrality of the choice frame makes it possible to provide evidence to inform stakeholders with divergent political positions.

Reframing the Inquiry

In this chapter, we treat the following as an initial, intermediate understanding: *Individuals—administrators, teachers, and parents—make choices in situated contexts*. Although this restatement of the choice perspective, may provide a more complete explanation for the patterns of strategic adaptation than the alternative frames previously explored, the inherent political neutrality of the initial argument was too limiting. In order to explore further the political aspects of the adaptation process within schools, this analysis explored the situated context of choice relative to two political arguments:

- *Innovation as Outcome of Choice: A New Progressive Interpretation*. In a sense, the new conservative political interests have argued that school choice is in the interest of all families because it is more likely to promote innovations in ways that enable more children to achieve in schools. This argument carries forward elements of social attainment theory, which argues for cross-generation improvement in status (Blau and Duncan 1967; Alexander and Eckland 1978). It also carries forward the new rationale that market forces induce innovation in schools that are stimulated by parent's aspirations for their children (Chubb and Moe 1990). This argument links gains in cross-generation attainment to innovations attributable to the introduction of market forces.
- *Cultural Reproduction as Outcome of Choice: A Critical-Social Interpretation*. Bourdieu's theory of practice (1977, 1990) provides a lens for viewing situated choices that focuses on forces in cultural contexts that reinforce culture and class. Bourdieu distinguishes between economic capital (with focus on money), symbolic capital (with a focus on symbols of social status), and cultural capital (with a focus on education). This perspective suggests that choice schemes could be limited to cultural reproduction—and indeed to largely symbolic gains in capital—unless the innovation has an influence on the formation of cultural capital in the family.

In this analysis of parent and teacher interviews, we are interested in exploring these two alternative notions of the underlying social forces that influence the choices people make, once a choice scheme is put in motion. In the concluding section, we explore how these lenses inform our collective understanding of the consequences of introducing new open choice schemes into urban communities.

Research Approach

We wanted to examine schools holistically and uncover the dynamics of change as revealed naturally by the voices of those in the schools, revelations that we could not anticipate. Therefore, we used a qualitative research approach. Interviews and observations were our predominant data collection strategies.

Identifying schools as sites for study was based on several factors: those schools parents would or would not want to leave based on prior information and shifting enrollment patterns; those schools into which we would be given access; finally, our interest in schools that had relatively high and low numbers of PFSP applicants and that could be matched on an instructional theme. We were interested in exploring whether or not differences might exist among those schools from which a relatively large proportion of parents would want to withdraw their children and those schools where fewer parents would demonstrate such desire. There was, therefore, much negotiation in identifying sites for study. Several face-to-face meetings between school administrators and the research team built a foundation of reciprocity on which the first year of the study was begun (Marshall and Rossman 1989). All findings, for example, would be shared with the schools before they were sent to other audiences. Access to building sites, dates of data collection at individual schools, and all other logistical matters were agreed to by the schools and the university team. Informed consent procedures were put in place.

In the baseline year (1997–98), eight schools were sites for study, four public schools and four private schools. In the second year of the study (1998–99), two public schools were added. Because the baseline year was based on "applications" and the second year was based on "takers," it was impossible in the baseline year to predict from which schools applicants would be selected by the lottery. For the baseline study, two City Elementary Schools with (in March 1998) high numbers of applicants (N=48 or 7.9% and N=44 or 6.8%) were selected as well as two City Elementary Schools with low application numbers (N=11 or 3.0% and N=17 or 4.0%). The two City Schools with low application numbers were selected to match instructional themes of the two City Schools with high application numbers. Four private schools were selected based on two criteria. The first was selecting schools that historically have attracted high numbers of low-income students in the area of The City. The second criterion was selecting schools that expressed the intent to actively recruit PFSP students.

In the second year, the same four private schools were studied but there were six public schools studied. To the original four CPS, two additional City schools were added that had two of the highest proportions of scholarship recipients and "takers": 2.3 percent and 3.1 percent of their enrolled students left with the PFSP. A third, one of the original City case schools, had a substantial proportion of "takers": 1.2 percent. According to Armor and Peiser (1998), in Massachusetts, school change resulted when in excess of 2 percent of a school population left; thus, our second year selection of schools to study was justified. The bulk of the interpretation in this paper (all the data other than the senior level administrators) is based on these schools during the second year, the year when any impacts would likely take place.

Two intense periods of data collection characterized the first year of the study. First senior level administrators were queried in face-to-face interviews in late fall 1997 and early winter 1998 at the earliest stages of the PFSP's publicity. The second period was when school-based researchers spent between one and three weeks in each of the eight schools during spring 1998, with each researcher exclusively focusing on the schools he/she was studying.

Between May and June 1998 four researchers spent between one and three weeks on site in the eight schools. In year two, four researchers carried out the same procedures but were on site for a longer period of time, usually over four or five weeks during Winter–Spring 1999. Researchers were not so intimately involved as members of their respective school settings that they could adopt the insider perspective on school life. One constraint was the short period of time between the announcement of the PFSP program and the end of the school year, which limited the duration of possible time in the schools. Throughout the research team discussions of spring and fall 1998, the research team worked under the assumption proffered by Guba and Lincoln (1981) that they had not captured the culture of the school in all its complexities and layers; instead the data "masquerade[d] as a whole when in fact they are but a part—a slice of life" (377). The brief time span on-site was augmented with planning meetings with principals and group debriefing meetings before, during and following the data collection period. As peripheral agents to the schools they studied, they did not actively engage as members of the school family but instead interacted closely enough to enable them to make valid meaning about school culture, what Adler and Adler (1994) would label a role as a "peripheral member."

On-site, the researchers collected several kinds of data. First, they completed statistical profiles of each building, including demography, curriculum descriptions, and school environment variables. Secondly, they interviewed the principal and a sample of teachers and parents. A limitation to interpreting the findings is the fact that the teachers and the parents who were interviewed were those selected by the principal.

The emphases in these interviews were on the school as it was in the past, as it is currently, and factors that have influenced change in the school (Spradley 1979). Semistructured interviews (Fetterman 1989) allowed the interviewers to tap into the reality of each informant in a fairly open way, but, at the same time, to stay focused on the meaning of school life and change within it. Researchers asked informants to address: relationships with external authorities (the school system in public schools and churches and other authorities in private schools); school leadership; curriculum and instructional practices; the role of the faculty; and parents and community involvement in the school.

An interpretive stance to interviewing (Rubin and Rubin 1995) would best characterize the research team's strategy. Actively participating in the interview, the researchers attempted to evoke meaning not in isolation but within a context. In other words, as "accounts," the researchers invited these interviews as socially meaningful text (Coffey and Atkinson 1996). Each informant was offered a pseudonym and almost all interviews were tape-recorded. Transcripts were prepared. Each informant was sent his/her typed interview transcript so that changes, if any, might be made to record each one's ideas and attitudes about the schools in the most valid way. The principal selected the parents we interviewed as parents who have "an active voice" in school matters. The interviews focused on family characteristics and background, daily school-related activities, and parent involvement in their children's schools. In religious schools questions included a focus on family religious practices and religious education. The procedures related to use of pseudonyms, audio taping, returning transcripts to informants for revisions, and analysis were the same as were the procedures described for the teacher and administrator informants.

Third, researchers conducted systematic classroom observations as well as informal observations of school life. Lastly, they collected a variety of documents that represented the school's mission and operation. Researchers kept field notes on-site that described what they were observing and experiencing while in the schools. Each researcher kept a reflective journal as well, a record of thoughts, insights, and interpretations after leaving the school building, a strategy recommended by Emerson, Fretz, and Shaw (1995).

Coding the interview transcripts and field notes began with phrases or sections of text which the researcher identified with labels that maintained, as much as possible, the language of the informant. The coded "units of meaning" were sorted into categories and resorted and integrated into themes. In other words, our intent was to first reduce the text and then expand the text into newly organized themes of meaning (Tesch 1990).

The Voices of Teachers and Parents

How did educators and parents in public and private respond to changes in policy and choice opportunities? The labyrinthine complexity of the choice environment increased the more we learned of the cultures of these two educational settings. The voices we listened to told of forces of change brought about by increased parental choice that were both similar and different in public and private schools. Within both sets of schools, for example, came evidence of withstanding the results of highly transitory leadership. A priority in both contexts was to find leaders that could bring "orderliness" to the schools. Establishing the tenets of the competition argument for school choice rendered moot any one-to-one comparisons (public-to-private comparisons). For instance, resources were more plentiful in the public schools but the private schools offered the benefits of smaller school size. (Class sizes were no different between the public and private settings.) The public schools offered substantial extracurricular opportunities and aids for special needs students the private schools lacked.

With these "apples and oranges" examples as an initial backdrop, we found that adaptations in the lives of teachers and parents occurring within the buildings exposed a mix of current tensions. These disclosures also included what might, in a more positive light, be seen as signs of growth toward deeper understanding of how high the stakes are for urban children's success. We characterize these complicated conditions within three dominant themes, each of which unearths a sort of "duality": threats to cultural coherence created by exiting and entering students in these urban schools, dual tensions created by standardized testing and urban family needs, and generally competing (and conflicting) attitudes toward choice that potentially position parents and teachers against one another.

Threats to Cultural Coherence within School Buildings

Organizational clarity and systemic processes that governed day-to-day life were more present in the private schools. The religious base of the private schools appears to provide the gate-keeping anchor that the public schools lack. The administrative structure of private schools may be less important as a consequence. That is, the principal is not the only one responsible for defining a focus. The religious purpose and mission of private schools in some respects transcend the principal's administrative style. Public schools, on the other hand, showed less evidence of organizational coherence, a dynamic perhaps similar to what Rothstein, Carnoy, and Benveniste (1999) reported on in their study of public schools in California as seemingly "incoherent" operations when compared to private schools. Unlike a private school, they claim, a public school is "often subject to conflict . . . because it tries to do so many things at once" (Rothstein, Carnoy, and Benveniste 1999, 5).

Cultural coherence in the religious schools might be threatened when students come from public schools as a result of choice programs. One Rose Lane teacher expressed that dynamic by referring both to religious aspects of the culture and children with special needs who the school might not be equipped to serve. When asked about what concerns teachers have,

> Personally I would say . . . amongst the staff there are probably still a few children that go here that [don't] quote unquote comply to a philosophy. The Catholic philosophy. And . . . you're trying to have an open door policy and cater to all children . . . the behavior and handicapped and everything like that. And that . . . may put some stress on some teachers . . . you have to deal with it . . . to [have] the new . . . open enrollment policy.

A parent at Hayes Hill, another Catholic school, commented on the changes in the school as a result of "open enrollment," and the resulting increasing size of the school and the increasing range of problems she perceives that has caused:

Q: Have you noticed anything that may have changed [in this school] from a few years back?

A: The only thing they've done is have open enrollment.

Q: Do you think that [is] a good thing or a bad thing?

A: I don't think it was very good. . . . Well it's just things my daughter has told me. . . . They've got more kids in here that just don't listen and [they]cause problems. . . . My daughter said she'd had a lot of stuff stolen from her in the last couple years.

Q: She'd never had that [happen before]?

A: Yeah, only since they had the open enrollment . . . the kids complained a lot to me about stuff like that. I guess just 'cause [new students] weren't used to it. . . . For so many years it was just mostly Catholics here and then they had the open enrollment. And, . . . it's a little bit more crowded now than what it used to be."

One private school principal remarked about the change in school size and school culture:

> Our non-Catholic population might go up a bit as it did in the past when we . . . made a real concerted effort to bring in lots of students. . . . I think that was our biggest change because we went from a hundred and seventy kids to two hundred and thirty-five, in one year. And we weren't prepared for that many kids. . . . We got some kids who had not been used to a smaller, quieter school. . . . I don't think they knew how to act . . . and they . . . didn't understand that these are your friends here, you don't have to . . . put on a show. . . . They'd "shout" that you [the teacher] didn't care. And now we do more screening in the beginning . . . [when students apply.]

Catholic schools are experiencing increasing pressure to strengthen Catholic identity in this era of diminishing numbers of vowed religious on their staffs. Increasing diversity of students, as a result of choice, exacerbate that identity problem while lessening the problem of economic survival of these schools, especially in urban neighborhoods. Added enrollments were increasing school sizes, exacerbating the struggle to maintain coherence. Several teachers at private schools were concerned that the weakening emphasis on religious identity was occurring at the same time that parents of new students were beginning to object to school policies about orderliness and discipline. In the Christian schools, too, teachers were concerned about a weakening school mission. For example some teachers were questioning the conviction of PFSP parents who signed the obligatory faith statements perhaps, they mused, only to assure their children's admission. In addition to these suspicions, one teacher remarked that students transferring into the school brought "bad habits that are ignored in public school settings."

The extent to which teachers in the daily life of the private schools are able to meet the needs of both larger numbers of students as well as students from more diverse backgrounds is reflective of their adaptability. Likewise, public school teachers faced not totally dissimilar challenges—primarily from testing and family needs in a rapidly changing cultural milieu.

Pressures from Standardized Testing and Distinctive Needs of Many Urban Families

Urban public schools face daily pressure from a range of sources. Market competition might only exacerbate pressures on these same schools that already are facing transitory families, densely populated impoverished neighborhoods, and a declining tax base. Two dominant sources of stress were thematic from the voices of those with whom we talked in the schools: growing emphases on mandated state tests and the unique needs of urban families. In some sense meeting one of these needs might diminish the likelihood of meeting the other; in other words, addressing the first pulls resources away from addressing the second. Furthermore, conditions under which families attempt to best provide for their children can often work against their children's likely success on these mandated tests.

A first-grade teacher at Embassy School expressed a sentiment echoed by many teachers when she described the strong emphasis on higher state test scores:

> I've known a lot [of the teachers] for the sixteen years that I've been here and . . . it seems to me like everybody's trying to do their best and to do their job and to get the children to pass these [state] tests which is our basic goal, I guess you know. It seems like that one little goal . . . one test . . . why one test to put all this emphasis on one test. . . . I don't know. I think everybody's [feeling] an awful lot of pressure. I think teachers [say to themselves] 'Will we pass this [state] test?' and that's the thing that's . . . in your mind the whole year." She described the pressure as a first-grade teacher because the "off year" [state] tests are becoming as important as those that the state system requires.

Increasing weight on mandated state tests interacts with some urban family situations, according to this same teacher, to create a detrimental impact on school improvement. Ironically, even when teaching innovations are successful, families' circumstances can override that success. When a family moves children from one school to another, monitoring children's progress is almost impossible. Mrs. Evans spoke despairingly of successful outcomes she and another teacher had with reducing the number of objectives in reading in their direct-instruction classrooms, an effort to improve the instructional focus to ultimately glean higher test scores. Not only were she and her partner unable to account for individual student learning progress, they were prevented from showing evaluative evidence of positive program outcomes.

> I think this [has] worked . . . a lot with this direct instruction . . . it goes very slow[ly] but what it does go over, they really do learn. . . . We just have everybody do it. . . . Well, I'll tell you the unfortunate thing about it is [after we]first taught . . . we haven't been able to track our kids. They've been going to different schools; and that [is] really, really bad. We have not been able to track the children that have started in kindergarten and have gone. We have a very few that are left. . . . And then people think that it's not working and that's really not the case. We haven't been able to keep track of the children.

In addition to the theme of state tests pressures, a second dominant theme emerged from the distinctive needs frequently surrounding urban families. At Walton School one teacher responded to questions about factors that inhibit parent interaction with the school by saying, "Well, I think . . . first of all that some of our students live very far away. . . . And I'm not sure all the parents have access to getting, to a way of getting here." At Embassy School, too, a parent remarked on transportation difficulties facing parents:

> I think that that's part of the parental problem is the busing. Because, you know, we do have parents who don't have a way to get here and they're not motivated enough to know that they could take the city bus but if we were a neighborhood school they would be in walking distance they could just, you know, walk out their front door and get here."

Parents at Frazer School told a story of another family, their former "next-door neighbors:

> I don't think it's a lack of choice. . . . One of our next-door neighbors, we used to have a rental unit, she rented from

> us. She had two kids in City Public Schools. She's a single mom struggling hard to get on her feet. Okay? Her kids were right at that age level where they were too young to be home. But, you know, school choice allowed her to send them to Anderson School . . . which was for her a better option for them because it's a little more, uh, structured. Making her way through the school system was the biggest problem. It wasn't, she had her kids in the kind of school she wanted them to. But conferences were always during work hours, you know. She was constantly getting called in or talked to during times when she needed to be at work. She had a fragile enough work history to begin with. The school system itself does not adjust to the needs of working families. It just doesn't.

These same parents had the attitude that choice challenges urban families by confronting them with complex circumstances to exercise their choice:

> . . . . make a lot more simple. Like to register for the magnet program, the magnet lottery, you have to go over to [the central administration building] during their work hours. . . . So if you work eight to five and you don't have any flexibility in it, what are you going to do? . . . you can't just mail this stuff in. And it happens almost a year before the child actually attends. . . . [CPS] is not accommodating families' needs and not trying very hard to, you know, help adjust for the, the problems. Those who can scratch their way to the top get there."

Thus, choice complicates the urban school environment—without a resulting simple yes-no answer as to its whether its effects are positive or not. Families and teachers both face, at times, insurmountable obstacles in meeting the learning needs of students, particularly high stakes testing. Families face hurdles in gaining easy access to the schools their children attend, and parents face demands other than schooling demands to successfully parent their children. Explaining the complicated factors that might lead families, for example, to enroll their children in a new school only to, a year later, return to the original school might be grounded in the multiple and complicated demands these families face.

Choosing from the magnet schools internal to the district was quite a different dynamic than was participating in the PFSP. What is complicated about drawing inferences from these dynamics is the fact that parents were making, at best, an indirect choice, at least insofar as the PFSP was concerned. Parents were not participating in a process to directly choose a school. They were participating in registering for a lottery. A large proportion of parents, then, were participating in a process that would never lead to the opportunity to choose a school. And they recognized that during the process. If selected, by chance, from the pool of applicants, then parents made their choice, often for a school that was unavailable. Furthermore, the voucher was insufficient to cover the total costs of private school tuition, in most cases.

Parents and Teachers Hold Opposing Views on Choice

The competition theory underlying certain views of school choice presents the image of winners and losers, an adversarial montage. Similarly, teachers' voices defended an antichoice sentiment that matched the pro-choice feelings from parents, according to our interviews. We heard language that suggested that growing market forces in The City were shaping not only the realities of these two constituencies, but were instructive about the different ways of knowing about schools that the two groups employed. While not exhaustive of our data, but strongly thematic, was the fact that teachers experienced a feeling of threat and fear and parents experienced confusion and empowerment. Such disparate realities might restrain their ability to collaborate in the best interests of children they hold in common trust.

Several teachers and parents expressed sentiments that were shared by the bulk of informants. A teacher at Johnson School, for instance, responded to queries about what she expected PFSP might portend with what we referred to earlier as "skimming." And, the very fact that one of the elementary schools (not in our study) with the highest level of state tests scores had the one of the highest percentages of parents applying for the PFSP bears out this fear. Of even deeper interest, moreover, was this teacher's frustration, as a Montessori-trained teacher, that the exclusively public-to-private choice being exercised in the PFSP might inadvertently persuade others that Montessori instruction is undesirable. In other words, the choice bias favors the private schools not the public Montessori schools. She said:

> I don't like it . . . not because I think public schools are better but what you're going to get is every parent in the world is going to want to send their kids to this private school. And

> those private schools are going [to] pick and choose who they want. And the . . . severe behavior problem kids are going to come here and they'll be stuck in the public school system. And then they're going to start going after [us with questions like why] can't you teach them . . . I don't think it's fair that the cream of the crop go to a specific school . . . my classroom works well because I've got kids who . . . work from kindergarten [and] four DH students all the way up [to] a first grader who reads at a sixth grade level. You know . . . classrooms like that work. They do work. My kids help each other all the time. . . . If you just take the cream of the crop, you put them into a private school, I don't think you're going to get the type of cooperation that you get here.

Mr. Fritz, a teacher at Frazer School, reflected on teachers' fears about choice when he remarked, "I feel that, you know, it is always so aggravating that they always try to put it on the teacher. We are the scapegoats . . . for everything that's happening in society. Education. It's the quality of education. . . ." To the researcher's following inquiry as to whether teachers were worried about the charter schools and the voucher program, Mr. Fritz continued, "I think we were last year. I think all the teachers were more worried. They talked about it a lot. More last year. We haven't heard more favorable comments about [the new charter school] . . . and . . . friends of ours who work there aren't saying [whether] they're getting the discipline problems."

A parent at Frazer School, the public Montessori setting, came from another public school district north of The City. Not a PFSP recipient, she had exercised a different type of choice in that she paid cross-district tuition to remove her son from a private preschool and enroll him at Frazer. Her motivation demonstrates the niche that Frazer provides within the changing market. She remarked, "Because I live out of the [CPS] District the price that I pay for the public compared to the private school is almost the same. I know I'm unique. I would love [if that scholarship was available for the public school]." This mother described her local options as unsatisfactory. The limited time her son would be in school would require supplemental day care arrangements. . . ." [It] would cost more money for me to send him to that particular school and only have three hours of academic . . . because you have to include lunch . . . I didn't like that, not one bit. And it's based on your income so, to me, this one here [Frazer] is not based on your income." Her preschool-aged son fit well into the youngest levels at Frazer School, an option in CPS that even more completely met her needs, she said, because it is a year-round school.

Thus, the positionalities of families and teachers are quite different, leading them to draw conclusions about school choice from different value structures and sets of assumptions. Although parents might celebrate the empowerment choice seems to provide, teachers seemed be equally disempowered with the spectacle of unstable enrollments. The potential presented by the PFSP was different than the implementation of the PFSP. Although parents might initially hope for attractive options for their children, they might find daunting the reality of the process for realizing that option. Strong identity within a school community might exacerbate the conflicting views of parents and teachers. One principal with whom we spoke literally guaranteed that no matter what amount of money parents whose children attended her school were offered, and no matter what the level of state test scores were, parents would not leave because they so strongly identified with the school.

Understanding the Underlying Forces in School Communities

The complexity of the change process within school buildings overwhelms simple explanations offered by traditional arguments about school choice. Although the structural argument about skimming is echoed in the voices of educators, this perspective overlooks the complexities facing teachers in public schools. In particular, the heavy emphasis on testing—and the common response of aligning curriculum—constrains the capacity of public school teachers who attempt to innovate, to educate in ways consonant with their new missions or to respond to the very real needs of their students. This argument, as articulated by teachers, often overlooks the fact that much of the new competition comes from within the public system.

And, although parents seemed to value the prospect of making school choices, a position aligned with market arguments, many were not happy with the realities of the new choice environment. Parents in public schools experience the public school choice process as complex and time consuming, whereas parents who considered or made private school choices realized that they really had few options for their children. Further, the extent of discernable improvement was constrained by the complexities of testing in public schools and the slowness to respond to new clientele in private schools. Thus, whereas the PFSP students who actually changed schools may have realized a slightly better learning environment, as measured by standardized test scores, students who were already enrolled may not have experience changes that improved their learning opportunities.

Finally, the choice perspective provides an explanation for what happened, but the explanation it provides may not satisfy either the opponents or advocates of choice schemes:

- *Family choices were constrained by the circumstances of urban schools.* Parents voice real concerns about the constraints of their choices and the complexities of changing schools in the public system. The structural conditions that constrained choice opportunities for urban families include an unwillingness of some public and private schools to admit PFSP students and the complexities of introducing choice into a public system.
- *Innovation in public schools was constrained by the high emphasis on testing and curriculum alignment.* Although public school administrators were emphasizing new educational strategies that promoted choice, the constraints of school reform imposed by the new testing environment limited opportunities for teachers to move toward these new goals. Early studies of the outcomes of charter schools suggest that teachers free from prior constraints of their practice might still fall back on proven pedagogical practice due to high stakes testing in these schools (Lasley et al. 1999).
- *The quality of education for previously enrolled students in the private schools that responded to the PFSP was somewhat constrained by the complexities created by bringing high-need students into these schools.* The critics of voucher schemes that include private schools argue that private schools will exclude students with extreme learning needs. They may overlook the fact that private schools are changed by the levels of need voucher students bring to those schools. Yet proponents of these programs tend to overlook that the quality of education for students who were already enrolled—as measured by class size, shared values, and time on task—can be influenced by these developments. For example, one recent study found the Catholic schools placed an emphasis on evangelization when a large number of private scholarship students entered Catholic schools (Watras and St. John 1998).

These observations support the idea that it is important to view the circumstances that constrain or enable educators and parents to make educational choices. They also reveal that implementing school choice into urban schools introduces new complexities that are overlooked by the rationales currently being used by the proponents and opponents of private school choice. At the very least, there is a clear need for more studies that systematically examine the ways teachers and parents respond to choice schemes within schools.

Conclusions

The study has examined the experiences of teachers and parents in public and private schools in an urban community while private scholarships were implemented. The findings indicate that while the educational systems adapted relatively rapidly to the new context (St. John and Ridenour 2000), the new environment creates new challenges for educators. Below we explore the implications of this research from the two interpretive lenses—innovation as outcome, and reproduction as outcome—and also consider the practical implications of this inquiry.

Reinterpreting the Impact of Choice

Although this study provides apparently contradictory evidence relative to the two interpretive frames outlined earlier, using the two lenses helps untangle further the implications of the movement toward private schools choice in urban settings.

On the one hand, the desire from cross-generation uplift on the part of parents of urban school children is strong. Indeed, these interviews capture parent attitudes that are deeply preferential toward having a choice. In fact, differences in the value placed on choice are the more evident differences in attitudes between teachers and parents. This value would seem to favor cross-generation gains in attainment and would seem to be supported by the desire of teachers in both public and private schools to respond to the learning needs of children. On a superficial level, these findings seem to support the claims of proponents of choice schemes. These phenomena would seem to support the new political rationale.

However, innovation at the classroom level was remarkably constrained in both public and private schools during the first year of this urban experiment. Innovations by teachers in public schools were constrained by a pervasive influence of testing whereas innovation was per se was not evident in private schools.

On the other hand, arguments about cultural reproduction would seem to explain why many of the suburban public schools and elite private schools did not open their doors to the voucher students. Faced with such constraints, parents may have favored having a choice, but their actual choices were severely constrained. Having more economic capital—in the form of a voucher—did little to expand the range of schools these parents could choose from for their children. Thus, we agree with McDonnough's (1997) conclusion that the social contexts of urban communities seem to reinforce cultural and class reproduction.

Yet, we are struck by the extent to which parents desired better options for their children. Clearly it would be an over simplification to argue that class reproduction happens because of a lack of family support. Indeed, this study reinforces other research that indicates that parents of minority children have exceptionally high aspirations for their children (St. John, Griffith, and Allen-Haynes 1997).

Thus, the politics of situated choices in urban schools are not easily untangled. It would be too simple to argue against the value of introducing choice schemes because the politics of schools constrain choices by students from poor families. Rather, the opponents of schools choice need to take the interests of parents more seriously and find ways to improve schools to meet the educational yearnings of parents of urban school children. At the same time, it is overly simplistic to argue that simply providing a voucher to a poor student enables greater attainment by school children or fosters innovation in schools. Rather, vouchers tend to reinforce class differences and social inequity as much as or more than they foster innovation, particularly when the vouchers cover only a portion of the expense of attending a private school. If vouchers have any hope of expanding opportunity for poor children in inner cities, there is a need to make fundamental changes in the systems used to screen and admit students in private schools, as well as in the accountability schemes being used in public schools.

Practical Implications

First, *the constraints created by public accountability systems can limit innovation as an outcome of school choice.* The urban public educators we interviewed felt pressures to improve test scores and these pressures increased with implementation of the scholarship program. Similar pressures were not evident in private schools, which created a form of inequity in the situations facing teachers in the two systems. Whether this new set of incentives actually can influence improvement in test scores in some schools will remain an open question. For even if test scores improve in some of the highly impacted schools, it would be difficult to discern the cause. Further, if the question were "has the introduction of market forces improved learning opportunities for urban children?" then an answer would be especially hard to ascertain. Further studies of change processes in public and private schools impacted by PFSPs are needed to build an understanding of the consequences of this new turn in education politics.

Second, *there is more freedom to innovate in private schools than public schools, but introducing new demand into private schools can constrain innovation*. The introduction of private scholarships provided educators with the opportunity to build communicative relationships with families, involving families in schools. The opportunity to choose schools and to be involved in schools increased parental satisfaction, but it also generated confusion among parents, and hope for their children's future. Educators had faced declining trends of parent involvement and now were increasingly faced with parents' need for information and clarity, even when such needs are not expressed. Serving new groups of students with needs they had not previously faced challenged teachers in private schools. The fact that new ways of organizational accountability are needed, in the face of the demands of competition and the consequences of transitory families, are being realized by public school teachers. Private school teachers meanwhile try to hold on to a cultural and spiritual tradition.

Third, *no common standards ground the assessment of the two sets of schools, public and private*. A dilemma (perhaps supportive of the dynamic of skimming) rests on the fact that families, in what was a more effective public school, showed relatively more interest in the PFSP than did families in less effective schools. A fear that choice schemes might be part of a trend toward the "social sorting" of students and families (Sykes, Plank, and Arsen 2000) may not be an unreasonable one. From the public school perspective, that choice can serve to better the weaker schools does not seem borne out by this first year of data. The study here is only an initial look over a relatively short time at City schools undergoing the changes wrought by school choice. Further examinations of these schools are needed before firm conclusions are warranted. The fact that public and private schools face vastly different accountability standards seems to accentuate differences between public and private schools and bias the results of these experiments in the favor of private schools. Indeed, differences in these system influences could explain the minor difference in student outcomes observed in the research of scholarship and voucher programs.

Note

Financial support from the Smith Richardson Foundation, Walton Family Foundation, D and D Foundation, Lynde and Harry Bradley Foundation, and Thomas B. Fordham Foundation is gratefully acknowledged. This paper presents the authors' interpretations and does not represent official policies or positions of funding agencies. The authors gratefully acknowledge contributions made to this study by researchers: Katie Kinnucan-Welsch, Will Place, Mary Anne Angel, Reva Cosby, Melva Cookie Newsom, Kelli Thomas, Jeff Wimer, and Connie Monroe. We also acknowledge the assistance of Louise Moore, Principal, and the faculty and staff of Holy Angels School who graciously allowed us to conduct training and pilot studies in their school.

References

Adler, P. A. and P. Adler. 1994. Observational techniques. In *Handbook of qualitative research*, edited by N. K. Denzin and Y. S. Lincoln. Thousand Oaks, Calif.: Sage.

Alexander, K. L. and B. K. Eckland. 1978. Basic attainment processes: A replication and extension. *Sociology of Education* 48: 457–95.

Armor, D. J., and B. M. Peiser. 1998. Interdistrict choice in Massachusetts. In *Learning from school choice*, edited by P. Peterson and B. C. Hassel. Washington, D.C.: Brookings Institution.

Blau, P. and O. D. Duncan. 1967. *The American Occupational Structure*. New York: Wiley.

Bourdieu, P. 1977. *The outline of a theory of practice*. Cambridge: Cambridge University Press.

———. 1990. *The logic of practice*. Stanford, Calif.: Stanford University Press.

Chubb, J. E., and T. M. Moe. 1990. *Politics, markets and America's schools*. Washington, D.C.: The Brookings Institution.

———. 1991. Schools in a marketplace: Chubb and Moe argue their bold proposal. *School Administrator* 48(1): 18, 20, 22, 25.

Coffey, A., and P. Atkinson. 1996. *Making sense of qualitative data*. Thousand Oaks, Calif.: Sage.

Emerson, R. M., R. I. Fretz, and L. L. Shaw. 1995. *Writing ethnographic field notes*. Chicago: University of Chicago Press.

Fettermam, D. M. 1989. *Ethnography: Step by step*. Newbury Park, Calif.: Sage.

Finnan, C., E. P. St. John, S. P. Slovacek, and J. McCarthy, eds. 1996. *Accelerated schools in action: Lessons from the field*. Thousand Oaks, Calif.: Corwin Press.

Fossey, R. E. 1998. Desegregation is not enough: Facing the truth about urban schools. In *Race, the courts, and equal education: The limits of the law*, ed. R. E. Fossey. Reading on Equal Education, vol. 15. New York: AMS.

Glen, C. L. 1991. Controlled choice in Massachusetts public schools. *Public Interest* 103: 88–105.

Guba, E. G., and Y. S. Lincoln. 1981. *Effective evaluation*. San Francisco: Jossey-Bass.

Hussar, W. J., and D. E. Gerald. 1996. *Projections of education statistics to 2006*. Washington, D.C.: U.S. Government Printing Office.

Jencks, C., and P. E. Peterson, eds. 1991. *The Urban Underclass*. Washington, D.C.: Brookings Institution.

Kozol, J. 1992. I dislike the idea of choice and I want to tell you why. *Educational Leadership* 50(3): 90–92.

Lasley, T. J., C. S. Ridenour, C. Talbert-Johnson, and C. Raisch. 1999. Charters: A value added opportunity for urban teachers? *Education and Urban Society* 31(4): 499–511.

Marshall, C., and G. B. Rossman. 1989. *Designing qualitative research*. Newbury Park, Calif.: Sage.

McDonnough, P. 1997. *Choosing colleges: How social class and schools structure opportunity*. Albany: State University of New York Press.

Metcalf, K. K., W. J. Boone, F. K. Stage, T. L. Chilton, P. Muller, and P. Tait. 1998. *A Comparative Evaluation of the Cleveland Scholarship and Tutoring Program. Year One: 1996–97*. Bloomington, Ind.: Junior Achievement Evaluation Project.

Peterson, P. E. 1998. School choice: A report card. In *Learning from school choice*, edited by P. Peterson and B. C. Hassel. Washington, D.C.: Brookings Institution.

Rose, L. C., A. M. Gallup, and S. M. Elam. 1997. The 19th annual Phi Delta Kappa/Gallup poll of the public's attitudes toward public schools. *Phi Delta Kappan* 79(1): 41–56.

Rose, L. C., and A. M. Gallup. 2000. The 32nd annual Phi Delta Kappa/Gallup poll of the public's attitudes toward the public schools. *Phi Delta Kappan* 82(1): 41–58.

Rothstein, R., M. Carnoy, and L. Benveniste. 1999. *Can public schools learn from private schools: Case studies in the public and private nonprofit sectors*. Washington, D.C.: Economic Policy Institute and The Aspen Institute's Nonprofit Sector Research Fund.

Rubin, H. J., and I. S. Rubin. 1995. *Qualitative interviewing: The art of hearing data*. Thousand Oaks, Calif.: Sage.

Spradley, J. P. 1979. *The ethnographic interview*. New York: Holt, Rinehart, and Winston.

St. John, E. P. (1991). What really influence minority attendance? Sequential analyses of the high school and beyond sophomore cohort. *Research in Higher Education* 32: 141–58.

———. 1994. *Prices, productivity, and investment: Assessing financial strategies in higher education*. Washington, D.C.: George Washington University.

———. 1995. Rethinking tuition and student aid strategies. In *Rethinking tuition and student aid strategies*, edited by E. P. St. John. New Directions for Higher Education no. 89. San Francisco: Jossey-Bass.

St. John, E. P., and R. J. Elliott. 1994. Reframing policy research. In *Higher Education: Handbook of theory and research*, edited by J. C Smart. New York: Agathon.

St. John, E. P., A. I. Griffith, and L. Allen-Haynes. 1997. *Families in schools: A chorus of voices in restructuring*. Portsmouth, N.H.: Heinemann.

St. John, E. P., and D. Hossler. 1998. Desegregation in the post-*Fordice* legal environment: A critical-empirical perspective. In *Race, the courts, and equal education: The limits of the law*, edited by R. Fossey. Reading on Equal Education, vol. 15. New York: AMS.

St. John, E. P., and C. Ridenour. 2000. *Market forces and strategic adaptation: The influence of private scholarships on educational improvement*. Dayton, Ohio: University of Dayton School of Education and Applied Professions.

Sykes, G., D. Plank, and D. Arsen. 2000. The Michigan experience: School choice and school change. *Education Week*, February 9.

Tesch, R. 1990. *Qualitative research: Analysis types and software tools*. London: Falmer.

Witte, J. F. 1998. The Milwaukee Voucher Experiment. *Educational Evaluation and Policy Analysis* 20(4): 229–52.

Watras, J., and E. P. St. John. 1998. Choice and schools: An analysis of free markets and educational values. *Catholic Education* 1: 400–13.

Part IV

Community-Based Reforms

Chapter 9

Parental and Community Empowerment: The Chicago Model

Kathryn Nakagawa

One of the major school-reform experiments using parent and community involvement was created by the Chicago School Reform Act of 1988. The Act created a number of changes to a centralized system, among the most important being the creation of "local school councils" (LSCs) at each of the nearly 600 public schools in Chicago. Each LSC is comprised of six elected parents, two elected community members, two teachers, the principal, and, at high schools, one student representative. The LSCs were given much more authority than had ever been tried with other attempts at local control. In the 1988 Act, the LSCs were given responsibility for hiring and firing principals, designing and approving budgets (particularly overseeing discretionary funds), and creating local school improvement plans (Hess 1991).

Many proponents and observers of the Chicago school reform lauded it as a historically significant reform (e.g., Elmore 1991; Fine 1995), as seen in its description by Katz, Fine, and Simon (1997):

> Reform represented a historic achievement—the most radical restructuring of an urban school system and its relation to its communities in a century. Reformers in the city had created an unprecedented multiracial, cross-class coalition dedicated to school improvement through democracy. (132)

It is not an overstatement to note that the overriding discourse of the Chicago school reform was one marking it as a momentous change in school policy. This discourse arose both from the process through which the reform was created and from the amount of control given to parents and community members in the reform.

Does the Chicago reform live up to its reputation? This chapter considers the creation of the Chicago school reform and its outcomes thus far. In particular, the chapter asks, How did the LSCs operate, and to what extent did parents and community members become substantive partners in the process of school reform? Using the "critical-empirical" method, I argue that, to judge the historical significance of this reform, it is important to understand whether and how the primary mechanism for reform—parent and community involvement—worked. To do so, I contrast the underlying theory of the "empowered" parent/community role mandated by the Chicago reform with the more traditional parent/community role, one of "enablement" (Lewis and Nakagawa 1995).

Parent Empowerment versus Parent Enablement

Parent empowerment is one way that active parent participation is being promoted in the schools. In particular, Concha Delgado-Gaitan (1991) discusses parent empowerment as the key for minority parents to have a role in the schools. In her work, she traces the development of a group of Mexican immigrant parents in California and how they worked together to gain an active, vocal, knowledgeable role in the schools. Her work serves to exemplify how parents, working separately from the school, can become empowered in their parent role.

However in some instances a greater role for the parents, one that should promote a more empowered role, is mandated by legislation. The belief is that by bringing parents into the system and "empowering" them with more control over how the school functions, reform will occur. This is what the Chicago reform did. Does such a mandated role, one that allows parents more voice in the school system and more rights to help decide curriculum, budget, and hiring, actually empower? With respect to parents and schools, much of the legislation that mandates parent involvement is to make it possible for ethnic-minority and lower income parents to have greater voice in the school system. That is, for those groups that have been poorly served by the public schools, parent participation is seen as crucial to rectifying the situation. For instance, Title I requires home-school compacts and parent involvement in schools that receive such funding (Improving America's Schools Act 1994), and some charter school legislation also requires a parent involvement component as part of the school charter (Becker, Nakagawa, and Corwin 1997).

The Chicago School Reform, based on an ideology of participatory democracy, was seen as an opportunity for improving schools for those who were least well-served. As Hess (1995) wrote, "The Chicago School Reform Act empowered the parents of 'at-risk' students by giving them the opportunity to win democratic control of local school councils governing their schools and by providing extra resources to the schools enrolling the most low-income students" (21–22).

However, the empowerment role is difficult to encourage, in part because traditional parent roles in the school offer few such empowering decision making or governance opportunities. The typical parent role might be considered an *enablement* role. It is one in which the parent supports the school system with little opportunity to influence change in how the school operates. In the enablement model, involvement has the purpose of molding the parents to fit school needs—equipping parents with the knowledge, skills, and abilities to help the child do better in school (Coleman 1990). Parents are not seen as involved in running the schools; instead, they are seen as necessary resources for the schools to do their jobs adequately. The activities typically associated with the enablement model are parent education programs and school volunteer organizations, activities that reinforce the controlling authority of the school over parents (Lightfoot 1978).

Educators and school officials generally state their preference for enablement roles, perhaps because they do not challenge their authority. For example, in a nationwide survey done at the time the Chicago School Reform Act was taking effect, Snider (1990) found that more than 60 percent of teachers felt it would be valuable to improve communication with parents, and 60 percent thought it was important for parents to help out in the school or work on fund-raisers. But just 26 percent of the teachers polled thought it would be very valuable for parents to serve on policy-making teams, and just 18 percent felt it was important for parents to be on curriculum committees. Similarly, much of the recent push for more parent involvement in schools often requires that parents sign contracts or home-school compacts that call for helping out at the school and supporting the school's goals at home; little emphasis is placed on having parents involved in meaningful school governance (Nakagawa 2000).

The tension between a traditional enablement role and an empowerment role for parents suggests potential problems in the Chicago school reform, although the law itself created much opportunity for change. Reformers and some observers of the reform held high hopes for the influence that participatory democracy might have for improving school achievement; the next section offers a brief history of how the hope of the Chicago school reform evolved.

The Creation and Ideology of the Chicago School Reform Act

Katz (1995) classifies the Chicago school reform not only as a "legislative act" and a "process" of reform but also as a "social movement." Katz writes, "As a social movement, Chicago school reform means the mobilization of communities around the cause of educational reform, the democratization of relations in school governance, and the revitalization of the public sphere" (as quoted in Katz, Fine, and Simon 1997, 121). Thus, to situate the Chicago school reform historically, he and others consider it as part of a broader social movement in democratic pluralism. In addition, as others have noted (Katz, Fine, and Simon 1997; Mirel 1993), Chicago's political history makes this attempt at democratic pluralism an especially notable feat.

Although the story of the Chicago School Reform Act is varied (Katz, Fine, and Simon 1997), there is some agreement on the key elements that led to this policy. Among the most important factors in its creation were the educational summits organized by Mayor Harold Washington, a growing body of research from community and research organizations about the poor state of the Chicago public schools, and the Chicago Teachers Union (CTU) strike of 1987 (Bryk et al. 1998; Hess 1991; Katz, Fine, and Simon 1997; O'Connell 1991).

The history of school reform was part of a major change in Chicago politics, beginning with the election of Chicago's first African-American mayor, Harold Washington, in 1983. Until Washington's election, Chicago was primarily characterized by a machine politics and dominated by whites (Mirel 1993). But Washington was elected mayor by putting together a "Black-Hispanic-liberal coalition," with one of its defining issues being school reform (Mirel 1993, 123). Washington understood that for the African-American population in particular—the majority group in the Chicago public schools—educational improvement was critical. He organized multiethnic coalitions and brought together diverse interest groups to work on changing the public schools. Throughout Washington's tenure, public distress with the Chicago public schools grew. For instance, reports by community groups such as the Chicago Panel on School Policy and Designs for Change documented the dismal state of those schools: Just 3 percent of high schools reported scores above the national average in reading; nearly 50 percent of the students who started ninth grade failed to graduate from high school; and students at risk of dropping out were being segregated into the worst schools (Bryk et al. 1998; Hess 1991, 1995; Niemiec and Walberg 1993).

In 1987, after the CTU strike of nineteen days (and after U.S. Secretary of Education William Bennett called Chicago schools the "worst in the nation"), Mayor Washington took advantage of the resulting public outrage over education to reconvene a special educational summit group he had created in 1986. In contrast to the earlier summit, however, the mayor now charged the summit with proposing a means for complete school restructuring. The summit, which included parents and community members as well as teachers, business leaders, principals, administrators, and board members, had as its goal the creation of a document that could be submitted as legislation to the Illinois legislature. Although the summit document was not, ultimately, the prototype for the reform legislation, it did bring parents and community members into the process in a systematic way.

However, a few months after the summit convened, Mayor Washington died suddenly, creating a split in the African American community. The new mayor, Eugene Sawyer, deemphasized education. Sawyer was thought to be the candidate of the old-time machine politicians, and, although he was African American, he did not represent the multiethnic coalition that Washington had created (Mirel 1993). Although the summit finalized its recommendations, little happened when the document was passed on to the mayor's office to be translated into legislative language. By that time, it was spring 1988, nearing the end of the state legislature's session, and many of the community groups that had worked on the summit believed that their document would not reach the legislature.

Because the perception was that the mayor's office was not going to move toward school reform, other organizations worked with state legislators to introduce school reform bills. One in particular was supported by a broad-based coalition of business and community organizations called the Alliance for Better Chicago Schools, led by the community group Designs for Change. Designs for Change had been working on its own version of school reform before the summit, and many ideas from its document were used to create Senate Bill 1839, the precursor to the Chicago School Reform Act.

In the meantime, the Chicago Board of Education and other groups also took reform proposals to the state legislature to be submitted as bills. The document the mayor's summit originally created also was submitted eventually, but it had been modified and weakened by the mayor's office and received little attention or support in the state legislature. Speaker of the House Michael Madigan (a legislator from Chicago) convened a number of meetings in which representatives from each of the interested parties were invited to air their concerns over the bill. However, some parent organizations and groups representing the African-American community felt left out of the process (Lewis and Nakagawa 1995; Mirel 1993). Despite this, Senate Bill 1839 was passed in July 1988 with the support of most community coalitions, but excluding the Board of Education, the CTU, and the Principals' Association. Then-Illinois Governor James Thompson used his amendatory veto power to rewrite portions of the bill. After further negotiations involving various legislators and different interest groups, Senate Bill 1840 was approved by the legislature and signed into law, becoming Public Act 85-1418.

Liberal ideology drove the broad democratic participation element of the reform and old-time Saul Alinsky-style organizing formed the basis of methods for mobilizing parents and community members (Lewis and Nakagawa 1995). From the inception of the Chicago reform, a liberal ideology emphasizing participatory democracy through parent and community involvement was seen to be crucial to its success. In a memo urging support of alternative governance structures for school reform, Don Moore, founder of Designs for Change and one of the architects of the Chicago reform, marshaled "evidence concerning the effect of parent involvement on student achievement" (Moore 1988, 1). He cited a report that stated parents "must be involved at all levels of the school" in advocating the idea that parents should have a role in school decision-making. The hope was that each individual school community would take the opportunity created by the reform to cultivate effective school practices at its school site and thus raise the level of achievement. Reformers in Chicago believed it was necessary to mandate a majority of parent and community involvement on the councils because, historically, voluntary models had not proven successful in allowing sufficient voice for lay members on similar councils (e.g., Malen and Ogawa 1988). Reformers also believed that Chicago administrators would never agree to "power-share" with parents and community members (Hess 1991).

But parent and community control was also supported by more conservative interests. For instance, the political and financial backing of business groups was crucial to passage of the reform (Shipps 1997). Business interests ensured that greater accountability measures were put into place, that the central bureaucracy was limited, and that no new funding was given to the schools. Conservatives supported the reform not only because they believed that schools were not turning out the "workers" businesses needed (Mirel 1993) but also because they were hoping for greater parental choice in education. In a book coauthored by a prominent Republican, the "cure" for the Chicago school "crisis" was elaborated

> We believe we have found the cure. It requires taking control of the schools from a remote and too-powerful bureaucracy and returning it to principals, teachers, and local community representatives. It requires giving the parents of students enrolled in each school a voice in the selection of its principal and the establishment of school policies. And it requires allowing parents to choose which schools their children attend. (Walberg et al. 1988, 111)

As the above quote suggests, some liberals were concerned that the backing of conservative interests meant that the Chicago reform was a precursor to school choice and vouchers in Chicago (Mirel 1993).

Hess (1995) discusses how both liberals and conservatives were excited and dismayed by the reform. He points out how some liberal writers, such as Jonathon Kozol, believed that school restructuring reforms such as Chicago's might improve the "efficiency" of schools but do little to correct fundamental inequities. On the other hand, some conservative observers such as Chester Finn believed the reform was a radical departure from previous attempts at school restructuring; however, Finn was also a proponent of school choice and vouchers. Hess believes that the reform had its "roots" in the "egalitarian and compassionate soil of the traditional liberal perspective" (135). But, he acknowledges that the reform itself was "fashioned more pragmatically than ideologically" (Hess 1995, 135).

Was the reform, as Hess (1995) asks, "left-over liberalism or neo-conservative conspiracy?" Part of the answer lies in what happened in subsequent years. The reform underwent a few constitutional challenges in the first two years. Most notably, although the original reform required that only parents vote for parent members of the LSCs, in December 1990, this portion of the reform was deemed unconstitutional by the Illinois Supreme Court and was rewritten by the state legislature. The new wording allowed community members surrounding a school also to vote for the parent members. A few years later, in 1995, in an effort to improve the financial solvency of the schools and to get more accountability, Mayor Richard M. Daley "covertly joined forces with the state's Republican leaders to revise the School Reform Act of 1988" (Lenz 1997, 1). The legislature created revisions in the Act that allowed the mayor to name a chief executive officer (CEO) for the schools and gave the mayor complete control over appointing the school board (a five-member "super board" until 1999 and thereafter a seven-member board with four-year terms). In turn, the CEO was given power to remove or replace LSCs, principals, and faculty in schools that were "failing" or found to be in "educational crisis" ("The new law" 1995). Paul Vallas, Mayor Daley's budget director, was named as CEO. Vallas implemented many new programs and policies, most notably a strict accountability system that put the "failing" schools with low test scores on probation and retention of students who did not meet grade level math and reading test scores (Lenz 1997).

For the LSCs, although the initial powers were not substantially changed, neither were new resources put into better training or support of their work. The emphasis shifted from participatory democracy as a mechanism for school reform to accountability and testing as a means of reform. "Phase II" of the reform did not result in a voucher plan, as some were concerned would happen. But the process by which it was fashioned, the parties who were involved, and the greater emphasis on accountability mark this reform as in line with more conservative, rather than liberal, interests. The LSCs still existed, but in the absence of city leadership that believed in the power of parent and community empowerment, with growing deficits in educational funding, and without immediate improvements in student achievement, participatory democracy as a means of change faded.

Assessing the Reform: Achievement and Democratic Participation

The main goal of the Chicago reform was to raise student achievement. And in the original Chicago School Reform Act the means by which this goal was to be achieved was by allowing more parent and community involvement into the school system. In terms of achievement, the reform stated:

> First priority should be given to . . . assuring that students achieve proficiency in reading, writing, mathematics and higher order thinking that equals or surpasses national norms; assuring that students attend school regularly and graduate from high school at rates that equal or surpass national norms. (34–101)

The Chicago reform also clearly explained how this priority would be met:

> The General Assembly intends to make the individual local school the essential unit for educational governance and improvement and to establish a process for placing the primary responsibility for school governance and improvement in furtherance of such goals in the hands of parents, community residents, teachers, and the school principal at the school level. (26)

Although reformers and early observers of the reform expected participatory democracy to result in great changes in student achievement and in school operations, the empirical link between parent and community empowerment and school improvement was not strong. The reform was established to allow for greater parent and community control, but this involvement was to be an instrument for higher student achievement. As with parent involvement in an enablement model, parents in the Chicago school reform were being used to meet the needs of the school. In order to assess the reform, it is important to look at whether the "first priority" of increased student achievement was reached and, secondarily, if changes in participatory democracy occurred and were related to improved achievement.

Student achievement. On this goal, as might be expected, the results are mixed. An early assessment of achievement by Niemiec and Walberg (1993) found that, over the first three years of reform, the percentage of students scoring at or above the national norms in reading and math declined. For instance, across elementary schools, the average percentage of students scoring at or above the national norm in reading for the 1989–90 school year was 23.4 percent; in 1991–92, it had fallen to 22.6 percent. Similarly, in mathematics, the rate went from 31.5 percent in 1989–90 to 29.2 percent in 1991–92.

However, subsequent data showed that rates began to climb after that. Hess (1999) reported that, for grades three through eight, the average percentage of students scoring at or above national norms in reading rose from 26.8 percent in 1992–93 to 34.7 percent in 1997–98. The average percentage of students scoring at or above national norms in mathematics showed a similar increase, from 25.4 percent in 1992–93 to 39.6 percent in 1997–98. In high school, percentages of students scoring at or above national norms generally declined in reading and improved in mathematics. Although the increases are encouraging, it should be noted that, ten years into the reform, more than 60 percent of students across grades still score below the national norms on reading and mathematics.

Graduation and drop-out rates also showed mixed results. Niemiec and Walberg (1993) reported that, three years into reform, graduation rates had decreased from 47 percent in 1989–90 to 43.7 percent in 1991–92. The annual drop-out rate (the percentage of students who started in the first week of school but left during the year) was at about 13.2 percent for each year. Drop-out rates in more recent years rose slightly to between 15 percent to 17 percent, and a 1998 report found that more than 40 percent of students who began ninth grade had dropped out of the system four years later (Catalyst 2000). Clearly, achievement and enrollment data demonstrate that the reform has a long way to go before reaching its goal.

Improving participatory democracy. As others have stated (Bryk et al. 1998; Hess 1995; Mirel 1993), this was not a community control initiative as had been tried in the 1960s in New York. This was a restructuring that attempted to put control of the local schools directly into the hands of those closest to the school: the parents, community members, and teachers at the school site. The ideology behind this portion of the reform was one of participatory democracy at the local school site, what Bryk and his colleagues termed *democratic localism*.

One way of assessing the success of the reform on this point is to look at involvement in the process of electing individuals to the LSCs. The first LSC election did generate a good deal of involvement from parents. Held in October 1989, more than 17,256 individuals ran for the LSCs, with 9,500 parents running for the approximately 3,200 LSC parent positions (Designs for Change 1989). The average school had eighteen parents running for the six parent positions. Schools with a higher percentage of low-income students had slightly fewer parent candidates than did schools with lower numbers of low-income students (e.g., schools with 99% to 100% low-income students had an average of seventeen parent candidates, whereas schools with fewer than 39% low-income students had an average of twenty candidates). A study by the Chicago Urban League (Lewis and Taylor 1990) reported similar results.

Other findings from both the Designs for Change report and the Chicago Urban League study showed that schools with a higher percentage of Latino/a students tended to have fewer candidates than did other schools. Schools with higher percentages of African-American parents had more candidates overall than did schools with higher percentages of whites or Latino/as. Although schools with a greater African-American population had the most candidates, the

Chicago Urban League study found that those schools also had the lowest voter turnout (Lewis and Taylor 1990). More white parents won seats than would have been expected based on the racial makeup of the schools. In the first election, 55 percent of parent LSC members were African American, 20 percent were white, 23 percent were Latino/a, and 20 percent were Other (Designs for Change 1989; Lewis and Taylor 1990).

Subsequent elections did not have the level of interest generated by the first LSC election. The second election, held in 1991, had about 8,200 parents, teachers, and community members running for the 5,400 open seats on the councils (Bradley 1991). Later elections in 1993 and 1996 each had fewer than 8,000 individuals running for open seats; about 60 percent were parents ("Local School Council Elections" 1996).

In terms of the running of the LSCs, the Chicago Panel on Public School Policy studied participation at LSC meetings for twelve different schools (Easton et al. 1990). In the first year of reform, they found that of all LSC members, parents (not including the chairperson, who was also a parent) were the least likely to speak in meetings. However, case studies of schools (Rollow and Bennett 1996; Yanguas and Rollow 1996) demonstrate that changing traditional patterns of interaction between school personnel and parents was a slow process. Five years into the reform parents were better at working with principals and were better able to effectively voice their positions.

Bryk and his colleagues (1998), in a broad study looking at the "lower-performing" elementary schools in the Chicago (86% of all schools fit into this group) and at longitudinal case studies of twenty-two schools echoed these results. Four years into the reform they estimated that about one-third of schools were "actively restructuring," another third were undertaking some moderate restructuring, and another third had little changed. They identified four different types of school politics: adversarial, consolidated principal power, strong democracy, and mixed. The third of the schools that were actively restructuring and seemed to be improving were those with strong democracy and "balanced" governance (Eason and Storey 1994). However, between 37 and 44 percent of the schools were classified as having consolidated principal power and were sites where "LSCs were likely to be inactive" (84). Thus, Bryk and his colleagues demonstrated some relationship between participatory democracy and school improvement. They were impressed with the results they saw in the strong democracy schools, despite few external supports for training.

Hess (1999) also looked closely at the workings of fourteen LSCs and linked the work that they did with achievement changes. Hess found that about a third of the schools in his study also demonstrated balanced governance but he found less of a relationship between the governance type and school improvement. Although Hess (1999) believed that LSCs served as an important "public focal point" for evaluating principals' work and the school improvement process, his conclusion was more nuanced:

> If what reformers were expecting to see was LSCs actively leading the drive to reform individual schools through LSC-generated proposals, active committee investigation of alternatives, and adoption of directions that would be implemented by school staffs, then the picture of reform in Chicago schools falls short in most schools that we studied. (80)

In sum, it seems that the LSCs generated more initial public interest and activity in school reform. It appears, however, that generating sustained school improvement and interest through participatory democracy is more elusive.

Achievement or democracy? As the above literature suggests, neither the goal of improved student achievement nor the goal of democracy was clearly reached. Although there were some initial gains in student achievement, the overall picture is little improvement in student outcomes. Similarly, despite the fact that more parents and community members became involved in the schools, the involvement was not clearly sustained, nor did it fundamentally change the way most schools operated. Finally, although Bryk and his colleagues (1998) established some connection between those schools with stronger democracy/participation and increased school achievement, this was prior to "Phase II" of the Chicago School Reform. The new emphasis on oversight and accountability through testing establishes an environment where local control is less important than meeting centralized requirements.

Perhaps the problem is that goals of achievement are difficult to reach through democratic means. As some researchers have documented, the local school councils (the heart of the participatory democracy process) were messy (Easton and Storey 1994; Lewis and Nakagawa 1995). Parents fought with other parents, they disagreed with the principal and teachers, or they did not have enough training or resources to make important decisions about how the schools should change. In Chicago, democracy did not result in quick changes to student outcomes, making it more difficult to believe in its power to change the schools. Furthermore, the traditional enablement roles parents play in the schools are hard to dismiss. Such roles do not threaten the authority of principals and teachers, and they bring parents into the schools in already sanctioned ways. And, as Lewis and Nakagawa (1995) found, many Chicago parents felt much more comfortable with a supportive school role and found it difficult to change the ways they interacted with the school even with the new authority they gained through the reform. Ultimately, the Phase II changes in the Chicago school reform seem to have facilitated the enablement role of parent involvement—it renewed the importance of professional authority and principal and teacher training, it provided no additional resources for helping parents to become empowered in their governance roles, and it clearly made parent and community involvement instrumental to the goal of achievement.

Conclusion: Unintended Consequences

The Chicago school reform has a reputation as the most "radical educational experiment in the United States" (Niemiec and Walberg 1993, 1), "one of the most dramatic restructuring initiatives ever undertaken in American education" (Mirel 1993, 116), and "a novel and far-reaching educational reform" (Elmore 1991, vii). Living up to that reputation cannot be easy. And yet it is precisely this discourse, one that marked the Chicago school reform experiment as historical prior to any outcomes, that is one important element in understanding this reform:

> Embodied in Chicago school reform is a very democratic ideal. It is the democracy of shared responsibility that makes, in part, the reform experiment so attractive and uniquely American. In a modern republic, instances of participatory decision making among the electorate are rare. It appears that no one wants the reform to fail. (Niemiec and Walberg 1993, 103)

In some ways, the Chicago school reform lives up to its "historic" reputation. Especially in terms of the process by which it came about, it created unique coalitions of different classes and ethnicities, community members and businesses, interests both liberal and conservative. But, some ten years after the passage of the original reform, the evaluations of student achievement, even by those who were strong champions of the reform, remain mixed. Many point to the need for greater teacher training and professionalization as key, as Bryk and his colleagues (1998) concluded

> We are convinced that the Chicago Public Schools will not become fundamentally better over the long term unless greater professionalization occurs. Marginal changes can be effected in other ways, but the deep changes required to reach "world class standards for all" remain unlikely. (307)

The broad democratic participation and empowerment that also marked the Chicago school reform as historical show similarly mixed results. The reform has helped to draw more individuals into active participation in the schools, but this empowerment process has been limited in its success. Often, typical patterns of control and power are difficult to change because they are inherent to both the practices and history of the institution and the makeup of the individual (Bourdieu 1981). To embrace the empowerment role, Chicago parents and community members had to move beyond the traditional enablement positions in the school and the concomitant expectations for how they should act. But this is not easy, given that it is often in the schools' and the parents' best interest to work in enablement positions. Lareau (1989) illustrated that although teachers may state that they want a "partnership" with parents, they frequently desire involvement in very specified ways, ways that are not equal to a partnership model. Furthermore, Lareau found that those parents who did what the school asked received better support for their children. This is one way the conventional, customary relationship between parents and schools is reinforced and reproduced, and one reason it may be difficult to mandate an empowerment role, as was done in Chicago.

Commentaries by Epstein (1993) and Wasley (1993) point out that what parents often desire most is more information and more communication. To the extent that reforms like Chicago's open up the possibilities for such improvements, they should be commended. However, the original legislation and the 1995 amendments provided few means of cultivating parental and community authority and voice; it appeared the reform was more likely to "enable" parents and community members rather than "empower" them. The possibility of radical changes through reforms like Chicago's are directly tied to the reforming of the relationship between parents, community members, and the school. As Bryk and his colleagues (1998) demonstrated, such changes occurred in fewer than half the schools in their study. And, in looking closely at the functioning of LSCs in fourteen schools, Hess (1999) found that few LSCs were truly active in reforming their schools.

The Chicago reform created the opportunity for parents to gain authority in the schools by mandating a majority of parent members on each LSC and allowing them decision-making power on substantial school issues. But in order to use this authority and become empowered, parents needed to establish authority with other members of the LSC, particularly the school personnel, and with other members of the general school community, such as parents. The question of *how* parents may establish their authority in school governance councils is crucial.

Lightfoot (1978) uses Weber's categories of "positional authority" and "personal authority" in considering how teachers gain legitimacy and respect with parents and students. Lightfoot states that a teacher may maintain authority either by virtue of "the structure she represents," that is, "the socially recognized position she holds (positional authority)" or through her own "individual qualities of expertise, charisma, and personality (personal authority)" (30). Teachers who are less competent will depend on institutional support (positional authority), rather than personal talents (personal authority), for their power. For the parents on the local school councils, the school reform law endowed them with some "positional authority" as elected representatives of the school community and through mandated duties on the councils. But it seems positional authority was not enough to change how parents, teachers, and principals interacted. Personal authority, which comes from experience and knowledge, were hard to come by. Often, parents were given neither the time nor the support to establish this personal authority (Lewis and Nakagawa 1995).

The process of empowerment takes time, as other researchers have documented. For instance, St. John, Griffith, and Allen-Haynes (1997) found that parents were welcomed and empowered only after the entire school staff changed their way of thinking. Rather than utilizing parent involvement as a means of reaching their own goals (as with enablement roles), principals and teachers had to recognize parents as partners in the process of school change. Furthermore, teachers needed to feel a sense of power and control over their own practices in order to welcome parents into the school. The Chicago school reform, although creating a potential environment for empowerment, did little to facilitate a change in principal and teacher thinking. The overarching goal of student improvement also necessarily made parent and community involvement instrumental to many school and administration decisions, more of an enablement kind of involvement than empowerment.

As St. John and his colleagues' work indicates, true empowerment roles for parents and community members might be better established in a number of ways: through the emphasis on partnership and egalitarian roles in the school (e.g., Epstein 1987, 1993; St. John, Griffith, and Allen-Haynes 1997) or by establishing a parent context for involvement separate from the school environment (Delgado-Gaitan 1991). Epstein's work demonstrates how to create family-school partnerships that acknowledge the strengths and capabilities in both institutions and that change the ways in which they interact. She and her colleagues use a model of "overlapping" responsibilities between families and schools to detail the various ways in which family-school partnerships can be built and maintained. St. John and his colleagues find that empowerment necessitates "rethinking the meaning of leadership" and suggests a process for how parents, teachers, and principals can engage in such work. Alternatively, Delgado-Gaitan describes an instance of empowerment established by parents and community members, not by schools or reformers or legislators. The Latino parents in her study organized a parent group outside of school and then were able to cooperate with the school in terms of what the parents expected, not what the school expected. In the end, the school had to change its expectations for how parents could and should be involved. The work of these researchers offer other models of empowerment that would fundamentally change parent-school relationships and reform schools.

In Chicago-type reforms, however, will policies based on an assumption of empowerment-through-governance ultimately result in radical reform in the schools or in the lives of parents and children? In an earlier experiment in "egalitarian" means of governance, Gruber and Trickett (1987) outlined many roadblocks to empowerment at an organizational level. In their study, a policy council—composed of equal numbers of parents, students, and teachers—performed school governance. Gruber and Trickett specifically studied empowerment or, as they defined it, "how much decision-making power people actually wield in an organization" (354). They found that parents had very little decision-making power because of inherent inequities: "inequality of knowledge, expertise, and access to policy implementation" (360). The inequalities, combined with the organizational difficulties of trying to establish and maintain the new governance structure, resulted in teacher control. Gruber and Trickett found that the power structure changed very little, and the policy-making council eventually was viewed as having little importance in the school governance process.

Finally, although parent involvement is thought to be important for all children, it is often used as a policy mechanism for change only in areas where there is a large population of lower income minority families, and often in place of other policy supports for changing schools. Confronting the "economic inequalities in our cities" that militate against the availability of resources and maintain the lack of opportunity in "job creation, housing, [and] health care," Apple (1993) centered "realistically on the question of whether more local control of schools, finance, and curricula can compensate for these conditions" (39). Apple's work helps us to understand some of the potential unintended consequences of reforms like Chicago's, ones where democratic ideals are championed without balancing these with basic economic needs of families. Are we setting lower income families up for further failure in the schools? And will that failure spell the end for serious attempts at empowered parent participation? Writing a few years after the creation of the Chicago school reform, Apple (1993) cautioned:

> The Chicago experiment can also serve less progressive purposes and may indeed lead later on to greater power being given to the conservative alliance. It can cause splits within communities at the school level, pitting one group against another unless we are very cautious. (39)

Although community splits at the school level were not widespread, in some ways the reform did lead to more power for conservative purposes. The 1995 amendments gave greater control over the schools to the mayor, downplaying the importance of participatory democracy, democratic interests, and broad-based coalitions.

There are stories of "successful" LSCs that suggest that policies like Chicago's at least create the hope for change. However, such hope may be based on faulty assumptions about the relationship between parents and schools as well as flawed notions on how power and authority can be redistributed. The Chicago school reform, as a grand experiment in hope, offers a unique instance of participatory democracy put to the test. However, as Morone (1990) stated in his book *The Democratic Wish*, the conviction that "somehow, power can be taken away from the state and restored directly to the people. . . . That ideal may be the most important false hope in American history" (30). What the Chicago school reform demonstrates is that even when some power is restored to the people, that power may not result in intended outcomes. Rather than having participatory democracy used in pursuit of achievement-oriented goals, participatory democracy is important enough to be pursued as a goal in and of itself.

References

Apple, M. 1993. *Official knowledge: Democratic education in a conservative age*. New York: Routledge.

Becker, H. J., K. Nakagawa, and R. Corwin. 1997. Parent involvement contracts in California's charter schools. *Teachers College Record* 98: 511–36.

Bourdieu, P. 1981. Men and machines. In *Advances in social theory: Toward an integration of micro- and macro-sociologies*, edited by K. Knorr-Cetina and A.V. Cicourel. Boston: Routledge and Kegan Paul.

Bryk, A. S., P. B. Sebring, D. Kerbow, S. Rollow, and J. Q. Easton. 1998. *Charting Chicago school reform: Democratic localism as a lever for change*. Boulder, Colo.: Westview.

Catalyst. 1996. Local school council elections. Available at http://www.catalyst-chicago.org/05-96/056upd83.htm. Accessed July 3, 2000.

———. 1995. The new law. Available at http://www.catalyst-chicago.org/09-95/095upd82.htm. Accessed July 15, 2000.

———. 2000. CPS dropout rates: Let me count the ways. Available at http://www.catalyst-chicago.org/06-00/0600letmecount.htm. Accessed July 1, 2000.

Delgado-Gaitan, C. 1991. Involving parents in the schools: A process of empowerment. *American Journal of Education* 100(1): 20–46.

Designs for Change. 1989. *Shattering the stereotypes: Candidate participation in the Chicago local school council elections*. Chicago: Author.

Easton, J. Q., and S. L. Storey. 1994. The development of local school councils. *Education and Urban Society* 26(3): 220–37.

Easton, J. Q., S. L. Storey, C. Johnson, J. Qualls, and D. Ford. 1990. *Local school council meetings during the first year of Chicago school reform*. Chicago: Chicago Panel on Public School Finance.

Elmore, R. F. 1991. Foreword. In *School restructuring, Chicago style*, edited by G. A. Hess. Newbury Park, Calif.: Corwin Press.

Epstein, J. L. 1993. A response [to [Ap]parent involvement]. *Teachers College Record* 94: 710–17.

Fine, M. 1995. Foreword. In *Restructuring urban schools: A Chicago perspective*, edited by G. A. Hess. New York: Teachers College Press.

Gruber, J., and E. J. Trickett. 1987. Can we empower others? The paradox of empowerment in the governing of an alternative public school. *American Journal of Community Psychology* 15: 353–71.

Hess, G. A. 1991. *School restructuring, Chicago style*. Newbury Park, Calif.: Corwin.

———. 1995. *Restructuring urban schools: A Chicago perspective*. New York: Teachers College Press.

———. 1999. Understanding achievement (and other) changes under Chicago school reform. *Educational Evaluation and Policy Analysis* 21(1): 67–83.

Improving America's Schools Act of 1994. Pub. L. 103–382, Oct. 20, 1994, 108 Stat. 3518. 1994.

Katz, M. B. 1992. Chicago school reform as history. *Teachers College Record* 94: 56–72.

Katz, M. B., M. Fine, and E. Simon. 1997. Poking around: Outsiders view Chicago school reform. *Teachers College Record* 99: 117–57.

Kozol, J. 1991. *Savage inequalities: Children in America's schools*. New York: Crown.

Lareau, A. 1989. *Home advantage: Social class and parental intervention in elementary education*. London: Falmer.

Lenz, L. 1997. Punching up reform. *Catalyst*. Available at http://www.catalyst-chicago.org/11-97/117punch.htm. Accessed July 12, 2000.

Lewis, D. A., and K. Nakagawa. 1995. *Race and educational reform in the American metropolis: A study of school decentralization*. Albany: State University of New York Press.

Lightfoot, S. L. 1978. *Worlds apart: Relationships between families and schools*. New York: Basic Books.

Malen, B., and R. Ogawa. 1988. Professional-patron influence on site-based governance councils: A confounding case study. *Educational Evaluation and Policy Analysis* 10(4): 251–70.

Marris, P., and M. Rein. 1967. *Dilemmas of social reform*. Chicago: University of Chicago Press.

Mirel, J. 1993. School reform, Chicago style: Educational innovation in a changing urban context, 1976–1991. *Urban Education* 28(2): 116–49.

Moore, D. 1988. *Memorandum to National Advisory Panel on School Reform on selected research pertinent to the Panel's assertion about the effects of alternative governance structures*, March 4. Chicago: Designs for Change.

Morone, J. A. 1990. *The democratic wish: Popular participation and the limits of American government*. New York: Basic Books.

Niemiec, R. P., and H. J. Walberg, eds. 1993. *Evaluating Chicago school reform*. San Francisco: Jossey-Bass.

O'Connell, M. 1991. *School reform Chicago style: How citizens organized to change public policy*. Chicago: Center for Neighborhood Technology.

Rollow, S. G., and M. Bennett. 1996. *Parents' participation and Chicago school reform: Issues of race, class, and expectations*. Madison, Wisc.: Center on Organization and Restructuring of Schools.

Snider, W. 1990. Parents as partners: Adding their voices to decisions on how schools are run. *Education Week*, November 21.

St. John, E. P., A. I. Griffith, and L. Allen-Haynes. 1997. *Families in schools: A chorus of voices in restructuring*. Portsmouth, N.H.: Heinemann.

Walberg, H. J., M. J. Bakalis, J. L. Bast, and S. Baer. 1988. *We can rescue our children: The cure for Chicago's public school crisis*. Chicago: URF Education Foundation.

Wasley, P. 1993. A response [to [Ap]parent involvement]. *Teachers College Record* 94: 720–27.

Yanguas, J., and S. G. Rollow. 1996. *The rise and fall of adversarial politics in the context of Chicago school reform: Parent participation in a Latino school community*. Madison, Wisc.: Center on Organization and Restructuring of Schools.

Chapter 10

Joint Ventures Between Public Schools and City Government: Implications for Community Development

Louis F. Mirón

School districts located in major urban centers throughout the United States appear to suffer from chronic underachievement. Although schools are expected to serve multiple functions ranging from implementing a curriculum aligned with state frameworks to providing after school care, they nonetheless elicit criticism when students do poorly on standardized achievement tests. Society holds schools and school districts accountable for academic achievement while also tending to blame principals and teachers for a variety of social ills when performance lags. These ills include unemployment, violent crime, and the lack of moral values owing to a curriculum and academic standards that are widely perceived as lacking discipline and high expectations. Implicitly, the wider society seems to extend the perceived failure in academic achievement with the public school sector to rampant social problems in the inner cities (Mirón 1996).

It is small wonder, then, that the mayors of large urban school districts have increasingly joined the national chorus for educational reform. For instance, the 1998 meeting of the Council of Great City Schools, as well as that of the U.S. Conference of Mayors, featured workshops and keynote addresses on the role of urban mayors in promoting reform. Historically mayors in cities like Boston, New York, and Chicago have maintained a firm, albeit sometimes implicit, grip over education governance and policies by virtue of their abilities to appoint members of the local school board or school finance committees. Moreover, the politics of local economic and community development, as Paul Peterson (1976) theorized in *City Limits*,[1] virtually necessitated in cities like Chicago a close linkage between ward-based community politics and educational policy. Both of these political processes were often controlled by mayors.

This paper examines the dynamics of mayoral involvement in urban education through a case study of "joint ventures." Joint ventures are formal collaborative relationships between institutions of government, for example school districts and cities. Historically they have operated under the auspices of the provisions of Home Rule, which was granted to many cities by their state constitutions. Informally joint ventures can consist of partnership arrangements among individuals engaged in activities such as mutual planning, facility sharing (public libraries and parks), and joint oversight committees.

Two cases will be presented, New Orleans, a city that in 1995 institutionalized joint ventures in its City Charter,[2] and Santa Ana, California, a city where the mayor took the symbolic initiative to name the city the "Education City." The latter symbolized an effort to link the economic progress of that city with the success of its public schools. The chapter focuses on the actual, as contrasted to the espoused, degree and quality of cooperation as manifested in the extant joint ventures. An analysis of multiple sources of data including interviews with mayors and superintendents (or their staff), public documents, and promotional materials will be presented. However, before beginning the analysis I will present a conceptual framework that seeks to merge political, organizational, and procedural dimensions of joint ventures.

New Institutional Configurations

In general terms joint ventures may be viewed as mutual responses by the various institutions of government to perceived isomorphism. That is, as society at large, and in particular those interest groups and institutions (taxpayer associations, the news media) that pride themselves as watchdogs of government bemoan the "fleecing of America," there is pressure for governmental agencies—including public education—to work together. The public holds a wide image of an inefficient government that does not cooperate among all of its sectors. As students of contemporary educational reform and governance have widely noted, public schools and school systems are notorious for their organizational isolation (Stone 1996).

The unstated theoretical assumption is that, however powerful, governmental organizations are incapable of controlling the global demands of their environment. Borrowing from the works of Stone (1993, 1996), Emery and Trist (1965) and others, Howell Baum

(1998) has proposed a conceptual framework for studying collaborative institutional relationships. Baum conceptualizes an interorganizational domain model "wherein organizations [are] becoming interdependent, and actions by one would set others into motion, in turn affecting still others in ways that no single entity could control." (1998, 3) These "interorganizational domains" provide the environmental contexts that engulf seeming autonomous organizations. Turbulence, uncertainty, and complexity mark their theoretical and normative contours. The unintended consequences of the newly rationalized behaviors of the actors in such organizational dynamics replace the assumptions of the rational theory of the firm. That theory was based on economic models.

Baum (1998) interprets the conceptual underpinnings of interorganizational domains along these twin trajectories: empirical and normative. Echoing Peterson's 1976 study of school politics in Chicago, organizations are perceived to have their own internal, yet potentially overlapping, interests and problems. Moreover, there exists "the potential for organizations to work deliberately to articulate a domain or field according to consensually accepted rules and to create a system" that works (3). Previous theoretical notions of the "relative autonomy" (Poulantzas 1978) of the state (and its sectors), self-regulation and self management give way to a more nuanced understanding of interdependence. Public institutions, following Foucault, are now decentered. Of central concern to our understanding of the isomorphism of the institution of public schooling is the notion that interdependent organizations now embark on new rules. What are these?

Normatively, cooperation, not competition or conflict, is key. New configurations invoke the organizational images of networks and coalitions. Furthermore, the institutional and marketing strategies of the "new capitalism" (Gee, Hull, and Lankshear 1996)—collaboration—are invoked. At heart is the recognition that resources, services, marketing, and indeed "power" itself are distributed across organizations. These precious holdings of organizations (among education professionals the very notion of teaching as dispenser of knowledge and information) are purviews of multiple organizations and actors. Foucault's thesis that power and knowledge are mutually constituting practices puts the issue abstractly.

Student Achievement as Community Concern

In a previous article (Mirón 1995) I hypothesized that, in urban centers beset by the disappearance of work, rampant violence, and overall social dislocation, student academic outcomes assume a broader social significance. Neighborhoods in urban communities are in need of much more than excellent student achievement from their public schools. Doubtlessly academic excellence is a matter of grave concern to families in these schools. However, it is not the only concern. For example, at Pio Pico Elementary School in Santa Ana, California, one of the cities in this study, the mainstay issue for parents was safety. When the current principal was hired, she began a practice of holding informal "chats" with parents. The parents were exhausted from the gang violence, vandalism, and the instability of their neighborhood, a major port of entry for immigrant families from Mexico and other Latin American countries. They wanted the principal to make the school a refuge for the neighborhood. The conceptualization of the school as serving more than an academic function required interorganizational collaboration with other public agencies such as the Santa Ana Police Department, as well as nonprofit groups like the Boys and Girls Club. The Club is located directly across from the school, and the director and the principal distribute resources freely across their organizations. Both formally with public and private agencies, as well as informally with parents, the school formed joint ventures.

Such institutional boundary spanning, moreover, results from a critical pragmatic, even moral and an ethical vision, that school environments "matter." These admissions do not come easily for public school educators, particularly school administrators and classroom teachers. In the case of Santa Ana, and as we shall see below New Orleans as well, coalition building with public schools was politically welcomed by mayors. The reverse seems to be true for superintendents, when then superintendent Morris Holmes of the New Orleans Public Schools told an audience of mayors, that the sole mission of the school district was "to raise academic achievement" (Mirón 1995, 108). Under intense pressure from actors in other environments, corporate leaders, editorial writers, school board members, and state departments of education to lift test scores above the national average, superintendents perceive it a luxury to engage in joint ventures such as full service schools, on site health clinics, and before- and after-school care. Ironically it is these concrete exemplars of joint ventures that would help shield superintendents from the inordinate political pressures from their elected and civic leadership demanding academic excellence. By establishing formal partnerships with other institutions, schools in distressed urban centers could relieve some of the social pressures cited above and perhaps concentrate more fully on raising student achievement.

Peterson remarked in *City Limits* that mayors and city council members would respond to pressures to grow broad economic development policies that would benefit the city as a whole. Here the superintendents' world view seems to run counter to the idea that academic achievement is only one piece of the puzzle to improve urban schools. That cities and local communities have broader needs that go beyond test scores is an idea that is difficult to grasp.

Crossing the Border: Planning for New Institutional Boundaries

I borrow the concept of the *border* from Henry Giroux's (1993) work on border pedagogy. In brief, Giroux argues that educators need a perspective from which they can view themselves as intellectual and cultural workers. In isolation, professional educators (teachers and principals) can do little to level the playing field of unequal schooling, and obviously, do less to make equitable and democratic the unequal society that in which the material practices of schooling (Popkewitz 1998) are situated. Ditto for city governments.

The institution of public schooling, as I have illustrated elsewhere (1997), can make an ally of local governments and cities generally. Historically their relations have been characterized as isomorphic owing to the divorce of "politics" from "education." Of course, no such split can be realized, and despite the apparent good intentions of education reformers in the progressive and subsequent eras, the practices of education are both *political and politicized*. They are political because they are effects of "power." This view of power follows closely Popkewitz' rejection of power as sovereign, meaning, "a question of who rules (or who is ruled) (17)." This notion of power effectively conceptualized power as a commodity (Mirón 1997), that is as a thing, that can be distributed from the ruler to the subject under rule. The conception advanced here is relational: power is an interaction among, and between, unequal relations and the meaning the actors within those fields ascribe to these relations (Cherryholmes 1988). Education is also politicized in the more conventional notion on the distribution of resources and the allocation of values, in other words, who gets what, when, why, and how.

Thus urban educators can potentially cross the isomorphic borders of public schooling into the interorganizational domain of the city itself, in particular city government and its agencies. In a nutshell these border crossings constitute the theoretical underpinnings of joint ventures. They are *joint* because of more substantive reasons than merely collaborative. Operating in the field of interorganizational domain, these collaborative relationships between the city and schools construct new social spaces that *may* give rise to alternate organizational realities which in turn create possible visions of a better quality of life for the children and residents that schools and city governments purportedly serve. In a word, they can foster local community development. The question before us, therefore, is what is the nature of these spaces in the context of urban schools and urban centers? More theoretically stated, what are the phenomenological qualities of these joint ventures as new social spaces forged by mayors and superintendents?

Methods and Data Collection

In this study, data were collected in cities and urban school districts across the country. These included Albuquerque, Los Angeles, New Orleans, San Diego, Santa Ana, California (Orange County), and Santa Fe, New Mexico. A team of faculty and doctoral students interviewed the mayors (or their education advisors), superintendents of schools (or governmental relations staff) in these cities and urban school districts. In addition, we collected archival material about school-city partnerships, business alliances, promotional materials, and curriculum. The purpose of data collection was to ascertain the quality of the actual joint venture, whether or not formally inscribed in law or public policy such as the City Charter.

Below I present an analysis of two cases, New Orleans and Santa Ana, California. The juxtaposition is both empirically and theoretically significant in that both contexts are populated with heavy minority students and residents, experiencing significant economic transformations as a result of the global economy, and like most school districts located in or near urban centers, suffering from chronic underachievement and weakened public confidence. These perceptions approach a near universal judgment of "failure." The differences between the two cities, in addition to geography, is in its history: New Orleans' culture was constructed along the social and political dimensions of the African-American experience as well as that of the Caribbean. Santa Ana is almost exclusively Mexican-American, or Chicano. I begin with New Orleans.

New Orleans: "Never the Twain Shall Meet"?

New Orleans, a city that is over 60 percent African American, and nearly 40 percent poor, has been dominated by regime politics that are polarized along racial lines. The city has been led for over twenty years by an African-American mayor, beginning with Ernest "Dutch" Morial (the first African-American politician elected to Congress in Louisiana) and continued with his son, Marc Morial. The school district has been governed by a majority African-American school board and led by an African-American superintendent for approximately the same amount of time. City politics, then, has been characterized as dominated by a majority African-American governing body (city council and board of education) mayors and superintendents of schools. These politicians have competed for political power with the mostly white business and civic elite (Mirón 1992; Whelan, Young, and Lauria 1994). This regime politics echoes Stone's (1989) framework with one difference: the regime is dominated by, not subordinate to, the social group whose political constituents are the poor and minority. These conditions have served many urban centers, for example, Washington, D.C., and Baltimore, where African-American middle class professionals and politicians have successfully mobilized their majority-minority population and white upper-class progressives to obtain, and largely sustain, elected office. This social-political landscape undergirds the analysis of the case study data presented below.

When Marc Morial assumed office in 1994, he pledged to establish an education liaison in city government. Marc Morial had run his campaign for implicitly as an education mayor for New Orleans. For example, the largest broad-based citizen task forces he formed after the election was the fifty member strong Education Task Force. Polls commissioned by the *Times-Picayune* during the election had uncovered an astonishing fact: 25 percent of the respondents offered *unsolicited suggestions* as to how to improve the perceived dismal performance of the public schools.

The Education Task Force was co-chaired by two of the most powerful politicians in the African-American community, the head of the teacher's union (United Teachers of New Orleans) and the president of the school board. The Task Force recommended that an education office, headed by an education liaison, be established and funded. On March 31, 1994, a draft of its mission statement read:

> The Education Task Force seeks innovation for our educational system. By establishing a liaison with the members of city government and with all concerned citizens, we can unite to achieve quality education in New Orleans. Therefore, a coalition of educators, government officials, and other citizens can combine in a joint effort to improve public education [for the citizens of New Orleans] (Minutes 1994).

The education liaison office would be located in the Office of the Mayor. Its functions were to promote more effective communication between city hall (and thus city government) and the school district, especially the local school board. In addition, the Task Force recommended that a permanent Education Advisory Committee to the Mayor be established.

Symbolic Steps

In what was widely perceived by the news media and community activists as a historical precedent, Morial appeared in May 1994, before a public meeting of the newly elected school board. This was the first time in recent memory that a sitting mayor had ever publicly addressed the school board and pledge cooperation—on its own turf. The mayor reiterated his pledge to join the board as an active partner for the betterment of public education and the children of New Orleans. In subsequent interviews with members of his executive staff, it was gleaned that the mayor was merely following through on his campaign promises for public education. In particular, the mayor was keen on the furtherance of joint ventures between the city and the school system. These collaborations were designed to:

1. "Continue and expand coordinated capital budget planning processes between the city and the school board *in order to encourage further joint-use facilities such as the New Orleans Public Library branch in the new Martin Luther King Elementary School*" (emphasis added);

2. "Direct the police department to create a 'security zone' on and around school grounds in order to assure the safety of students arriving, attending, and leaving school facilities";

3. "Develop a cooperative effort among New Orleans Public Schools security, the New Orleans Police Department, parents, students and the community to improve security within schools. Develop alternative schools for violent students presently dispersed among the general student population";

4. Assign a ranking officer to work with the superintendent to develop a school facilities security program at each school; *the school board does not need to incur the cost of*

outside security consultants when the expertise necessary to perform this function resides within our own municipal police department" (emphasis added);[3]

5. "Encourage the New Orleans Public Schools to work with juvenile justice experts, university personnel, and city officials to develop a model comprehensive violence reduction and delinquency prevention strategy for elementary, junior high, and senior high students, going beyond traditional delinquency prevention programs by involving the family and the community in identifying 'at risk' youth, monitoring their progress, and intervening with effective programs at critical times in the youth's development";
6. Finally, the following recommendation paralleled the one offered by the Task Force on Education (see below). "Establish an Office of Education to provide {a} liaison between city government and the Orleans parish public schools, colleges and universities, police, religious leaders and business leaders" (Campaign Committee 1994).

Of course, the reforms advanced by the Education Task Force for the proposed education liaison and Advisory Committee had the potential to undermine the overall good feelings enjoyed by the mayor and a new school board. First, the new superintendent of schools, Dr. Morris Holmes, was not keen on the idea of an education staff in the Office of the Mayor. As noted above, at a conference focusing on the mayor's role in urban education reform, the superintendent admonished the audience, reminding participants that the sole mission of the district was to raise academic achievement. Second, one of the co-chairs of the Task Force, the president of the school board, urged the group at its final meeting (when it formally adopted recommendations to present to the mayor) to drop the liaison and advisory committee items. (The school board president was under pressure from a white business developer, a member of the civic elite, to merge the Education Task Force Recommendations with his group. The developer was seeking funding from the city and the school district to establish a commission on children and families.)

From Morial's perspective, the mayor offered more than symbolic gestures. Informal interviews held with his staff and advisors, including the chairman of the Charter Revision Committee, (see below) confirmed that Morial was sincere. The mayor realized that, despite the political problems for the city, he should honor his pledge to be an active partner with the school board and offered to help the school district campaign for passage of a near $500 million bond measure and other sources of revenue to repair dilapidated, dysfunctional, and non-air-conditioned buildings. In meeting between a joint committee of the City Council and the school board held September 29, 1994, the spirit of cooperation also seemed apparent. The minutes of the Orleans Parish School Board read:

> [A member of the school board] explained that as a result of the priorities set in the 1992 election, the Board members would work collaboratively with the City even though they are governed by separate bodies. The Board solicited the Council's assistance on the $492 million dollars needed to repair its aging schools. The schools are plagued with many problems ranging from plumbing to serious termite damage. Few of the schools in Orleans Parish are able to pass fire code inspections. The Council had requested information regarding the conditions of the buildings and the related cost. It was suggested that the Council visit some of the schools to see first-hand the deteriorating conditions. Members of the group expressed pleasure with the collaboration that was going on between the Orleans Parish School Board and the New Orleans City Council.[4]

Although the superintendent publicly endorsed the broad goals of the emerging city-district interorganizational alliance, he nonetheless had previously noted that the keynote address of the conference on city-school partnerships "contained nothing new." Insiders from the school district then commented that Superintendent Holmes had grown wary of all of the unfunded governmental mandates. Dr. Holmes had apparently viewed the emerging call for joint ventures to ameliorate both the social ills and, possibly, the problem of underachievement as mayoral meddling in his, the school system's internal affairs.

Thus, within these minor, largely symbolic gestures we note the institutional constraints impeding interorganizational coalitions (joint ventures). Moreover, the racialized conflicts engulfing the formulation of potential local community development (Peterson 1985) goals and proposals—ones such as an education liaison and a commission on children and families—become racialized, as actors from different social positions advocate for their own interests.

Institutionalizing Joint Ventures

Finally, the mayor moved beyond symbolism to enact collaborative, joint ventures into a city ordinance. The vehicle was the revision of the *Home Rule Charter of the City of New Orleans*. David Marcello, the legal architect and chief political strategist for the revision of the City Charter, (the previous attempt by former mayor Sidney Barthelemy had failed) was no stranger to Marc Morial and City Hall. He was the former chief legal counsel to Marc Morial's father, Dutch Morial mentioned above.

Marcello assembled an impressive array of citizens, professionals, academics, and citizen-activists to mobilize the community to seek a consensus for a new charter. Moreover, Marcello went much further than producing a new legal document. He mobilized the New Orleans community to win broad public support for passage of the new charter in the April, 1994, elections. In the new document was a proposal to establish "Cooperative Endeavor Agreements."

> Under Section 9–314 the City of New Orleans, through the Office of the Mayor, shall engage in cooperative endeavors with the state and its political subdivisions, the United States or its agencies, or with any public or private association, corporation or individual. Such cooperative endeavors may include but not be limited to agreements regarding joint planning of capital projects, joint use of facilities, joint research and program implementation activities, joint funding initiatives, and other similar activities to further public education, community development, housing rehabilitation, economic growth, and other public purposes.

Ultimately, Morial delivered on his pledge to work in partnership with the School Board (and indirectly, the City Council). Largely as a result of his political support and overwhelming popularity with most of the citizens, the School Board won passage of a $400 million plus bond issue (the amounts were reduced) to rehabilitate and air-condition the public schools. Several years later, however, owing in part to his frustration with the school board, and in particular Superintendent Holmes, Morial made gestures to take over the school system, much like Mayor Richard Daly had done in Chicago under the provisions of the Amendatory Reform Act passed by the Illinois Legislature in July 1995. This may explain the reason that, according to city officials, no evidence of an application for a cooperative endeavor under the provisions of the new charter was ever submitted during Morials' first term in office. As we shall see, the case study data suggests that little beyond joint capital planning and revenue raising exists in the city of Santa Ana, California, and the Santa Ana Unified School District.

In summary, the historical separation of school districts and city government in New Orleans (ensconced in the state constitution) reproduced isomorphic relations between the two. Kipling's adage, "East is East and West is West, and never the twain shall meet" appears to be correct in this case. The school board's and the city's brief successful coalescing around capital needs (the $400 million school bond issue) was, apparently, short lived. Indeed, interviews with parents upset with the school board's recent (1998) attempts to "dismantle" the system of magnet schools that have historically served a biracial mix of middle class families, suggest that the mayor is working behind the scenes to control the selection of the next superintendent after Holmes leaves the district in 1998. Subsequent superintendents continued to focus on improving student achievement (test scores). There was no systematic effort to promote the concept of Joint Ventures.

In the next section I take a brief comparative look at the case of Santa Ana, California, a city in Southern California, forty miles south of Los Angeles, widely known locally for being a major port of entry for Mexican immigrants of binational citizenry.

Santa Ana, California: "Education First" at the Crossroads

Santa Ana, California can be seen as a "transnational locale"—a locale that forms part of a multitude of transnational networks (see Mirón, Inda, and Aguirre 1998). Santa Ana, a community of 300,000 residents, is little known outside of southern California. Situated in northern Orange County, a sprawling suburb of nearly three million people located forty miles south of Los Angeles, it is unique in a number of ways, especially in the profound demographic changes it has undergone in the previous twenty-five years. Since 1970, the percentage of Latino/as in Orange County has grown from 8 percent of the total population to 27 percent. In Santa Ana these numbers are more dramatic: 69 percent of the population is Latino/a, and more than half are foreign born, mostly from Mexico. Dubbed by the 1990 U.S. Census as one of the most impoverished cities in the nation, Santa Ana has also been designated as one of two youth capitals in the United States, second only to El Paso, Texas. In one square mile of the city alone live approximately 26,000 youths, ages 18 and under, many of whom are undocumented residents (U.S. Census 1990). In effect, Santa Ana has become a young Latino/a city; people come here from communities all over Mexico and other parts of Latin America, reinventing themselves along with the city. As a consequence of such migrations, Santa Ana has been transformed from a strictly national space to what may be called a translocality (see Appadurai 1996).

Generally speaking, a translocality belongs in one sense to particular nation-states, because it occupies their territorially defined spaces. But at the same time, because it is traversed by a multitude of processes, that is, because it forms a node in a multitude of transnational circuits, thus connecting it to elsewhere beyond the nation, a translocality also transcends, to some extent, the nation-state. In other words, a translocality is a space of which the nation-state is not in complete command, weaving together, as it does, various "circulating" populations with various kinds of "locals" (Appadurai 1996, 192).

It is in this space, this translocality, that the lives of thousands of immigrant students take place.[5] It is a space of flows, a node in multifarious transnational migrant circuits. It is also a space, however, entwined with vehement attacks on bilingual education. Orange County is at the forefront in the state, if not the nation, of the fledgling "English-only" grassroots movement discussed earlier, of this movement whose principal aims are: (1) to eliminate all bilingual education in California; (2) to institutionalize English "immersion" programs (in elementary school, programs that would force foreign born and native born students who speak little English to "sink" or "swim," using English as the language of instruction); (3) and finally, to deny—in pedagogical practice—Mexicans and other immigrants access to their culture by prohibiting instruction and conversation in Spanish or the mother tongue. So Santa Ana is caught at the crossroads of those national processes that attempt to regulate the conduct of subjects in the interests of the nation-state and those transnational ones that prevent this regulation from fully taking place. It is at such crossroads that we attempt to understand the construction of joint ventures.

Interviews with the mayor of Santa Ana and administrators in the school district reveal that the relations between the two echo those in New Orleans. Calls for collaboration and the formation of school-business partnerships between the two institutions (and others, for example business) are largely rhetorical. The exception is on capital needs. According to the mayor, the city helped the district fund the construction of seven new schools. The city was able to use federal redevelopment funds to advance the vision of Mayor Miguel Pulido for Santa Ana as "Education First." In 1991 the city launched a redevelopment initiative in partnership with the Santa Ana Unified School District to

> . . . take dollars that had accrued through redevelopment funds and in essence advance them to the school district so that they in turn could engage in some of the pre-construction costs that are affiliated with building new schools. Of course what Sacramento had [the state legislature] was a program where they (the state) would reimburse school districts that were building schools. But if you didn't have the money to start it up and build it in the first place, you're never going to get it reimbursed. So we took $30 million and ended up building, I believe, 11 schools in about seven years. It's more than any other city in California. This partnership has resulted in a new high school, intermediate schools, elementary schools and it's been a tremendous boost to Santa Ana Unified. (Pulido 1997)

Apparently the partnership, the limited joint venture, ended after these schools were built. Population demands (a 41% increase since 1988) took its toll on the resources of the city (see above). In addition to Proposition 227, the voters initiative to do away with bilingual education in California (see above)—a method of instruction the local district had employed for at least a decade—Santa Ana Unified School District was saturated with attempts to deal with a school violence problem, and the new superintendent of schools embarked on an ambitious system of reform to increase student achievement known as "Above the Mean." (System wide test scores on basic skill such as mathematics, reading, and language use had lagged at the twenty-fifth percentile for the pervious decade.)

After the capital program ended, the city-wide effort to build partnerships with the school district extended beyond the mayor's office. Known as Santa Ana 2000, it consisted of vision setting for public education among the private, higher education, business and industry councils, such as the Chamber of Commerce, and the nonprofit sectors. "Santa Ana 2000 is an interagency coalition consisting of hundreds of individuals working collectively. Its mission is to make the city of Santa Ana an even better and a more rewarding community in which to live that works, succeeds in school, and nurtures a family" (Davies 1997). In the parlance of this paper it seeks to foster local community development. The purpose of the Santa Ana consortium is to provide a "mechanism to continue periodically to update and address and talk about issues. Now it's not to say that we do everything because we don't or that there are no gaps. We could be doing more. But it's at least to say that there's a group that talks about what we can do as partners. And we have a very strong partnership with our educational partnerships with the city (Pulido 1997).

As will be seen below, however, the goal of fostering broadly conceptualized community development (Mirón 1995) was virtually impossible to attain. Too much discussion and too many local, narrowly defined, economic development goals (such as economic growth and job creation) could more readily be accomplished. This pattern follows Peterson's model (cited above) that development policies (economic growth, also see Mirón 1992) will supersede more redistributive policies that may benefit neighborhoods. These would include joint ventures between schools and city governments around locally defined issues such as crime prevention, free tutoring programs and before- and after-school learning opportunities. There is plenty of evidence to suggest that individual schools such as Pio Pico Elementary, a two-way bilingual school, and Davis Elementary (a newly built school with abundant community support) successfully established interorganizational coalitions—joint ventures—to pursue mutually constituted academic, economic, and community development goals. However, the preliminary judgment is that these accomplishments, much like New Orleans, failed to take institutional root *system wide and city wide*. These findings confirm previous research (see Mirón 1997) that found city government in New Orleans rallying with the school district to help build the nationally recognized high school for the performing arts, the New Orleans Center for the Creative Arts (NOCCAA). Two administrations, under mayors Barthelemy and Morial, sought help from the state legislature in Louisiana to obtain $22 million in capital outlay funds to relocate the school from an affluent uptown neighborhood to one experiencing urban blight. The project was funded largely with the perception that it would help revitalize a neighborhood along the riverfront, thus promoting safety, small businesses, and community pride, in a word fostering community development.

The Social Relations of Community Development

Between the school districts and city governments in these comparative case studies are social relations that appear to undermine community development goals. In New Orleans racial conflicts between the public and civic sectors, and within the public sectors, embed the push toward collaboration. For example, the recommendation from a white developer to halt the formation of an office of education liaison broke the consensus within the Education Task Force. Also when the draft language for cooperative agreements surfaced, members of the subcommittee who represented the work of nonprofit civic elite objected to the use of the word "capital" (see Mirón 1997). In Santa Ana the state wide effort to eliminate bilingual education doubtlessly forged divisions within the loosely organized Santa Ana 2000 consortium. Not insignificant as well was the perception that illegal—and illiterate—immigrants from Mexico were pulling down test scores. Under these difficult political and social conditions joint ventures other than siting of new school buildings (a largely economic outcome) become problematic.

Conclusion

In this chapter I have attempted to explore the feasibility of establishing joint ventures in urban social contexts. Although these contexts predictably share common characteristics, and conditions across locales, the cases presented here differ substantially. The obvious first level of difference is in the populations that reside in New Orleans and Santa Ana, California. New Orleans is approximately 60 percent African-American, Santa Ana over 60 percent Latino/a, primarily Mexican-American, or Chicano. These "populational reasonings" (Popkewitz 1998) do not constitute the principal basis of comparison in this exploratory study. However, these differences in ethnic affiliation and identity are not inconsequential.

In New Orleans, a strong tradition of civil rights seemingly enables the mayor, the city council, and the local school board to forge coalitions at the site of simplest and most direct impact: bond elections for school construction. This level of engagement among governmental partners—the infrastructure level—parallels the movement among school partners that begin with building improvement, the most accessible, and end with curriculum reform, the most isomorphically remote (see Mirón and Wimpelberg 1992). This coalescing around a common political interest during short term political campaigns may result in substantial improvements to the capital inventory: strong mayoral coalition building and institutional formation embodied in the *City Charter*. Apparently, however, it does not result in a practice of institutional networking (Baum 1998) around a common vision. School systems' tendencies to reproduce their social structures, discursive practices, and organizational territorial imperatives seriously undermine such networks in places like New Orleans.

Santa Ana, too, was able to build on civic goodwill and the accessibility of revenues for school construction to build eleven new schools with state funds. This is no small accomplishment. An absence of a civil rights tradition embodied in mayoral leadership, and perhaps its transformation into a translocal city, makes difficult the conversion of rhetorical strategies (Santa Ana 2000) into a discursive practice of networks. Santa Ana, like New Orleans, is enmeshed in a host of social problems like crime, gang violence, and chronic underachievement among its students. Both superintendents of schools focus on lifting academic achievement as the primary mission of the school district. At the same time each school chief readily accepts the gifts of the city in the way of revenue to support school construction. The difference seemingly lies solely in the leadership exhibited by Morial and his citizen activists to ensconce these new boundaries into city government. In neither case, however, do we find evidence on behalf of the school districts beyond rhetorical strategies to redraw boundaries between them to improve the overall quality of life in local communities and neighborhoods. Community development, a noble abstract goal, continues to elude the imaginations of school districts. Such possible new futures give way to existing systems of reason and discursive practices, as Popkewitz elegantly theorizes.

Notes

1. Elsewhere I have defined community development as a hybrid of economic and social policies that promote both economic growth and quality of life. See Mirón, Louis F. (1995) "Pushing the Boundaries of Urban School Reform: Linking Community Development to Student Outcomes." *Journal for a Just and Caring Education* 1(1): 98–114.

2. The Charter reads: "The City of New Orleans, through the Office of the Mayor, shall engage in cooperative endeavors with the state and its political subdivisions, the United States or its agencies, or with any public

or private association, corporation or individual." Effective May 1, 1954 (Amended January 1, 1996), Ordinance No. 17, 148 M.C.S.

3. In 1997, during a financial scandal exposed by the *Times-Picayune*, the school district's Director of Security accused the Superintendent of not disciplining security officers when school principals reported theft of money, computer equipment, television sets, and other school supplies. This exposé seemed to further the rift between the mayor and the school district, a dimension outside the scope of this article.

4. This open spirit of cooperation stood in stark contrast to the animosity between the Council and the Board in years past. The New Orleans City Council was forced to declare schools a "non-use." This meant that the Council would have to give approval before any new schools could be located. This move forced the delay of the location of its premier public school, Benjamin Franklin High Schools, a magnet college preparatory school. Cooperative Endeavors, Article IX (Section 9–314), 127.

5. Like most school districts throughout the country, Santa Ana Unified provides mostly transitional forms of bilingual education with the goal of having 1.4 million limited English speakers in the state quickly assimilate into English and U.S. culture. See Nick Anderson, "Testing the limits of Bilingual Education." *Los Angeles Times*. August 8, 1997, A16.

References

Appadurai, A. 1996. *Modernity at large: Cultural dimensions of globalization*. Minneapolis: University of Minnesota Press.

Baum, H. 1998. Empowering the zone: Ad hoc development of an inter-organizational domain. Paper presented at the annual Association of Schools and Colleges of Planning Conference, Pasadena, CA.

Cherryholmes, C. 1988. *Power and criticism: Post structural investigation in education*. New York: Teachers College Press.

Davies, D. 1997. Crossing boundaries: How to create successful partnership with families and communities. *Early Childhood Education Journal* 25(1): 73–77.

Education Task Force. 1994. Minutes, March 31, 1994. New Orleans, LA.

Emery, F. E., and E. L. Trist. 1965. The causal texture of organizational environments. *Human Relations* 18: 21–32.

Gee, J. P., G. Hull, and C. Lankshear. 1996. *The new work order: Behind the language of the new capitalism*. Boulder, Colo.: Westview Press.

Giroux, H. 1993. *Border crossings: Cultural workers and the politics of education*. New York: Routledge and Kegan Paul.

Mirón, L. F. 1992. Impact of school leadership on state policy. In *Educational policy for school administrators*, edited by P. F. First. Boston: Allyn and Bacon.

———. 1995. Pushing the boundaries of urban school reform: Linking student outcomes to community development. *Journal of a Just and Caring Education* 1(1): 98–114.

———. 1996. *The social construction of urban schooling: Situating the crisis.* Cresskill, N.J.: Hampton Press.

———. 1997. *Resisting discrimination: Affirmative strategies for principals and teachers*. Newbury Park, Calif.: Corwin Press.

Mirón, L. F., J. Inda, and J. Aguirre. 1998. Transnational migrants, cultural citizenship, and the politics of language in California. *Educational Policy* 12(6): 659–81.

Mirón, L. F., and R. Wimpelberg. 1992. The role of school boards in the governance of education. In *Schoolboards: Changing local control*, edited by P. F. First and H. J. Walberg. San Pablo, Calif.: McCutchan.

Peterson, P. 1976. *School politics, Chicago style*. Chicago: University of Chicago Press.

———. 1985. *Politics of school reform, 1870–1940*. Chicago: University of Chicago Press.

———. 1981. *City limits*. Chicago: University of Chicago Press.

Poulantzas, N. 1978. *Classes in contemporary capitalism*. London: New Left Books.

Popkewitz, T. S. 1998. *Struggling for the soul: The politics of schooling and the construction of the teacher*. New York: Teachers College Press.

Stone, C. N. 1989. *Regime politics: Governing Atlanta, 1946–1948.* Lawrence: University Press of Kansas.

———. 1993. Urban regimes and the capacity to govern: A political economy approach. *Journal of Urban Affairs* 15: 1–28.

———. 1996. *The politics of urban school reform: Civic capacity, social capital and the intergroup context*. Paper presented at the annual meeting of the American Political Science Association, San Francisco.

United States Census. 1990. Available at http:venus.census.gov/cdrom/lookup_doc.html.

Whelan, R. K., A. H. Young, and M. Lauria. 1994. Urban regimes and racial politics in New Orleans. *Journal of Urban Affairs* 16(1): 1–21.

Chapter 11

Rediscovering the African-American Tradition: Restructuring in Post-Desegregation Urban Schools

Leetta Allen-Haynes, Edward P. St. John, and Joseph Cadray

The desegregation of racially isolated educational systems did not result in integrated schools as many social reformers had envisioned. The dream shared by many was of racially integrated schools with African Americans, European Americans, and children of other races learning together, in just environments that promoted racial harmony (e.g., Blum 1993; King 1986). However, the reality has been different than the dream. After nearly a half century of court-mandated desegregation, a larger percentage of African-American children attend predominantly African-American public schools than did before the Supreme Court's *Brown* decision in 1954. A new wave of reformers has concluded: "[W]e must abandon the pretense that urban school districts are functioning systems that can deliver equal opportunities if relatively simple interventions—cross-district desegregation plans, magnet schools, better court supervision, more money, etc.—are put in place" (Fossey 1998, 16). Unfortunately, in the newly emerging post-desegregation period many urban schools will probably remain racially isolated.

If the ultimate aim of the desegregation process was to create integrated schools that are more just and caring for children of all races, then it is important to ponder the types of learning environments that support the growth, development, and learning processes of African-American children. Given that many urban schools remain racially isolated, it is vitally important for urban educators to understand the learning styles and developmental needs of African-American children. The African-American tradition, which emphasizes care and community (Dempsey and Noblit 1993; Irvine and Irvine 1985; Walker 1996; Ward 1995), provides an important foundation for creating just and caring learning environments in post-desegregation urban schools. Indeed, it is time to explore ways of integrating restructuring processes in urban schools. This is an important issue at the present time because Comprehensive School Reforms (CSR) show some promise of improving educational outcomes in some urban schools (chapter 7).

This chapter explores strategies for integrating the African-American education tradition into school restructuring in post-desegregation urban schools. First we review the ways desegregation has been viewed, both as a policy issue and as a process that influences educational practice. We consider the status of desegregation litigation in the United States, then reflect on ways the literature on moral education can inform restructuring. Second, based on this review we consider what desegregation policy omitted: preservation of the African-American tradition of education. We hypothesize that integrating an emphasis on the African-American tradition into a CSR restructuring process could provide a way of improving learning environments for children in urban schools. Third, we examine two case studies of restructuring schools, with a focus on aspects of the African-American tradition that emerged as part of the process. These cases provide evidence to ponder related to our hypothesis, but we recognize this inquiry is exploratory rather than confirmatory. Finally, we consider the implications of this review and the case studies for urban schools that are contemplating the various school restructuring models.

Desegregation Reconsidered

When reviewing progress on desegregation, it is essential to distinguish between three concepts as they will be utilized in the framework of this chapter. *Desegregation* refers to the legal process intended to result in the integration of schools and colleges that have historically been racially isolated. *Integration* refers to both the affirmative processes of balancing races within educational institutions and to creating just and caring learning environments for diverse children. *Postdesegregation* refers to school systems after legally mandated desegregation processes have been completed. Although the process of desegregating educational systems has proceeded through several stages of litigation, integration has proven to be an illusive goal. Rather than focusing on the illusive goal of integrating schools, we take a step back and reexamine the meaning of the desegregation process, as it relates to the learning experiences of children.

Desegregation at a Crossroads

The desegregation of public schools began in earnest in the southern United States with the Supreme Court's *Brown* decision which ruled that de jure systems of separate but equal were illegal. The initial wave of desegregation decisions began with the process of redefining enrollment boundaries for school buildings so that schools that were formerly racially isolated would improve their racial balance. This involved increasing the use of busing, given that neighborhoods were often segregated, as well as reconfiguring schools in different ways to make it easier to achieve a racial balance (e.g., mandating K–2 and 3–6 schools to replace the formerly segregated K–6 schools).

The second wave of school desegregation involved litigation against de facto segregation, systems of education in northern cities that were segregated by virtue of the patterns of housing rather than on the principle of "separate but equal." The desegregation of northern cities introduced new structural mechanisms, including magnet schools, to the arsenal of strategies used by the courts, as the focus of the courts shifted to findings ways to induce more families to choose diverse schools for their children.

Although the desegregation mandates were usually implemented in ways similar to what had been prescribed by the courts, these remedies did not, however, lead to integration of schools, especially urban schools (Fossey 1998; Orfield and Easton 1996; Teddlie 1998). Many whites either moved to the suburbs or enrolled their children in private schools. In a growing number of U.S. cities, desegregation has come to a legal end (i.e., Indianapolis, Boston): the courts are concluding that urban schools are desegregated. Now we are entering a postdesegregation period in many urban communities. Therefore it is important to consider how we can take affirmative approaches to improve the learning experiences of all students in this new context. Specifically, the *ethic of care* that was once central to African-American schooling in the United States was almost lost as a result of desegregation.

To a large extent, this *ethic of care* that was experienced in African-American schools prior to 1954, had its origin in the neighborhood school concept through which everyone in the school shared a common view of the world. African Americans remember those schools as fostering a strong sense of "community" and family cooperation. For the most part, during segregation, teachers lived and worked in their own neighborhoods and the school, like the church, functioned as the center of social activity in African-American neighborhoods. Parents' sense of association, identification, communication, and trust were facilitated by their everyday proximity to school personnel. Where a teacher sought to enlist the aid of a parent in solving a classroom problem (behavioral or academic) or assist with a school activity, it was as simple as stopping at the students homes while walking to and from school, or as mentioning to the parent while at church on Sunday.

This same phenomenon has likely been experienced within other ethnic groups where neighborhood schools existed. However, it was without warning or preparation that desegregation tactics such as busing abruptly displaced both African-American teachers and their students. Most African-American students were placed into schools where the ratio of minority students to minority teacher was severely diminished or nonexistent. Integration was attempted at the expense of African-American students' removal from their neighborhood schools and their alienation from the *ethic of care* associated with being taught by their own teachers. Although separated in a system labeled separate but equal, some African Americans report experiencing greater racial isolation as the result of school desegregation efforts.

Today, as courts back away from desegregation, it is important to recognize that inner-city schools often remain racially isolated. This new pattern is more than a bit ironic, given that urban educators increasingly work in racially isolated schools that courts have designated as desegregated. In pursuit of excellence, during the past two decades, federal and state educational policies have placed a greater emphasis on standardized tests, national educational standards, and the alignment of curriculum and standards. Further, many of the urban universities have attempted to provide teacher education programs aimed at responding to national and state reform initiatives, including these new "excellence" mandates, without explicitly considering the educational needs of urban children. Yet in the postdesegregation urban context, we need more educators to consider the learning needs of African-American children who comprise the majority of "desegregated" urban school systems. Thus, it is important to begin the conversation about how to integrate with justice and care, especially in urban universities that educate teachers who work in urban schools.

As we reflect on this history, it appears that desegregation in the United States is at a crossroads. The process of litigating for desegregation has led to a set of decisions and remedies that have been implemented. Yet the underlying problem of racial isolation has not been remedied in a way that seems just, especially if we use the paradigm of racial integration to judge the success of desegregation efforts. This new context should be of concern to all educators, and especially to educators in urban public schools and to teacher educators in colleges that prepare urban teachers.

Desegregation as Justice

The question of how to approach desegregation in this new context poses an especially troubling question from the perspective of moral education. Kohlberg (1981, 1984) posed a moral development lens that emphasized justice. When we use Kohlberg's stages of moral reasoning to view the desegregation puzzle, an interesting picture emerges. First, it is apparent that the reformers, including Martin Luther King, Jr., who led efforts to desegregate public and private systems of all types, were acting on postconventional principles, placing universal values for all humanity above the legal system. Indeed, Kohlberg (1981, 1984) consistently uses Martin Luther King, Jr.'s writings as an example of stage six moral reasoning. However, the process of litigating for the desegregation of schools involves working within the conventional legal system to find constitutional reasons for desegregation, which was the case for *Brown* and *Adams*. Perhaps stage four moral thinkers who value socially and legally constructed norms can look at desegregation with a clear conscience. However, if we take a step back and ponder the reasons why desegregation was not successful, it seems possible that some of those who espoused preconventional attitudes toward the new laws either chose to resist by moving from cities or placing their children in private schools. Specifically, some of the proponents of Martin Luther King, Jr.'s postconventional ethics lacked his ego strength and also placed their children in private preparatory schools.

Thus, those who hold postconventional values at an *espoused* level (i.e., as a stated belief) may need to reflect on the meaning of these values for their practice. Indeed, it is easier for most advocates of social justice to claim that we would take a virtuous path in a difficult situation, than to take this path when actually confronted by the genuine situation. The issue of where parents send their children to school is complex and potentially troubling precisely because it involves making choices that affect children. However, if we really believe in these espoused values, then we need to find ways to act on them. For example, it may be possible for some families to structure their time so one parent can volunteer in their public schools, rather than working longer hours to pay for private schools. This type of personal action (i.e., *theory in use*) would be more consonant with espoused values that favor integration. After all, an unintended consequence of working more is having less time with their children. In addition, when parents work as volunteers in schools, they can help schools become more just and caring (St. John, Griffith, and Allen-Haynes 1997).

For Kohlberg, universal conceptions of justice provided the basis for the more advanced moral stages: "At advanced stages, the most basic principle of justice is equality; treat every person's claim equally, regardless of the person" (1981, 144). He also argued that schools had a vital role to play in promoting moral development: "Social environments or institutions not only facilitate moral development by providing role-taking opportunities, but their justice structure is also an important determinant of role-taking opportunities and consequent moral development" (1981, 144). Thus, finding ways to desegregate schools that promote moral development represents a fundamental challenge within this construct of moral development.

The goal of creating meaningful integration is complicated by the need to include the voices of African Americans. It is interesting that the integration goal proved difficult to realize through the "just-community–schools" framework that was developed by Kohlberg and his colleagues (Powers, Higgins, and Kohlberg 1989). The just-community–schools approach to school restructuring may include features that promote integration, but it may not include all of the requisite features and philosophies necessary to create an environment that supports the development of all children. As a means of building a further understanding of possible strategies for promoting integration, it is appropriate to also consider how the concept of care, as part of the African-American tradition of education, might inform efforts to create more just and caring community schools.

Desegregation with Care

Carol Gilligan's (1977, 1982) critical examination of Kohlberg's theory revealed Kohlberg's lack of sustained attention to the ethical voice of care. Specifically, she examined how women responded to questions included in the instrument Kohlberg used on men to measure stages of moral development. She argued that:

> Women's construction of the moral problem as a problem of care and responsibility in relationships rather than as one of

> rights and rule ties the development of their moral thinking to changes in their understanding of responsibility and relationships, just as the conception of morality as justice ties development to the logic of equality and reciprocity (1982, 73).

Using this concept as a basis for examining the evolution of moral thinking in women revealed care as an alternative construct for moral thinking:

> As we have listened for centuries to the voices of men and the theories of development that their experience informs, so we have come more recently to notice not only the silence of women but the difficulty in hearing what they say when they speak. Yet in the different voice of women lies the truth of an ethic of care, the tie between relationship and responsibility, the origins of aggression in the failure of connection. The failure to see the different reality of women's lives and to hear the differences in their voices stems in part from the assumption that there is a single mode of social experience and interpretation. (1982, 173)

These constructs of relationship (or connectivity) and care provide a different lens for viewing the culture of schools and discerning possible images of successful schools for African-American children. The African-American education tradition placed a strong emphasis on care and community, qualities that were enhanced by African-American control of schools (Irvine and Irvine 1983). The evolution of this tradition in the context of school desegregation merits more attention. In particular, we are struck by the contrast between three images:

- the caring community in a segregated African-American high school in North Carolina before desegregation (Walker 1996);
- the description of the decline in a culture of care in a southern school system as an outgrowth of desegregation (Dempsey and Noblit 1993); and
- the recreation of caring environments in desegregated schools in Louisiana that were involved in the Accelerated Schools Project, a democratic restructuring process (St. John, Griffith, and Allen-Haynes 1997).

First, the concept of care was integral to the concept of quality education in African-American schools before desegregation (Irvine and Irvine 1983; Walker 1996). Vanessa Walker's (1996) study of the history of an exceptional African-American high school in North Carolina prior to desegregation revealed a caring school culture. The school not only had teachers with higher levels of education than surrounding schools for whites, but also had a deep culture of care, a commitment to the development of children and to finding resources from the community to support the children. For example, in recorded comments, the voices of former teachers and students told how the community had found money to support travel for the children, as well as to support extensive extracurricular programs. This example illustrates a form of local democracy that is based on commitment, relationships and care. However, this school was closed as a result of desegregation.

Second, the desegregation process systematically favored the majority's conception of school quality over the African American tradition (Irvine and Irvine 1983; Dempsey and Noblit 1993). In a case study of a desegregation process in a southern community, Dempsey and Noblit (1993) examined the different perceptions of "good" schools held by whites and African Americans. Among the African-American schools, most had a strong tradition of teachers working together in ways that demonstrated care and responsibility for the development of children, families and neighborhoods. In contrast, the white community was concerned about test scores and less concerned about the community aspects of schools. However the white community dominated the school board, which led to the closing of the school that had been perceived as being a "good" school by African Americans, along with the release of the teachers formerly employed by the African-American school studied. They further describe how the closure of the historically African-American school influenced a decline in the close-knit relationships within the neighborhood surrounding the former school.

Third, school restructuring can create a broader conception of education that embraces critical aspects of the African-American tradition. Stories of care similar to those described by Walker (1996) were also evident in some of the exemplary Accelerated Schools included in a recent study of family involvement in schools (St. John, Griffith, and Allen-Haynes 1997). In one school that had been an African American school before desegregation, a white teacher described how she had used her church's bus to take poor children (African-American and white) from the school on field trips for school activities. An African-American parent in the same school described how she had been involved in planning for the pilot test of a conflict resolution process that had helped create a climate of care on the playgrounds. In another historically African-American school, one in an inner city that was almost exclusively African-American, parents described how their neighborhood pride had been raised by the school's multicultural education program. This second school had also proven more effective at raising achievement for nontransient students between third and fifth grade than were other Accelerated Schools in the same urban area that had not taken a multicultural approach (Slack and St. John 1999). In a third historically African-American school, an African-American teacher commented that she had learned she could care for all children, whites as well as African-American, as a result of her experience with Accelerated Schools Project. When teachers began to share their feelings with each other, the racial divisions within schools began to break down (St. John, Griffith, and Allen-Haynes 1997). Thus *caring communities* of educators committed to the development of all children, their families, and neighborhoods had been created in these schools. In these cases, this new caring community model built on the African-American traditions in these schools.

In combination, these examples point to the possibility that within the African-American tradition there is a strong culture of care that can be built upon efforts to restructure urban schools (e.g., Comer et al. 1996; Finnan et al. 1996). Indeed, this review suggests the possibly of creating *just and caring school communities* that combine aspects of the just community school concept, broadened to include important aspects of the caring community concept that emerges from an examination of schools that have restructured within the African-American tradition. The ethic of care and relationship may be an important balance to the more conventional patterns of academic achievement that dominate the majority schools. The decline in this underlying culture of care in African-American schools could also contribute to the perceptions of problems in the new urban schools recreated under the mandates of desegregation and in response to recent, test-driven reform mandates.

The idea that care and collectivity provide an alternative basis for thinking about moral maturity, an understanding that emanates from Gilligan's feminist critique of Kohlberg's theory, provides an alternative construct from which to view desegregation and integration. Specifically, some African-American schools and colleges with a strong tradition of care and supportive relationships involving families appear to be able to support integration with majority students. By expanding our understanding of integration to include the culture of care and collectivity, it is possible to illuminate some of the qualities of the African-American tradition of education that could add to the foundations used in teacher education.

What Desegregation Overlooked

This review of the moral aspect of school desegregation provides insight into what was overlooked in the efforts to achieve desegregation of public schools. Desegregation was approached within a narrow vision of integration that emphasized numeric integration. The conventional, legal system of justice reinforced this narrow view. Thus it is extremely ironic that schools are now more segregated than they were before *Brown;* however, the human dimension of integration—the goal of creating just and caring learning environments for all children—was overlooked in the legally mandated desegregation process. As a result the African-American tradition of care was forced out of schools in favor of the new emphasis on excellence. Therefore, it is important to refocus integration efforts on the human dimension of the process.

Rethinking Reform

Desegregation overlooked the importance of preserving and enhancing the African-American tradition of education. Indeed, placing more emphasis on this tradition can potentially bring a better balance between justice and care for all students. The desegregation remedies constructed by the courts did not live up to the ideal posed by the integration dream, a dream that values equality in education and social institutions.

Although Kohlberg's advanced stages are based on universal principles of social equity and justice, the concept of just community schools has not proven to provide a workable basis for achieving the integration ideal. Creating just community schools based on the Western concepts of justice (e.g., Power et al. 1999) seems to have overlooked the concepts of collectivity and care that are integral to the African-American education tradition (Walker 1996). Thus the alternative of a broader construct, one that creates more room for care and collectivity, seems to hold promise. Education in the African-American tradition has something important to add to efforts to create more complete images of systemic desegregation and integration within schools. The image of African American education that emerges from this review is that of schools as learning environments with supportive relationships and a commitment to caring for all children.

Kohlberg (1981) argued the progressive tradition was an essential foundation of school reform:

> The progressive position appears idealistic rather than pragmatic, industrial-vocational or adjustment oriented, as is often charged by critics of progressivism who view it as ignoring "excellence." But Dewey's idealism is supported by Piagetian psychological findings [the foundation of Kohlberg's early stages], which indicate all children, not only well-born college students, are "philosophers" intent on organizing their lives into universal patterns. . . . Our educational system currently faces a choice between two forms of injustice, the first an imposition of an arbitrary academic education on all, the second a division into superior academic track and an inferior vocational track. The developmental conception remains the only rationale for solving these injustices and for providing the basis for a truly democratic education process. (95–96)

For the past two decades the excellence notion of education improvement has predominated while the conditions of many urban systems have remained troubled. Although we agree that an alternative paradigm is needed, perhaps even one that builds on older progressive traditions, we think that this new image needs to be open to the tradition of care that was central to African-American education before desegregation. Gilligan's arguments about care and collectivity opened the door to defining moral development and education in new ways that include the voices of women and people of color (1998). At the very least this open door needs to be widened a bit more to include voices from the African-American tradition, along with the progressive foundations of the U.S. common school, as integral aspects of urban education in this new era of "desegregated" schools.

Integrating the African American in Restructuring

As we ponder this the emergence of this new postdesegregation period, we hypothesize that it is crucial to explore ways of integrating an emphasis on the African-American tradition with the new emphasis on excellence, as a part of comprehensive structuring processes. To integrate new philosophies into a structuring process, it s necessary for the reform model to be process oriented. Although many of the models approved by the states and the federal government for CSR are emphasize process over curriculum, not all have the flexibility needed to integrate a new philosophy. However, many of these models, such as Hudson's Modern Red Schoolhouse, use back mapping from educational standards to curriculum as a central feature of their process (St. John et al. in preparation), which limits the capacity of educators to integrate a new philosophy. Based on a detailed review of the CSR models (St. John et al. in preparation), we conclude that two CSR models seem compatible with an integration of the African-American tradition. Comer's School Development Process emphasizes a community mental health approach that is compatible with this tradition (Comer et al. 1996). Also, the process approach in accelerated schools enables educators to develop their own school visions (Hopefenberg, Levin, and Associates 1993), which means it is compatible with this approach. In this section, we examine a couple of Accelerated Schools that developed approaches to reform that exhibited features of the African-American tradition.

Cresent Park Elementary School

"I am the dream!" There was standing room only in the State Department of Education's auditorium that morning as each person in the audience looked both pleased and surprised that such an exceptionally commanding voice emanated from such a brief structure. Marc stood on a chair at the podium and still had to tiptoe to get near the microphone:

> I wear a necktie to school each day to remind myself and my schoolmates that we are gentlemen who can settle our differences with respect and without fighting. Each morning as I straighten that necktie in the mirror, I feel proud of myself and my friends . . . and when my teacher calls me "Mr. Hicks," I feel proud to be living Dr. King's dream.

By the time Marc was finished, there were few dry eyes amid those offering him a standing ovation. And, although the applause continued for several minutes, with lights flashing and cameras clicking, Marc stepped down and returned to his mother's side, looking totally unaware that very few third-grade boys like himself had earned such an honor. Marc had won first place in the elementary school category of his school district's Annual Martin Luther King Essay Contest. A state board of education official had heard him deliver his essay at the award ceremony and invited him, his mother, his teacher, and the school principal to the state department's budget hearing that morning to demonstrate ". . . our money at work."

The principal, Jan Woods, has worked hard over the past seventeen years at recognizing and seizing such opportunities. Recalling her appointment as the principal of Cresent Park Elementary, she recalled that she had seen it as an opportunity to ". . . change the learning outcomes in a school that had not yet accepted academic failure as its status quo." She went on to admit that she had been scared "out of my wits" because she knew that she would be getting a veteran faculty in every sense of the word. She knew that change would not be easy because for many in the school and the community, the current reality had not caught up with the school's once excellent reputation.

Making a decision to begin slowly, the first thing Jan did was to put together an administrative team to explore school problems and advise her on decisions. The team met once a month and consisted of upper, lower, and special education chairpersons, a ranking teacher, and a building representative of the teachers' union. By 1990, they had begun a full-scale self-assessment process which led them to a unanimous agreement regarding the school's need to change. They found that Cresent Park's enrollment, which was 99 percent African-American, had remained relatively stable between 405 and 439 students in grades prekindergarten through sixth between 1985 and 1990. But their demographic profile had changed: 60 percent of the students now qualified for free lunch; and although the school's age/grade distributions showed no significant abnormalities, there had been a steady decline in reading interest and proficiency at all levels. In fact, the overall results on standardized tests for 1989–90 showed that more than 25 percent of the students were reading below grade level (36.4% of the boys and 28.7% of the girls in grades one through three).

Once they had been notified that their school had been selected as the pilot restructuring site, Jan chose seven teachers, the administrative team and two others, to join her that summer in participating in a week of training at the University of New Orleans. These were persons she had come to trust and depend upon. Their enthusiasm was very high by the end of the week, and they immediately set a date to get together to plan the training format for the rest of the Cresent Park faculty and staff. It was agreed that the principal should ask faculty to voluntarily come into the school three days before their official starting date for the training. Most of the faculty and staff responded positively and attended all three days. By the end of the third day, the faculty had completed plans for implementing the process beginning the first day of school. Cadres were identified, everyone had volunteered for one of them, and plans were underway for bringing students and parents into the start-up process.

However, on the first day of the next school year, the teacher's union voted its membership into an official job action. Seventy-five percent of the teachers at Cresent Park Elementary School were out on strike that first day, with the number steadily growing towards the end of the first week. You can almost see Jan Woods shudder as she recalls her feelings during that first week of school:

> The district was demanding that we keep the schools open as usual. . . . Parents were calling and coming in with concerns about the safety of their children and the quality of the substitutes. . . . Teachers were marching outside the school with angry signs and shouting hostile slogans. . . . Most of my key people in the [restructuring] process turned out to be union organizers on the strike line. All but two of those who attended the summer training with me were not out on the picket line. . . . It was a nightmare, not at all like I'd pictured the opening of school that year.

Jan recalled that she felt sick most of the time but had to keep going, she had a school to run and the welfare of the children to ensure. The strike lasted twenty-two days, and during that period the unity of the school's faculty was seriously diminished. Teachers who did not go out on strike suffered harsh verbal harassment on a daily basis, and there were a few instances of personal property damage inflicted on them by persons with whom they had worked for years. Within the school, the principal reported that three distinct factions existed after the strike: those teachers who did not strike, a few teachers who were on strike but who were able to put the strike and its issues behind them once they returned to school, and those who went out on strike and returned to school very bitter and determined not to forget. They continued to speak out against the district for provoking the strike in the first place, the community because it didn't support the union's actions, and the principal who tried to show that business could go on as usual without them. Counting on the faculty's ability to work through these difficulties, Jan waited for time to heal their wounds. After a few weeks of trying to bridge this disjunction in her school, she began to realize that the tensions were increasing instead of diminishing. Most of the teachers she usually depended on and confided in had gone out on strike and were now very distant, if not openly hostile. During the strike she had come to rely on those teachers who remained in the school. And now the hostility which existed between those two groups left her with a sense of isolation:

> I had been a strong union supporter before I became a principal, so I understood their position when they went out. Once the strike was over, I called a faculty meeting and announced that I understood that they had to do what they had to do, that I had to do what I had to do. I asked them to join me in putting the strike behind us and getting back to work for our babies . . . it didn't work, they were too bitter.

She decided to meet with each of the three faction's informal leaders to obtain their thoughts on how best to restore unity within the school. Each of them expressed feelings that someone else should make the first move. Exasperated, Principal Woods turned to the staff on the restructuring process who recommended third-party intervention and healing facilitation.

A two-day workshop "Anger Management and Conflict Resolution" was arranged for the faculty. An experienced consultant was hired to conduct the workshop. He familiarized himself with the school's profile and the principles and values of the restructuring process in order to develop a format for working with the faculty. In the workshop, the faculty came to see conflict as the natural dynamic in the group change process. They managed to regain some of their original group self-confidence, and by the close of the workshop, the faculty had been exposed to concepts of self-managed teams, shared team control, adaptation to school change through conflict, and some techniques for identifying and solving problems in a group format. They later discovered that the literature refers to their workshop experiences as "capacity building"—achieving unity of purpose through conflict, inquiry, resolution, and application. In a traditional school teachers and administers would have had little or no opportunity for such a group experience and would have doubtfully ever built a capacity to work together with a unity of purpose. Most faculties never develop the skills for identifying and defining their own challenges.

Upon their return from the holiday break, all of the faculty and support staff resumed involvement in restructuring activities. New leadership emerged as members volunteered to chair committees and subcommittees; more and more teachers stepped forward to provide information and expertise that revealed talents and interests previously unshared. No one worked harder than Jan Woods, however. At first she had been stunned and very hurt by her faculty's accusations regarding her leadership; but the more she examined her own actions and questioned her own beliefs, the more she began to see the contradictions. Over and over she began to replay the words which Dr. Henry Levin had challenged the school community not only ". . . talk the talk but also walk the walk." Jan vowed to herself that she would regain the trust and confidence of her faculty. She constantly reflected on the principles and values of the restructuring process. Giving teachers responsibility and empowering them to make the decisions which she could, did not come easily. After all, she had distinguished herself as a leader in the district and was appointed to a principalship when she was in her early 30s because of her ability to take charge and lead others. Now she was struggling to learn a new set of behaviors and adopt a different style of leadership.

In retrospect, everyone came to agree that the implementation of the restructuring process may have been delayed by the strike, but it was not retarded by it. In fact, its progression and chances for success were enhanced by the strike. The aftermath of the strike produced situations of conflict sufficient to involve the entire school community in a collective posture of questioning, testing, and change seeking.

Michael Fullan (1999) describes meaningful educational change as the result of such significant conflict. He states that the first change occurs in the individuals as they each are forced to examine their personal values. These values then function to shape their professional beliefs and practices in a manner which facilitates joining with others for a collective action. During the controversial strike, several parents served as substitute teachers in the school. For many of them, this was their first time in a school since they themselves had been students. And, although the strike presented an unusual backdrop, all of these parents were afforded an opportunity to learn what actually goes on in a school during the course of a school day. Events and circumstances that emanated from the strike required almost constant collaboration and cooperation between the principal, the regular teachers, and these parent substitutes.

Parents' advice and suggestions were not only entertained by the regular school personnel, but in many instances they were also solicited. Therefore, after the strike, the involvement of parents evolved almost naturally. Many of the fathers who previously had not been past the front office began to inquire about the repair needs they returned on weekends with their own materials and supplies to make repairs. Within a short time, this group evolved into what is now known as the "Dads' Club," and they are credited with improving the school's physical environment. They worked diligently to rewire and air condition every room in the school except the cafeteria. The interior and exterior of the buildings were repainted, furniture was repaired, businesses were solicited to donate equipment and supplies, and talent was secured to decorate classrooms and hallways.

One of the first things a visitor notices about Cresent Park Elementary School upon entering the first building are the colorful wall murals depicting scenes and characters from African American history, traditional nursery rhymes, and contemporary children's cartoons. Children's work is displayed on the numerous boards, cases, and hanging lines that are situated all over the school.

At first discipline and safety were issues for parents. They began to take an active role in providing security for the school. Their presence had a positive impact on discipline. Service on the various cadres during the taking stock stage and the vision forging activities provided them with input into establishing an Afrocentric and multicultural curriculum base with self-esteem building as the major focus. Parents got involved in planning special events that not only provided cultural and historical exposure for the students, but in most instances brought in participants from the larger community.

Many local political and business personalities in the city at that time had grown up in that neighborhood and had attended Cresent Park Elementary. Media coverage and attention from members of the city council and school board officials during the Accelerated Schools implementation and vision celebrations provided more of an impetus for parent involvement with classroom processes than Jan Woods could have hoped for. School pride was high among parents and teachers as they worked together to improve student achievement. Teachers accepted parental input almost as if it was the natural way to work. Extra hands in the classrooms allowed teachers to plan lessons which they may not have dared a year before. It became obvious to everyone that having a retirement-aged community, with persons available during the day to come into the school, was one of Cresent Park's greatest strengths.

By the end of the first year of restructuring, the school had begun to distinguish itself in the school district. To address the reading and writing deficits in the school, the curriculum cadre secured consultants to come in and work with teachers and parents to begin a creative writing project. Teachers were trained in techniques for using writing across the curriculum, and parents were given techniques and advice about encouraging their children at home. The cadre also launched a project called DEAR—Drop Everything And Read—where everyone in the school departed from regular school work and read any literature of their choice for twenty minutes each day. During these periods parents came into the school and either read to small groups of children, read with their own children, or simply read something of their own choice alongside the children. Throughout the school, students could be observed lying on the floor in classes, halls, and outside breezeways. No calls were accepted in the school during this period, because even the clerical staff stopped to read. Reading materials and activities increased in the homes and within one year the reading scores took a significant jump up.

Jessie Owens Elementary School

Don Banks moves at two speeds, fast and faster. As soon as a decision is made in his school community, he's off to the telephone, making contacts, finding the resources to turn the decision into a reality. His daily routine includes repeated telephone interruptions from such persons as the city's district attorney, university deans, fire marshals, television personalities, and bank representatives. The list reads as if Don were the mayor of a big city.

Jessie Owens Elementary School is now referred to as Jessie Owens Accelerated City and Don Banks is the principal. Many of the people he must speak with on the phone each day are people he contacts in order to get support resources for a school project or on behalf of a family in need. His motto is "Ask! There can only be one of two answers." An example of this would be when the faculty decided to change the name and improve the school's appearance. Within weeks of the decision, the campus was being transformed.

Jessie Owens is on the north side of this Louisiana city which is still struggling to pull up from the economic decline caused after the bottom fell out of the oil industry. A great portion of the working population in that region of the state are now either fishermen or farmers. The school itself is situated in a low socioeconomic area, primarily composed of either working class or government assisted households. Ninety-seven percent of the students receive either free or reduced-cost lunches, placing them in relative poverty. Owens is the only school in the school district which serves all the government-funded housing projects. Enrollment is steady, approximately 945 students (90.96% African-American; 9% white, 0.04% Latino/a and other) in grades preschool through fifth. The school has one noncategorical preschool handicapped special education class, eight kindergarten classes, eight first-grade classes, seven second-grade classes, seven third-grade classes, six fourth-grade, and four fifth-grade classes. There are also three mildly mentally handicapped special education classes and a behavior-disordered special education class. In addition to fifty-seven regular classroom teachers, the faculty also consists of two full-time resource teachers, two full-time speech and language pathologists, four Title I teachers, two counselors, a librarian and library assistant, a physical education coach and an aid, and a computer proctor. A large portion of these personnel are located in seven portable buildings. The school was originally constructed in 1959, when the neighborhood was still a white middle-class single-family dwelling area, to accommodate a maximum of 600 students.

Along with Principal Banks, there are two assistant principals, a secretary and an office clerk who make up the administrative staff. Don says that he had to fight with the school district to get the third administrator when he took the job in 1990. Two years after they agreed to place another assistant principal at Owens, it became a district policy to place two assistant administrators in any school where the enrollment exceeds 600.

Don fought for the extra administrative help because he needed to make a difference in the school as soon as he got there. Tensions were high in the school and in the neighborhood when he was called from his principalship at a south side middle school and asked to go to Jessie Owens Elementary. The previous principal had been a dividing force among faculty and parents; teacher and student morale and attendance were extremely low, and discipline problems were extraordinarily high. One teacher, who predates all of the administrators at the school, characterized the state of the school as a "dumping ground." She explained that teachers who had problems at other schools were reassigned there; students who were on the road to expulsion were sent there; and other faculty and staff vacancies were generally filled with available applicants after all other schools had been staffed. Many of the competent teachers would leave the school as soon as they acquired the seniority to move to a better school. The school had scarce resources, no enrichment or extracurricular activities, and no parent involvement. Student achievement was the lowest in the school district.

At the initial training, the Owens group began planning and organizing implementation plans almost from the first day. This enthusiasm was evident in the rapid school transformation which followed. Each of the group members studied the process, reflected on its meaning and internalized it individually. They began the taking stock process with the rest of the school at the same time as they began experimenting in their own classrooms. Because they were such a large faculty, reorganizing into a more equitable and efficient governing structure gave everyone something to do. To keep everyone on the right track, the steering committee selected one person whose sole responsibility was to learn all the ins-and-outs of the restructuring process.

Jessie Owens pioneered new approaches that the rest of the schools in the state network took note of once they learned inquiry and began to use it; they developed check list and reporting forms for cadres to demonstrate that their decisions had been derived through the use of inquiry. Each cadre poured over sections of the taking stock data, and reported to steering and then to the school as a whole before any change actions were planned. Changing the exterior physical appearance of the school resulted from questionnaire data on how personnel, students, parents, and the larger community felt about it. Changes to the interior were accomplished through innovations occurring in the curricular practices of the teachers.

They realized that the grade-level building configuration of the school served to divide the students and teachers, stifle the flow of ideas across the faculty, and inhibit the creation of community. Through inquiry, buildings became multigrade neighborhoods, teachers began to plan multigrade units, and students of all ages and grades got to participate in the renovation and revitalization. In one building they selected the theme "We are the World." Curricular planning took on a global perspective, and as each class completed the study of a country and its people, they decorated the classes and hall with images and symbols representing it. Eventually a wall mural of the entire globe was depicted in the hall and every child could point to the exact portion she or he had painted. Attendance improved and discipline went down. Students dared not miss out on their turn at the wall.

Breaking through to get parents involved was much more difficult. Many times when students became ill at school, they had to either remain at school or be brought home by school personnel because parents either could not be contacted or did not respond. Don had many discussions with faculty regarding how to attack this problem. It was decided that if the parents would not come to the school, then they would go where the parents were. One day Don, a counselor, and two parents went to a large project (where 300 of the families lived).

Teachers designed parent in-service sessions to acquaint them with the process and the school, and specific assignments were posted for parents, including things which could be done at home.

When many parents protested that the lack of a bus route near the school posed an inconvenience in getting there, Don requested that the steering committee create an ad hoc committee to address the problem. The committee requested local merchants join the school in making these requests. Several months later a city bus stop was created within one block of the school.

Realizing the limited resources of his parents, Don approached the steering committee with the idea of offering incentives to parents to get them into the school. A cadre working on obtaining more business partners obtained a sponsor for bus tokens. Don offered a family assistance agency space in his school for their food distribution process that occurred four times a year. Before long, the neighborhood had come into the school—parents, agencies, adult education services, and universities for research and field placement opportunities. When the school district had to cut its janitorial and maintenance budget, all schools suffered except Jessie Owens Elementary.

Parent volunteers were encouraged to get district certification to become employed in the school. Title I and other grant money had increased the school technology program from one lab with no computers in the classrooms to four computer labs. A parent volunteer obtained her GED, then was certified as an assistant by the district, trained in computer literacy, and hired on a full-time basis as a proctor. A cadre of teachers who are responsible for scheduling in the school has scheduled thirty minutes a day for every child on a computer. The computer proctor is now assisted by a pool of parent volunteers. The parent coordinator, who was hired shortly after the faculty identified space on the campus, secured furniture and equipment donations as well as funds to pay the proctor. The coordinator had two children in the school, worked full time, but was always available to volunteer on her day off. Of her decision to take the job at Owens, she said:

> When he (Don) explained the position to me and offered it to me, I quit my job the same day to come here and work. Mr. Banks is very understanding, he's open-minded. He'll listen to any idea you may have and he'll tell you quick; if you think it can work, give it a try. . . . This is family. . . . There is no other school with a parent center of this magnitude with the materials we have, and I'm proud of that.

The center has distinguished itself across the state to the extent that school personnel now have to call in and are placed on a schedule for visits to observe how it works.

So much has improved at Jessie Owens, but Don is the first to tell you that it has not been easy and that there is still a lot to do:

> I've made mistakes, I mean I could just hit the ceilings. . . . my hairline is falling further back, you know. . . . I can still come here, laugh and smile . . . and hopefully for me I've had more good days here than bad days. The bulk of anything our kids get here comes from the faculty . . . still . . . you still got the drug addicts out there. I mean we found out right after the holidays here in January when we returned a 4th grader who was dressing his kindergarten sister and literally breaking out of the house to come to school. And they were walking up the . . . two-way highway coming to school in the morning because mama was trying to lock them in the house to stay home and take care of young brothers or sisters.

With these comments, Don revealed his personal commitment to working within the school to be a catalyst for change in the community. His efforts to bring adult education programs into the school had helped, but he knew there was still much more that needed to be done.

Restructuring and the African-American Tradition

The Crescent Park and Jessie Owens cases illustrate examples of integrating the African-American tradition of care into a restructuring process that aims to improve student learning outcomes. Based on the literature review, we hypothesized: *it is crucial to explore ways of integrating an emphasis on the African-American tradition with the new emphasis on excellence, as a part of comprehensive structuring processes*. These initial cases illuminate three aspects of the restructuring processes that merit note, as we reflect on this hypothesis.

First, connectivity to the community provides urban schools with support for integrating care into the restructuring. The research on the African-American tradition before desegregation reveals that connectivity to the community was a crucial part of enabling schools to support the development of children. In both of the cases, this emphasis was evident. At Crescent Park, a Dad's Club was formed from a group of fathers who had learned about the restructuring process. Their involvement was visible in every aspect of the school culture and was manifest in culture of the school. At Jessie Owen, building a strong link to the community proved difficult initially because metro bus routes did not go by the school and because of the history of treating children and parents as a "dumping" ground. However, by working with the city and local businesses a new structure was created that provided incentives and means for involvement. And a new culture did emerge in the school that was not only welcoming to parents, but that bought parents' love and care into the school.

Second, a caring attitude toward all teachers, all students, and all parents seems central to creating an involving restructuring process. The ethic of care is closely linked to the concept of connectivity in both Gilligan's feminist view and in the African-American tradition. As we reflect on these cases, it seems crucial that there be an emphasis on care for all involved in the school and its community. The union issues may have accentuated the need for communication and care among teachers at Crescent City, but there were also divisions among teachers at Jessie Owens. At these and other accelerated schools included in the Louisiana study, there was a need to heal divisions among teachers (St. John, Griffith, and Allen-Haynes 1997). Further, teachers seem to need a community of support among themselves as they reached out to parents. Understanding their own differences enabled teachers to reach out to and understand the voices of parents, to recognize their love and care for their children. For the parents, this welcoming environment was crucial. Once they felt welcome, they worked with their schools to create learning environments that support parent learning as well as child learning. Opportunities for parent education were created in both of these schools, as well as other Louisiana Accelerated Schools (St. John, Griffith, and Allen-Haynes 1997). Further, care for children, by teachers and parents, as well as among children was evident in these schools. The movement toward multigrade learning communities a Jessie Owens illustrates an overt effort to create a structural strategy to foster this climate.

Finally, the ultimate focus of restructuring is to create a caring environment that accelerates learning for every child. This concept is certainly related to the African-American concept that "it take a village to raise a child", as well as with Comer's School Development process (Comer et al. 1996) and Levin's Accelerated School Project (St. John et al. 1997). At Jessie Owens, the outreach and climate of care influence families to keep their children in the school, rather than to move on to find better schools. At Crescent Park, not only did a few children gain recognition for essays, but test scores also improved, especially for children who stayed in the school also increased, even compared to similar children in other Accelerated Schools (Slack and St. John 1999). This aspect of the African-American tradition is where the linkages to the intent of new conservative reformers can be found. Indeed, the CSR reforms (chapter 7), and early reading reforms (chapter 6), and voucher experiments (chapter 8) are rationalized on arguments about improving learning outcomes. As these cases illustrate, reform that carries forward key elements of the African-American tradition can also support these new ventures.

Interestingly, these principles, or intermediate hypothesizes, are not incompatible with the intent of other reformers. Although these cases stop short of providing empirical evidence of a confirmatory nature, we think they provide compelling evidence that merits reflection. That is, reform processes that build on African-American traditions can improve learning outcomes. Although we do not reduce these insights to a claim that implementing the African-American tradition, by itself, will improve student outcomes, we do think there are lessons here to ponder. Clearly reform and tradition are not incompatible. Indeed, quite the opposite appears to be the case. Therefore, we conclude by suggesting that it is important to explore methods of integrating these aspects of the African American tradition into restructuring and other reform processes.

References

Argyris, C. 1993. *Knowledge for action: A guide to overcoming barriers to organizational change*. San Francisco: Jossey-Bass.

Banks, J. A. 1991. A curriculum for empowerment, action, and change. In *Empowerment through multicultural education*, edited by C. E. Sleeter. Albany: State University of New York Press.

———. 1995. Multicultural education: Historical development, dimensions, and practice. In *Handbook of research on multicultural education*, edited by J. A. Banks and C. M. Banks. New York: Macmillan.

Blum, L. 1999. Race, community, and moral education: Kohlberg and Speilberg as civic educators. *Journal of Moral Education* 28: 125–43.

Cadray, J. P. 1996. Enhancing multiculturalism in a teacher preparation program: A reflective analysis of a practitioner's intervention. *Dissertation Abstracts International* 57(8): 330A. (University Microfilms No. 97-01563).

———. 1997. Deconstructing bias: Reframing the teacher preparation curriculum. *Journal for a Just and Caring Education* 3: 76–94.

Comer, J. P., N. M. Haynes, E. T. Joyner, and M. Ben-Avie, eds. 1996. *Rallying the whole village: The Comer process for reforming education*. New York: Teachers' College Press.

Conrad, C. F., E. M. Brier, and J. M. Braxton. 1997. Factors contributing to matriculation of white students in public HBCUs. *Journal for a Just and Caring Education* 3: 37–62.

Cross, B. E. 1993. How do we prepare teachers to improve race relations? *Educational Leadership* 50(May): 64–65.

Dempsey, V., and G. Noblit. 1993. The demise of caring in an African American community: One consequence of school desegregation. *Urban Review* 25: 47–61.

Doyle, W. 1990. Themes in teacher education. In *Handbook of research on teacher education: A project of the Association of Teacher Educators*, edited by W. R. Houston, M. Habermas, and J. Sikula. New York: Macmillan.

Feiman-Nemser, S. 1990. Teacher preparation: Structural and conceptual alternatives. In *Handbook of research on teacher education: A project of the Association of Teacher Educators*, edited by W. R. Houston, M. Habermas, and J. Sikula. New York: Macmillan.

Finnan, C., E. P. St. John, S. P. Slovacek, and J. McCarthy, eds. 1996. *Accelerated schools in action: Lessons from the field*. Thousand Oaks, Calif.: Corwin.

Fleming, J. 1984. *Blacks in college: A comparative study of students' success in black and white colleges*. San Francisco: Jossey Bass.

Fossey, R. 1998. Desegregation is not enough: Facing the truth about urban schools. In *Race, the courts, and equal education: The limits of the law*, edited by R. Fossey. New York: AMS Press.

Fullan, M. 1999. *Change forces: The sequel*. Philadelphia: Falmer Press.

Gilligan, C. 1977. In a different voice: Women's conceptions of self and of morality. *Harvard Educational Review* 47: 481–517.

———. 1982. *In a different voice: Psychological theory and women's development*. Cambridge, Mass.: Harvard University Press.

———. 1998. Remembering Larry. *Journal of Moral Education* 27: 125–40.

Hopfenberg, W. S., H. S. Levin, and associates. 1993. *Accelerated Schools resource guide*. San Francisco: Jossey-Bass.

Hossler, D. 1997. Historically black colleges and universities: Scholarly inquiry and personal reflections. *Journal for a Just and Caring Education* 3: 114–26.

Irvine, R. W., and J. J. Irvine. 1983. The impact of the desegregation process on the education of black students: Key variables. *Journal of Negro Education* 52: 410–21.

Joyce, B. 1975. Conceptions of man and their implications for teacher education. In *Teacher education*, edited by K. Ryan. Chicago: University of Chicago Press.

King, M. L. 1986 I have a dream. *Ebony*, January, 40–42.

Kohlberg, L. 1981. *The philosophy of moral development: Moral stages and the idea of justice*. Vol. I: *Essays on moral development*. San Francisco: Harper and Row.

———. 1984. *The psychology of moral development: The nature and validity of moral stages*. Vol. II: *Essays on moral development*. San Francisco: Harper and Row.

McDonough, P. M., A. L. Antonio, and J. W. Trent. 1997. Black students, black colleges: An African-American college choice model. *Journal for a Just and Caring Education* 3: 9–36.

Mirón, L. F., E. P. St. John, and B. Davidson. 1998. Implementing school restructuring in the inner city. *Urban Review* 30: 137–66.

Orfield, G. 1992. Money, equity, and college access. *Harvard Education Review* 62: 337–72.

Orfield, G., and S. F. Eaton. 1996. *Dismantling desegregation: The quiet reversal of Brown v. Board of Education*. New York: New Press.

Power, F. C., A. Higgins, and L. Kohlberg. 1989. *Lawrence Kohlberg's approach to moral education*. New York: Columbia University Press.

St. John, E. P. 1997. Desegregation at a cross-roads: Possible new directions. *Journal for a Just and Caring Education* 3: 127–34.

St. John, E. P., and L. D. Burlew. 1993. A developmental perspective on reflective practice: An application of Jung's theory of individuation. *Louisiana Journal of Counseling* 4: 9–24.

St. John, E. P., A. I. Griffith, and L. Allen-Haynes. 1997. *Families in schools: A chorus of voices in restructuring*. Portsmouth, N.H.: Heinemann.

St. John, E. P., S. Loescher, S. Jacob, O. Cekic, and associates. (In preparation).

Slack, J. B., and E. P. St. John. 1999. *A practical model for measuring the effect of school reform on the reading achievement of non-transient learners*. Presented at the Annual Meeting of the American Educational Research Association, April.

Schon, D. A. 1983. *The reflective practitioner*. New York: Basic Books.

Sleeter, C. E., and C. A. Grant. 1988. *Making choices for multicultural education: Five approaches to race, class and gender*. Columbus, Ohio: Merrill.

Teddlie, C. 1998. Four literatures associated with the study of equal education and desegregation in the United States. In *Race, the courts, and equal education: The limits of the law*, edited by R. Fossey. New York: AMS Press.

Tierney, W. G. 1989. *Curricular landscapes, democratic vistas: Transformative leadership in higher education*. New York: Praeger.

Walker, V. S. 1996. *Their highest potential: An African American school community in the segregated south*. Chapel Hill: University of North Carolina Press.

Ward, J. V. 1995. Cultivating a morality of care in African American adolescents: A cultural model of violence prevention. *Harvard Educational Review* 65: 175–88.

Williams, J. B. 1997a. *Race discrimination in public higher education: Interpreting federal civil rights enforcement, 1964–1996*. Westport, Conn.: Praeger.

———. 1997b. Systemwide desegregation of public higher education: A research agenda. *Journal for a Just and Caring Education* 3: 63–75.

Zeichner, K. M. 1983. Alternative paradigms of teacher education. *Journal of Teacher Education* 34: 3–9.

Zeichner, K. M., and D. P. Liston. 1990. Traditions of reform in U.S. teacher education. *Journal of Teacher Education* 41: 3–20.

Part V

A Critical-Empirical View

Chapter 12

A Critical-Empirical Perspective on Urban School Reform

Edward P. St. John and Louis Mirón

Urban schools continue to be at the center of controversy. There are many new initiatives, including reading and comprehensive reforms, which encourage urban schools to adopt "proven," "research-based" methods. There other new initiatives, including state and mayoral takeovers and efforts to push vouchers, which indicates that some policymakers apparently have given up on urban schools as they are currently structured. Given these complex and seemingly contradictory initiatives, it is imperative that the policy researchers and educators develop a better understanding of these reform initiates. The chapters in this volume, in combination, provide a basis for developing a critical-empirical perspective on urban school reform, a perspective that might better inform efforts to improve urban education. Toward this end, this chapter revisits the four questions that guided the inquiries in earlier chapters.

Situating Urban School Reform

How were the reforms situated historically? After nearly a half century of urban school reform efforts, it is an appropriate to reflect on the ways the history of urban school reform can inform a new generation of reform efforts. Since the Little Rock school desegregation decision in 1954, there has been a litany of efforts to "reform" and "transform" urban schools.

Race and Class are Central to Urban School Reform

Race and social class are central to urban school reform because of the great economic and racial diversity in U.S. cities. Since Little Rock, the efforts to reform urban schools have been preoccupied with issues of race, whether or not the role of race was explicit. To understand why race and class are central however, we need only ponder the role of the courts in urban school desegregation and school finance reform. However, racial differences also mean class differences in U.S. cities.

The mandates of the courts prior to the *Brown* decision were that schools could be separate, but they must be equal. The NAACP and other advocates for social justice had litigated on inequality in opportunity for decades before the *Brown* decision, why equal opportunity for a quality education became a social policy issue, especially after *Brown* (chapter 1). Initially the strategies that courts mandated in school desegregation cases in both the South and the North focused on diversity in the opportunity to attend desegregated schools and focused on redrawing district boundaries and busing students. These strategies rapidly ran into problems because not all schools were equal, nor did all schools have equal resources.

A number of the strategies used in the second wave of desegregation remedies essentially set the stage for the school reform efforts of the past two decades. In the 1970s, courts were mandating that urban school adopt themes and that they be open to students across urban districts, a form of remedy that not only piloted tested school choice (Willie 1991), but that had many of the features of charter schools. Over time, the efforts to desegregate schools in urban setting became early experiments in urban school reform.

Inequities in school finance are also linked to race and social class in U.S. society. In spite of the new mandate to desegregate urban schools, the economic differences between urban schools and suburban schools became more evident and urban education became more central to finance reform (chapter 2). Because class and race are so inexorably linked in U.S. society, it is too easy to reduce the problem to social class difference. Not only are there wide class disparities between most urban schools, but there are even more substantial race differences. Therefore, it would be a mistake to ignore the role racial differences has played in education reform.

Indeed, as the reviews of the Chicago (chapter 9) and Detroit (chapter 5) cases reveal, not only is poverty a crucial issue in urban communities, but race also plays a central role in the development and success of reform strategies. The politics of urban communities is related to race and the coalitions that develop to undertake new initiatives (chapter 10). This suggests that it is important to understanding the values of diverse groups when reform initiatives are being considered.

From Equalizing Opportunity to Mandating Excellence

The Elementary Secondary Education Act initiated a major new federal program under Title I that was aimed at equalizing opportunity by providing supplemental educational opportunity for children from economically disadvantaged backgrounds (chapter 3). Reducing the disparity in opportunity to learn has remained the focus of Title I, but the means advocated for achieving this end have changed fundamentally over time. Initially Title I provided supplemental resources to schools with high percentages of low-income students. As the program received criticism for lacking a focus on educational improvement, it became more focused on improvement in reading and mathematics outcomes. Then in the 1990s, schoolwide Title I programs were encouraged and eventually comprehensive reform emerged.

Of course the federal government lead the shift in emphasis for equalizing opportunity to mandating excellence, starting with "A Nation At Risk" and other reform initiatives in the 1980s (Finn, 1989). This shift from equalizing inputs to emphasizing tests as an outcome measure had a pervasive influence on urban schools. The emphasis on high stakes tests, for example, has undermined efforts to bring more students into the educational mainstream (chapter 4). As states have responded to the new national calls for excellence, the efficacy of efforts to mainstream students was undermined. Including more students with learning difficulties in the educational mainstream means lower average test scores which leads to more sever accountability measures. It becomes a cruel cycle, creating an impression that urban schools are worse than they really are.

Whether state and local governments *should* change the authority structures in urban schools is a different question. Local boards have served U.S. education well for more than a century. In the new context, state and federal programs and policy wield substantial influence and constrain innovation and teacher initiative. Whether local takeovers will improve education depends in part on whether they reforms focus on enabling teachers to improve education in their classrooms, as has been the case in Chicago, or on politics and finance, which appears to have been the case in Detroit. Clearly the educational aspect of the challenge should not be lost in arguments over authority structures.

Increasing State Influence

Although schools are historically a local enterprise and the federal government was the first to take an active interest in reform, states are increasingly the source of authority in efforts to reform urban schools. Not only do states play a central role in the high-stakes testing game, but state power has increased because they are increasingly important in school finance (chapter 2). The political power increasingly resides in states and local reformers must address the state power base in order to undertake new initiatives.

The case of the Detroit schools takeover (chapter 5) clearly illustrates how local politicians must work state legislators if they aim to change the authority structure or internal accountability system in urban schools. Theobald (chapter 2) argues that it is crucial to work on informing coalitions of key players on issues, as a reform strategy. Thus state increasingly are in the power position when it comes to reform. This means that efforts to develop new strategies for improving urban schools may, by necessity, have to contend to state politics.

Conflict over the Locus of Reform Initiatives

However, although states may hold the power, they are not likely to be the locus of reform efforts in urban schools. In addition to state, the federal government, local schools, and their communities, there are frequently independent reformers in urban settings who have a stake in urban school reform. Many urban communities across the country now have private donors funding scholarship programs that enable children from poor families to attend private schools (chapter 8). However, these new initiatives also serve to undermine the role of local districts and educators in urban schools.

In this highly political context, urban school districts may lack the authority to be the locus of reform. Fending off, or responding to, the many externally mandated reform initiatives may be the primary source of power in these districts. And this is a negative power—a capacity to resist or comply—rather than a mandate to reform schools. The terrain of urban school reform is politically contested to an extent that seems to inhibit authentic improvement.

There were certainly examples in these chapters of initiatives intended to improve local input to reform. Mirón (chapter 10) described how joint ventures between school districts, local political entities, and local schools could be a force for improvement. However, when efforts are made to mandate local involvement, the democratic aspects of the reforms seem to be dominated by the mandates for academic excellence that are also embedded in these reforms (chapter 9).

Ideological Beliefs about Urban Schools

What ideologies underlie reform efforts? Political ideologies play a pervasive role in this politicized context for urban school reform. It is important to consider how the old political ideologies have broken down before considering how the new ideologies influence urban school reform.

Breakdown in the Old Consensus

From a century prior to the 1980s, a progressive political consensus held together diverse political interests in the support of public schools, including urban schools. This consensus revolved around a shared belief in the need for a *common school* experience in U.S. society and, more recently, that there should be *equal opportunity* for a quality education.

The Myth of the Common School. The common school movement in the United States took full force in the 1880s, as all states began to mandate schooling. Prior to this period schools had been widespread, but were modestly affiliated with churches. The commons school movement turned Protestant schools into public schools (Marsden 1994). Usually, urban communities preceded rural communities is the presence of common schools. Through the early twentieth century, the ideology of the "common school" across the country had a substantial influence. Although local boards officially controlled schools, an ethos about a common U.S. experience was an invisible force moving toward a common curriculum. However, there is reason to question whether there ever was a common school experience.

With the concentration of minorities and poverty in the inner cities, it has become increasingly apparent that the common school was a myth. Although there may be commonalties in curriculum within school districts, states, and even nationally, there is great disparity in the quality of education students receive. Wilson (date), Apple (1993), Mirón (1996) and others (Kozol 1991) have documented that urban schools faced massive challenges. Although in the first half of the twentieth century it was apparent that urban schools had greater resources, including more funding and more comprehensive schools, this was clearly no longer the case in the late twentieth century. In the last two decades of the twentieth century urban schools and rural schools lacked the capacity to teach students to read compared to schools in suburban districts and towns (Snow, Burns, and Griffin 1998).

Equal Opportunity as an Illusive Goal. An irony of this new set of circumstances facing urban schools is that after nearly five decades of social policy aimed at equalizing opportunity through desegregation, equalizing finance, and providing supplemental opportunity, these goals are fading for the policy agenda. The apparent failure of these strategies was central to the redesign of the federal role in the 1980s. The overhaul in educational policies is nearly complete, but it has proven no more effective in achieving the goal of equalizing educational opportunity. At the turn of the century, the term "urban schools" has become a way of speaking indirectly about racially isolated schools (Fossey 1998, chapter 1).

Rather than abandon equal opportunity as a goal, it is important to consider whether the new strategies have helped us achieve the goal. *Has the testing the implementation of stricter accountability systems enabled urban schools to improve?* The answer is not clear. In Chicago (chapter 9) there has been a great deal of emphasis on achievement, but the evidence is not yet compelling. In Detroit, the case was far worse: policies focused on structure and finances but seemed to have ignored the educational mission of urban schools (chapter 5). More generally, the stories embedded in all of these chapters were that the accountability systems have illuminated the disparity between urban and suburban schools more than they have resolved it.

Have these new approaches enabled more students from urban schools to achieve academically and graduate high school? There is some evidence that the newest wave of reform—reading interventions (chapter 6), comprehensive reform (chapter 7), and school choice (chapter 8)—that there are some gains from specially targeted reforms. These reforms merit more careful study, but they are hardly evidence that we have moved any closer to equalizing opportunity.

New Ideology of the Accountability and the Market

The new conservatives replaced the emphasis on equalizing opportunity for a common education with a new valuing of accountability and market strategies. Although the Bush administration is pushing both of these initiatives with greater vigor than a Gore administration would have, it is apparent that both strategies enjoy wide public support, although not support by teachers (St. John and Clement 1999).

The new belief in accountability and testing has been pushed in reforms initiated by both Republican and Democratic presidents over the past two decades. The testing movement itself is of questionable value as a reform strategy. *Is there evidence that the new accountability systems have improved schools*? There is some evidence that college participation rates rose somewhat in the late 1990s, for both whites and African Americans (U. S. Department of Education 1998), but there was a decline in minority participation in the 1980s and it is only now reaching the level of the late 1970s. Thus, there was not substantial improvement in opportunity as an outcome of these reforms. There is little reason to assume that there would be real improvement in urban education as a result of increasing the emphasis on testing, as the new Bush initiatives would mandate.

The new market rationale has been unevenly implemented to date. Charter schools are now widely adopted, comprehensive reforms are pervasive, and school-choice schemes are still being litigated. However, there is reason to ponder whether these reforms will improve opportunity in urban schools. Some limited innovation does eventuate from school choice schemes (chapter 8), reading initiatives (chapter 6), and comprehensive school reforms (chapter 7). Each of these schemes gives schools more choices about the pathways they take toward improvement, however, which may be the most positive outcome of these new policies, at least for urban schools. However, the effects are modest and far from conclusive.

Thus, the new reform ideologies still lack compelling confirmatory evidence. They are being pushed by politicians who believe either that these reforms will work or that there they gain personal political capital by promoting them. The challenge remains to test whether these rationales hold up to research evidence. There may be opportunities to improve schools as a result of these new initiatives. The early evidence on reading and comprehensive reform is compelling, but it is more complex than these reform advocates suggest that it should be.

The Politics of Race are Central to Urban School Reform

What is overlooked in these efforts to construct grand rationales for reform? If we go back to the mid-twentieth century, schools were racially isolated by law in one part of the country (the South), and as an artifact of residential pattern in the rest of the country. In the old model of racial isolation, an ethos of cross-generation racial uplift, care for children, and community development is evident in schooling for African Americans (Walker 1996). In the desegregation process, these older ways were essentially lost. Instead the common school ideal was used as the ethos of equalization, a dream that was never fully realized.

The values of care and community that are central to the African-American tradition of education merit consideration in efforts to improve urban schools (chapter 11). These values are compatible with some of the comprehensive reform models, such as Comer's School Development Process of Levin's Accelerated School Project. More experimentation with values oriented change merit consideration in urban schools.

It is clear that the current debates about education reform emphasize ideologies but not values. As the common school dream has given way to beliefs about accountability and markets, it is evident that more value-centered approach may be needed. However, the fact that the politics of race play a role in the debates about values in urban schools (Gordon 1999), just as they do in the debates about the foundations of knowledge.

The Underlying Theory Problem

How does theory relate to these reform efforts? The problems confronting urban school reform are not limited to problems associated with the ideologies that drive reforms. There are also underlying theory problems confronting educators, educational researchers, and policy makers. Before considering remedies, it is important to consider the theory problem.

Changing Role of Economic Theory

Economic theory is generally used as a basis for decisions to invest in education and other areas. Human capital theory argued that individuals and society made decisions about investment in education based on cost-benefit calculation (Becker 1964). Society made investment decision based on judgement about both gains in economy and other social benefits. There is substantial evidence to support the underlying assumptions in human capital theory hold up when empirically tested (Paulsen 1998). However, it is difficult to move from research to policy solutions, especially in education.

The human capital rationale provided an appealing basis for arguments for public funding. Educators frequently use appeals to human capital to argue for funding (Slaughter 1991; Trammel and St. John, forthcoming). More recently there has been a shift in rationales, from arguing for investment in education in general, to arguments for investing in specific programs. For example, advocates of Reading Recovery frequently argue the program will reduce educational costs because it reduced retention in grade and special education referral (chapter 6). Thus, there is a shift from general human capital was frequently used as a rationale for public investment in the progressive period whereas new market rationales are now being used by new conservative and new liberals.

In the older model of urban school reform, the theory of human capital provided a rationale for public spending on education, a rationale that was easily adaptable to the goal of promoting equal opportunity. However, as Theobald (chapter 2) points out, the notions of equity have given way to a focus on outcomes, even in the debates about schools finance. Thus, although it is important that educational researchers continue to study the ways educational reforms influence educational opportunity, it is also evident that these arguments are not as widely valued in the education debates as they once were.

In the new model, the theory of the market seems to drive many of the reform initiative. The notions that accountability provides information on school outcomes and that new reform initiatives provide opportunities for schools to improve both rest on belief in the role of market forces. Increasingly the new conservatives argue that Title I funds should be portable, becoming more like vouchers (Finn, Manno, and Ravitch 2000), yet they continue to argue against providing adequate funding for the Pell grant program (Finn 2001). This raises the question: *if Title I becomes portable, will the adequacy of funding decline?*

As the section of independent reforms illustrates, it is possible to assess the impact of these reforms using equity-related measures (chapters 6 and 7). As states and the federal government respond to new conservative calls for "choice" they will probably place less emphasis on providing adequate funding, as has been the case in higher education. This means it will be important to develop better ways of assessing the impact of ally types of reforms on attainment/equity, as well as on student achievement. A better balance between the two types of outcome is needed.

The problem with both the uplift and reproduction theories is that other social forces that are beyond the lenses of these theories can impede or accelerated the formation of educational capital within families. The older model did not fully consider how these forces might impede cross-generation uplift for some disadvantaged groups. The newer model underestimates the constraints on innovation in some contexts (chapter 8). Therefore, we need to ponder the role of social theory.

Uplift and Reproduction

The two major social theories about educational attainment offer conflicting explanations about the potential and limitations of policy in promoting improvement equity of educational attainment: attainment and social reproduction. Both theories can inform efforts to reform urban schools.

The major social theory of educational and social attainment argues there is a pattern of *gross-generation uplift*, with gains in parent education and occupational status in one generation having a positive influence on the next generation (Blau and Duncan 1967). There is a growing body of research that indicates that this theory does help explain attainment processes within African-American populations even better than it does for whites (Carter 1999; St. John, Hu, Simmons, Carter, and Weber, 2001). Not only is a growing diversity in economic status and educational attainment within the African-American population, but there is evidence that social background and aspirations have a substantial influence on college attendance (St. John 1991) and college persistence (St. John, Hu, Simmons, Carter, and Weber 2001). The primary implication of this theory and research for school reform is that African-American families have aspirations for a better life for their children. There is also evidence from these chapters to suggest that there are high aspirations. For example, interviews with parents about school choice (chapter 7) reveal that urban parents are motivated to gain access to better schools. Thus, it clearly is not a lack of will that impedes the efficacy of school reform in educational settings.

Social reproduction theory offers another frame for viewing the consequences of and impediments to school reform. Bourdieu (1977, 1990) focuses attention on the situated contexts in which students and their families make educational choices. He argues that the lack of cultural capital—the lack of parental education and of exposure to alternative life patterns—can impede the aspirations for students. McDonnough (1997) found that the situated context of urban schools limits the exposure urban students have to experiences that might encourage students to complete school and to attend high quality colleges.

Several of the chapters in this volume illustrate how urban contexts can constrain opportunity and essentially promote social reproduction. Nakagawa (chapter 9) found that the forces of cultural reproduction impeded parental empowerment in Chicago schools, resulting in a more constrained image of "ennoblement." Franklin (chapter 5) documented the ways efforts to take over urban schools helped to remedy some of the financial problems, but did little to improve academic programs within urban schools. Ridenour and St. John (chapter 8) found that accountability policy constrained innovation in urban schools, even after choice schemes were implemented, and public school teachers were generally resistant to the concept of school choice. Thus, there is a very deep conflict within urban schools that impedes opportunity and essentially promotes the reproduction of poverty. Most policy remedies overlooks these very serious constraints in urban schools.

Contested Terrain of Educational Research

Interestingly, education research per se has had little influence on most educational reforms until recently. Instead, social and economic theories had a major influence on the Great Society education programs and most of the subsequent reauthorizations. The historical exception were the then new science and math programs introduced as a result of the National Defense Education Act of 1958. However, this legislation was not influenced by educational research but by the threat that the Soviets might win the space race.

In 1990s three major reform packages were introduced that can be viewed as "research based" in the sense that they were informed by educational research. The Reading Excellence Act introduced a state competition for new money for reading, requiring proposals that were based on educational research. The new Comprehensive Reform Demonstration Program provides money for schools to select research based reform models. And, GEAR UP, a federal program that provides categorical grants for postsecondary encouragement programs, was also based on research on college access. These developments bring education research into the policy arena in a new way.

These developments hold some promise for the education community in general and for urban schools in particular. The research included in this volume reveals that these new reforms show some potential. Urban schools that adopted both research-based reading programs (chapter 6) and comprehensive reforms (chapter 7) show evidence that these reforms can make a difference. By adopting research-based models, it is possible for urban schools to improve student outcomes. However, this is not as simple as it seems. Not all models are equal. Nor do any of the models work the same way in every setting. Therefore it is crucial to take steps forward in the research process that might inform schools on how to inform choices about reform strategies.

Currently the debates are too often constructed based on tautological, self-sealing premises. Just because research has shown that phonological awareness is linked to early reading (Snow, Burns, and Griffin, 1998), this does not mean that direct instruction approaches engage more students and keep more students in the educational mainstream. The problems are more complex and there is a need for more and ongoing systematic research on the success of different models in different contexts.

Educational Reform is Political

Although policy analysts persist in using rational models to depict the role that reforms should play in improving educational opportunity in urban settings, they tend to ignore the social and political aspects of policy. For many decades there has been a tension between rational policy models and political realities (First, Crucio, and Young 1994). There is clearly a need to think more critically and openly about the social and political aspects of reform and the chapters in this volume provide information to inform such efforts.

The chapters in the volume provide further evidence that school reform is political. Politics have constructed the urban reform process in Chicago (chapter 9) and Detroit chapter 5). Further, in finance (chapter 2) and desegregation (chapter 1) cases, the courts constructed political remedies. Thus, it is necessary to recognize the political aspects of reform. This means that efforts to build political coalitions that can work together in a cohesive reform process (chapter 10), or that use research to inform analysts with varying political interests (chapter 2), may be the best ways to craft political remedies.

However, social forces are also important in school reform. Clearly the values of different groups in urban communities influence the way they view reforms, a truism that applies to teachers and parents (chapter 8) as well as to school systems (chapters 5 and 9). Reforms that are situated in the values of social movements or of diverse communities (chapters 10 and 11) have potential of creating momentum in the reform process.

Lessons Learned About Urban School Reform

How does the evidence support the claims of reformers? With the conceptual foundations provided by these chapters, it is possible to derive a set of "lessons learned" that might help guide future reform efforts. These new understandings are summarized below.

Lesson 1. Most Urban Reforms Lack Compelling Confirmatory Evidence of Success.

After five decades of urban school reform there is remarkably little evidence that the reforms have worked as they were intended. From the earliest efforts to desegregate schools it has become evident that structural remedies seldom have their intended effects. After fifty years of desegregation efforts it is difficult to identify a set of strategies that have created sustained patterns of integrated schools or that have resulted in sustained improvements in the quality or urban schools (Fossey 1998, chapter 1). Rather, when we step back and use a historical perspective, it is evident that both urban centers and urban school are more segregated now than they were before and the desegregation remedies may have hastened both of these developments.

Even more troubling, many of the major reforms, such as Title I (chapter 3), have not had their intended effects. However, federal programs continue to evolve, in response to political and social forces. The most recent stage in the Title I program, the emphasis on schoolwide and comprehensive reforms, shows some potential, but still lacks substantial evidence of success.

Lesson 2. Contradictory Mandates Complicate Reform Efforts.

It is ironic and sad to find that not only do school reforms have contradictory effects, but that the mandates themselves often undermine each other. Manset and Washburn (chapter 4) provide clear evidence of this pattern. They documented how efforts to create inclusive special education in Indiana's urban schools was undermined by implementation of high-stakes graduation tests. The analyses of the effects of school vouchers (chapter 8) also reveal that implementation of a new reform idea can be undermined by other policy initiatives being simultaneously implemented.

These problematic patterns illustrate that reform advocates need to more explicitly consider the intersections with other programs when they introduce new reforms. This means that both analysts and policymakers should resist simple, ideologically driven solutions to the problems in schools. Although this is not an easy task, it is essential one. *At a minimum, the process of examining the impact of new reforms on existing state and federal programs should be required, as an educational impact statement, before new reforms are brought to legislative bodies for a vote.*

Lesson 3. Some of the New Reform Initiatives Have Potential.

There were hopeful signs in these studies. In particular, although not all of the research is confirmatory, there is evidence that the educational reform strategy has made a difference in Chicago (chapter 9). Indeed, Chicago and Kentucky may be the best national examples of sustained, systemic reform efforts. Theobald (chapter 2) also illustrated that it was possible to improvement equity in school finance, but that it was necessary to consider political interests to sustain an equitable school finance system.

In addition, the recent reading and comprehensive reforms (chapters 6 and 7) suggests that in new periods of research based reform could create a new context for urban school reform. By enabling educators to review reform models and to choose models they think will work in their schools, the new reforms have increased the chances of success for some schools. However, there were not uniform patterns of improvements even in these studies, so there is reason to be cautious about this new wave of reform, as well as to think critically about how these reform efforts can inform future efforts to improve urban schools.

Lesson 4. Social Cohesion and Professionalism are Crucial to School Reform.

Professional development opportunities were integral features of the new reading and comprehensive reforms. These new models take comprehensive and cohesive approaches, they require teacher collaboration, and teachers need opportunities to learn together about these new models. Thus, professional development opportunities are crucial to the success of these new reform models.

Further, the reform efforts also need to consider strategies for collaborating with parents and communities in reform efforts. As Nakagawa (chapter 9) illustrates, it is difficult to realize the potential of parent involvement in urban school because of cultural differences between parents and teachers. This means that leadership that promotes community development may be necessary for urban school reforms to be a success (chapter 11).

In addition to emphasizing the technical aspects of school reform, it is important to consider these professional and social aspects. It is important to create opportunities for teachers to learn about the cultures and traditions of their students. Comer's school development process represents a reform model that emphasizes professional development, community development, and improvements in educational practice based on research. This type of balance appears effective, at least in a few case studies (chapter 11) and merits consideration in future reform efforts.

Lesson 5. No Single Initiative will be Universally Successful.

One approach to reform is to identify successful model and to implement those models on a wide scale. It is possible to view the reading and comprehensive reforms in this way. However, when we take a more in-depth look at the research on these reforms, a different conclusion is evident: different models are successful at different times in different settings.

Consider the example of accelerated schools. In the Wisconsin study of comprehensive reform, Accelerated Schools stood out as methods that was associated with reductions in retention rates (chapter 7). Yet, as implemented in Indiana, Accelerated Schools was associated with higher retention rates (chapter 6). What explains these differences?

As we reflect on the status of Accelerated Schools in these states, we are aware that the early Accelerated Schools in Indiana have lacked substantial support in professional development. These models were implemented after a single national training, lacked ongoing professional development, and did not receive state funds through either CSR or the Early Literacy Intervention Grant Program. In contrast, the Wisconsin schools have a high level of ongoing support for professional development from the National Center for Accelerated Schools, funded by CSR. Thus, there were substantial differences in the support structures for the same reform model in the two states that might explain variability in success.

Further, in both of these empirical studies Success for All (SFA) was not significantly different from other schools in either the Wisconsin or Indiana studies. Thus, although the early SFA studies seem to indicate the model will have an impact if fully implemented, these student outcomes give reason to question this conclusion. Even with Success for All, the success of the model seems to depend on the context in which it is implemented.

This is not to argue for one reform model over other models. Rather, it is important to move from universal assumptions about reform models to more locally situated assumption. It is important to explore the reasons why reforms are successful in specific context. As illustrated by Allen-Haynes and her colleagues (chapter 12), some of the successful Accelerated Schools in Louisiana seem to have been successful because they took approaches that were consistent with the African American education tradition.

Lesson 6. Research Can Inform Policy and Local Choices.

Given the shifts in the policy context summarized above, it seems quite evident that government mandates have little influence on the education improvement process. There is little evidence that mandated desegregation, mandated testing, or that any other reform described in these pages had an unambiguous, positive influence on improvement in student outcomes in urban schools.

Instead, the successful examples of reform observed in the preceding chapters involved local choices about reform strategies. This included local initiatives in Chicago, some reading and comprehensive reforms, and joint ventures between local government, business and education. Each of these successful examples had two things in common: they involved local choices and were informed by research.

Thus, there is reason to conclude that researchers can inform policy makers about reform strategies and that research can inform policy choices. In this volume, Theobald (chapter 2) explicitly argues for a collaborative model of policy research informing policy development. This approach to collaboration between researchers and policymakers merits exploration and testing.

Lesson 7. States and the Federal Government Should Establish Frameworks and Incentives, Rather than Mandate Methods.

Based on these considerations, these analyses suggest that policymakers should provide developed frameworks that enable educators to make informed choices about educational improvement strategies, rather than prescribe specific reform methods.

With education rising in public attention, it has become a national priority. However, policymakers, researchers, and educators need to resist overly simplistic solutions to challenges facing schools, especially urban schools. This is not to minimize the enormity of the challenges facing educators in urban schools and elsewhere. Rather, it is important to recognize that urban educator are part of the solution to these challenges. This involves providing professional development opportunities for urban educators, providing frameworks that enable them to develop cohesive reform strategies, and providing incentives that enable them to implement workable reforms.

Interestingly, the comprehensive school reform and reading reform initiative reviewed earlier (chapters 6 and 7) include many of these features. Indeed, further study of the successes and failures of schools that adopt research-based reform models represent an important step for researchers and policymakers. The systematic study of these reform efforts nationwide—and in local contexts—can inform the further development of reform strategies.

References

Apple, M. 1993. *Official knowledge: Democratic education in a conservative age*. New York: Routledge.

Becker, G. S. 1964. *Human capital: A theoretical and empirical analysis with special reference to education*. New York: Columbia University Press.

Blau, P., and O. D. Duncan. 1967. *The American occupational structure*. New York: Wiley.

Bourdieu, P. 1977. *The outline of a theory of practice*. Cambridge: Cambridge University Press.

———. 1990. *The logic of practice*. Stanford, Calif.: Stanford University Press.

Carter, D. F. 1999. The impact of institutional choice and environments on African American and white student's degree expectations. *Research in Higher Education* 40: 571–93.

Finn, C. F. 1989. The biggest reform of all. *Phi Delta Kappan* (January): 584–92.

———. 2001. An opposing view: College isn't for everyone. *USA Today*, February 21, 14a.

Finn, C. F., B. V. Manno, and D. Ravitch. 2000. *Education 2001: Getting the job done: A memorandum to the President-elect and the 107th Congress*. Washington, D.C.: Fordham Foundation

First, P. F., J. L. Crucio, and D. L. Young. 1994. State full-service school initiatives: New notions of policy development. In *The politics of linking schools and social services*, edited by L. Adler and S. Gardner. Washington, D.C.: Falmer.

Fossey, R. E. 1998. Desegregation is not enough: Facing the truth about urban schools. In *Race, the courts, and equal education: The limits of the law*, edited by R. E. Fossey. Readings on equal education, vol. 15. New York: AMS Press.

Gordon, E. 1999. *Education and justice: View from the back of the bus*. New York: Teachers College Press.

Kozol, J. 1991. *Savage inequalities: Children in America's schools*. New York: Crown.

McDonnough, P. 1997. *Choosing colleges: How social class and schools structure opportunity*. Albany: State University of New York Press.

Marsden, G. M. 1994. *The soul of the American university*. New York: Oxford University Press.

Mirón, L. F. 1996. *The social construction of urban schooling*. Cresskill, N.J.: Hampton Press.

National Center for Education Statistics. 1998a. *The condition of education 1998*, by John Wirt, Tom Snyder, Jennifer Sable, Susan P. Choy, Yupin Bae, Janis Stennett, Allison Gruner, and Marianne Peire. Washington, D.C.: NCES.

Paulsen, M. B. In press. The economics of human capital and investment in higher education. In *The finance of higher education: Theory, research, policy, & practice*, ed. M. B. Paulsen and J. C. Smart. New York: Agathon.

Paulsen, M. B., E. P. St. John, and D. F. Carter. Forthcoming. *Diversity, college cots, and postsecondary opportunity: An examination of the financial nexus between college choice and persistence.*

St. John, E. P. 1991. What really influences minority attendance? *Research in Higher Education*.

———. Forthcoming. *Refinancing the college dream*. Baltimore: Johns Hopkins University Press.

St. John, E. P., and M. Clement. 1999. Public opinion and political contexts. In *Public relations in schools, 2 ed.*, ed. T. J. Kowalski. Upper Saddle River, N.J.: Merrill.

St. John, E. P., S. Hu, A. Simmons, D. F. Carter, and J. Weber. 2001. *What difference does a major make: The influence of college major filed on persistency by African American and White Students*. Policy Research Report 01-07. Bloomington: Indiana Education Policy Center.

Snow, C., M. Burns, and P. Griffin. 1998. *Preventing reading difficulties in young children*. Washington, D.C.: National Academy of Science.

Slaughter, S. 1991. The official 'ideology' of higher education: Ironies and inconsistencies. In *Culture and ideology in higher education*, ed. W. G. Tierney. New York: Prager.

Trammel, M. L., and E. P. St. John. Forthcoming. Reframing in the policy discourse. In *Policy funding of higher education: Changing contexts and new rationales*, edited by M. D. Parsons and E. P. St. John. Baltimore, Md.: Johns Hopkins University Press.

———. Forthcoming. Reconstructing rationales for public funding: A case study of the Louisiana education quality support fund. In *Public funding of higher education: Changing contexts and new rationales*, edited by M. Parsons and E. P. St. John. Baltimore, Md.: Johns Hopkins University Press.

Walker, V. S. 1996. *The highest potential: An African American school community in the segregated south*. Chapel Hill: University of North Carolina Press.

Willie, C. V. 1991. Controlled choice: An alternative desegregation plan for minorities who feel betrayed. *Education and Urban Society* 23(2): 200–207.

Chapter 13

Implications of the New Global Context for Urban Reform

Louis F. Mirón and Edward P. St. John

This book has admittedly been an ambitious undertaking, for in this project we have sought to present a new methodology for studying and arriving at tentative understandings of the impact of educational reform in inner city, public schools—the critical-empirical review method. In addition we have sought to turn the common sense understanding of the failure of inner city schools upside down. We posed the question: Has educational reform itself, that is the coherent set of educational ideologies, public policy, class interests, school finance patterns, and finally school-level practices, failed students in the inner city?

The Failure of Reform

Our analysis has proceeded systematically across three separate, though interrelated fronts. First we examined what we generally characterize as "externally driven" reform, that is, those imposed upon by the federal government mainly through its court-driven goal of school desegregation. Second, we looked at the other side of the spectrum and analyzed what happens in inner city schools when educational reform appears grounded in an empirical research base. Third, we investigated bottom up, that is, community-driven reform. The intention throughout all three levels of analysis is consistent. We seek to place in a new context—globalization—the impact of three markedly different types of urban schools reform. As stated in the introduction, by "globalization" we mean here those social, economic, and technological processes largely confined to urban centers characterized by "de- and reindustrialization, automation, revenue losses, brought on by middle-class taxpayer flight, and the emergence of new and urban multiethnic majorities." To Valle and Torres's largely political economy perspective (2001, 102) we would add Michael Smith's "transnational urbanism" (Smith 2001) cultural perspective (see also, Mirón, Inda, and Aguirre 1998). Each type of urban school reform is similar in its desired policy intent—increased student achievement and better life chances for students in urban centers across the United States. Yet each seems pointed in different directions with competing cultural or technical values—externally driven, bottom up or value neutral (empirically based). So what have the authors of the chapters in this volume found?

Resegregation

In its very ambitious policy agenda to desegregate urban public schools, the federal court system apparently has largely failed. Public schools are now more segregated than they were prior to the *Brown v. Board of Education* ruling (chapters 1 and 11). This is disturbing on a number of fronts. First, the noble moral aim of President Lyndon B. Johnson's Great Society program of the mid-1960s—social equality and societal integration—has been apparently lost in one of its principal institutional venues, the urban public school. Several reasons may account for the institutional phenomena of resegregation, ranging from white flight to inexpensive housing markets in the suburbs. Furthermore, the political resistance to busing and the subsequent federal government's implementation tool, masks itself in the new form of academic "tracking" (Green 1999). Whatever the causes, it now appears that for the vast numbers of poor students of color that populate inner city public schools across the United States, the social and economic forces of globalization (Sassen 1991; also, see Wilson 1987) now make it likely that these students are increasingly denied access to a quality public education. For example, they seem systematically excluded (see Mirón and Lauria 1998) from a challenging curriculum, teachers trained in the use of educational technology, and perhaps most damaging—as recent investigations of health hazards on school buses in Los Angeles as reported by NBC Nightly News has shown—a safe school environment and infrastructure. We believe that we would be remiss if we did not now ask a most controversial question: Are poor minority students actually worse off today in the context of the powerful forces of globalization, than they were when segregation was rampant before *Brown v. Board of Education in 1964*? (chapter 11) If the answer to this question is "yes," or even "possibly," then one fact is now made abundantly clear. That is, this form of urban school reform—court-mandated desegregation—has systematically failed in its primary mission of equalizing educational opportunities for poor students of color in urban centers.

Research-Based Reform

The prognosis and evaluation of this method of urban school reform is decidedly mixed. Programs such as Reading Recovery, which helped fund ELIGP in Indiana appeared to improve "educational opportunity in urban school districts" surveyed (chapter 7). With specific regard to rates of retention in urban school districts in Indiana, "program types (e.g., Reading Recovery, and Success for All) had little interaction" with variables such as the percentages of students on free and reduced lunch. These, not surprisingly, continue "to be positively associated with retention rates." Having said that, the researchers in this volume found that the "Literacy Collaborative" in Indiana was statistically significant in its effect on student retention. This program type was negatively associated with retention rates. The authors' explanation for this effect is worth repeating here: "It is apparent that a combination of Reading Recovery and closely aligned school-wide process represent a powerful force for [school] change." We will have more to say on how a "school wide" process should be reconceptualized.

Contradictions of Community-Based Reform

Chapters in this section indicate both the possibilities and inherent contradictions of community-driven school reform (chapters 9 and 10). The critical-empirical analysis of the Chicago model indicates that "mandated parental empowerment" is both conceptually flawed and organizationally vexing. Although the model mandated a majority representation of parents on the Local School Councils, parents were largely uncomfortable with their new substantive, potentially policy-influencing roles. Rather, these evolved into "enabling" roles, which often placed parents in a codependent relationship with the principal and teachers, the other elected members on the councils in addition to the single student representative. The elected parents' roles were not insignificant in that "the LSCs were given responsibility for hiring and firing principals, designing and approving budgets . . . and creating local school improvement plans" (chapter 9). These mandated community reform models, although driving the governance system via remote control (the Illinois legislature) toward participatory democracy often failed as a result of the organizational and ideological structures in place, for example, the ideology of professionalism and the lack of technical expertise among the elected parents.

Similarly, explicit community empowerment processes such as the city of Santa Ana, California's "Education First" community forums and the city of New Orleans's Mayor's Advisory Committee on Education and prior to that, the Empowerment Zone Planning process for public education (see Mirón 1995) are often problematically riddled with internal and political contradictions (chapter 10). For example, in both cities the mayor and superintendent used the planning process to fund infrastructure improvements—new school construction and air conditioning—yet apparently failed to allow for community needs identified in the planning process, such as the siting of new libraries adjacent to public schools, and the expansion of on site medical clinics in inner city high schools serving African-American students in New Orleans. It appears that broader social structures and processes—perhaps owing to globalization—caused the community goals to take a back seat to the furtherance of the academic aims to raise achievement on nationally standardized tests. Indeed, the recent phenomena of posting the results of standardized tests on the Internet and the imposition of high-stakes testing policies, such as high school exit examinations, indicate that community values may increasingly be made subordinate to a narrow technically defined academic mission.

Is there a way out of these dilemmas? We believe that there is, and in the remainder of this chapter offer new conceptual and institutional tools to resolve what appears to us as the paradoxes of school reform in the inner city during the prior twenty years and historically, since the beginnings of the public school system.

Reimaging the School–Community Relation

We want to argue that powerful economic, social, and cultural forces (see Smith 2001; Harvey 1990; Poster 1990) have apparently caused nearly unprecedented and rapid change in inner cities across this country. Doubtlessly these social transformations, including rapid demographic changes in states like California, which in its major cities and suburbs have become "majority minority" places, have had profound effects on teaching and learning in urban schools. Furthermore, the apparent "mismatch" (see Levin 1988) between the lived cultural lives of inner-city students and their more affluent suburban counterparts, the increasing inequalities between rich and poor, and the loss of a sense of community—all contribute to the enormous challenges facing any urban reform model. The "one best method" of reform is perhaps doomed to fail. We are calling for a revitalized sense of community and "place-building" (Smith 2001), as well as plurality in school design to allow reform to take deeper root.

Robert Crowson and his colleagues (see Crowson 2001) have perhaps best articulated the new school-community social relation that can help frame more vital approaches. Crowson succinctly captures this new conceptual and institutional configuration (see also Baum 1997; and chapter 10):

> There is much renewed interest, at present, in school outreach—with added services to children and families, strategies for enhanced parent-involvement, community partnerships, efforts to encourage more neighborhood-level participation in school governance. Among the most recent movements is a growing, but still nascent, effort to broaden school-community relationships *toward a key role for the local school in the very development or revitalization of the community itself.* (Crowson 2000, 1, emphasis added).

Although Crowson's heuristic conceptualization does not specifically address urban school reform, nor the multiple social relations between "school" and "community," his colleagues do focus on urban schools and school reform (see Crowson and Boyd 2001). Thus we would briefly like to extrapolate from this excerpt from a larger body of new work to suggest the following with regard to the reimagination of the school-community social relation. First, each separately conceived social institution is both socially and historically constructed. They are creations of history and thus of humanity. Second, these need not be conceived *in isolation*; indeed they can be viewed in partnership, that is, in conceptual and practical tandem (Baum 1997). Schools and community constitute a relation. Perhaps the most salient of their relational qualities, though we will leave this for another discussion, is their political inextricability. They are forever joined in the arena of politics, and thus a heightened sense of "localism" (Driscoll 2001), in the paradoxical context of the forces of globalization must be heeded. Finally, in order to mount the critical-pragmatic politics (Maxcy 1991), resulting in an awareness of community and the experience of a sense of place, new attention must be placed on matters of design (see Mirón 2001). Here we mention only three: architectural vitality (Shokes 2001), place-building in inner city schools (Baldwin 2001) and linking affordable housing with reform in inner city schools (Mirón 2001). These are but a few of the imaginative possibilities that for the moment we will call "improvisational." In the final section of this chapter we will outline a leadership process for setting in motion a new vision of urban school reform.

Critical–Pragmatism in Place

Educational leadership is a process whose meaning in public, inner-city schools lies in the enactment of values. Most critical of the array of community values emphasized here is the making of place (Smith 2001), "city building" (see Driscoll and Kerchner 1999) and community development (see Lauria et al. 2000). Below we outline the rudiments of a leadership process whose practical outcomes may result in more viable school-community partnerships aimed at the enactment of these community values (see Mirón 1997; St. John, Griffith, and Haynes 1997).[1]

Two Way Communication

The institutional realization of new school-community social relations involves the opening of communication that is "two way." By this we mean the following: (1) a practice of reflection, reflective practice, and critical inquiry, following John Dewey, that involves a continuous, on going discussion, debate, and dialogue about how the values of school and the values of local community both complement one another and potentially conflict (chapter 9); (2) following Habermas (1970) enacting a practice of communicative action whose reliance on "discursive-practices" in the multiple interactions between public inner-city schools and residents in local communities leads to the articulation of ideas, beliefs, and ways of knowing that are marked by substantive rationality (Weber 1968); (3) a dialogue about the relationships between the technical mission of the school (student achievement and learning) and the community values described above. This dialogue between the professionals in the school and the residents in the local community is especially critical in enacting a more substantial vision of urban school reform in that

[1]This section is adopted from Louis F. Mirón, *Resisting Discrimination: Affirmative Strategies for Principals and Teachers*. Thousand Oaks, Calif.: Corwin Press.

it potentially moves both beyond narrow, technical interests to more humanitarian aims, such as the furtherance of academic equality and social mobility. This overview of the two-way communication process needs elaboration.

The Discourses of Place-Making

According to Robert Starratt (1991, 1994), school leadership is marked by both *substantive* rationality and *technical* rationality (Weber 1968). Habermas's "communicative action" framework also stresses the distinctions among the technical, human, and moral interests of communities. In the construction of learning communities in inner city public schools in particular we believe it is essential that school-community partnerships pay close attention to *both* technical ends and human interests. The primary reason is that the multiple processes of globalization make the use of communication technologies salient in accounting for school academic performance. Thus inner city public schools, many of whom are located in what is now called "global cities" such as Los Angeles, New York, and on the world stage in Tokyo and London, are particularly vulnerable to the political use of the Internet to regulate the behaviors and practices of public school professionals (see Popkewitz 1999). For example, the widespread practice of newspapers to publish the results of standardized tests instantaneously creates a rank order of public schools from best to "worst performing." This vulnerability cannot be dismissed.

On the other hand, it is unlikely that a sense of place can be created if the discourse is primarily about raising test scores. A substantive rationality needs articulation. Here we will allude to those most evasive of concepts, the *vision* of the school. Defined simply, the process of school vision setting in relation to community-building lies in the imaginative painting of "a portrait of [their] ideal future" (Mirón 1997, 13). Concretely this means that communication the values of the local community—a prerequisite for establishing a discourse on the meaning of place in relation to schools in the inner city—is that the conversation moves beyond statements about means and ends, that is beyond the apparent core functions of the school—teaching and learning. An overarching artistic, and dare we say moral vision of the school and its local community, is recast in recognition that public schools are fundamentally concerned with the construction of virtue (Noblit and Dempsey 1996; also see Mirón, Bogotch, and Biesta 2001). What is pivotal in this process is that this vision aesthetically communicates the inherently social relations between urban school reform and the meaning of place in local communities (see Driscoll 2001), thus "releasing the imagination" of both institutions to produce a shared vision. As Baum (1997) has described, this is a process that is difficult to accomplish, but can be set in motion by a process of strategic planning. This places this process of establishing a shared vision in the context of the deepening of democracy in inner city schools. This process will, we hope, result in urban school reform that is rooted in community values.

Community as Participatory Democracy

Following Thomas Sergiovanni (1994), we define "community" as sets of cultural institutions (e.g., residents of a neighborhood) whose shared values achieve mutual goals. Local community involves those residents of neighborhoods who are bound together by place to preserve (or seek) a quality of life (see Mirón, Bogotch, and Biesta 2001). Prominent among these residents, although historically marginalized, are public high school students. The process of participatory democracy (see Apple and Beane 1995) politically transforms (Laclau 2000) professional values such that the seeming intransigent rigidity of public bureaucracies such as schools can be mediated. Participatory democracy provides an institutional mechanism in public schools (see Baum 1997; also chapter 10) whereby the condition of postmodern chaos and disorientation (Harvey 1990; Poster 1990) in the local community and indeed the wider society can be dealt with more effectively. What results, one hopes, are "communities of hope" (Baum 1997).

What we specifically mean here is that students, teachers, principals, and neighborhood residents work collaboratively to newly design inner city schools (see Baldwin 2001). The purpose of this design, at the very least, is the provision of sanctuaries where both the school community and the neighborhood can feel safe, respectful of each other and, ultimately, to achieve trust as equal partners (see Mirón, Bogotch, and Biesta 2001; also Starratt 1991). This is a necessarily paradoxical relationship, that is one marred in the "dialectics of place" (see Torres and Mirón 2001). Let us specify.

On the one hand it is vital that schools do not abdicate their responsibilities to improve quality of life in their neighborhoods. Indeed a fundamental assumption of the new school-community relation (Crowson 2001) is that public (inner-city schools) must play a pivotal role in the revitalization of daily life in local communities. What does this mean? At the very least it means holistically attending through partnerships with agencies such as the Boys and Girls

Club (see Lauria et al. 2000) to the vast array of community needs such as public health and safety, local economic development, and, in particular, the development of teachers who are sensitive to the needs of the community. In addition these teachers and site administrators ultimately may decide to reside in neighborhoods where students learn (at present housing markets seem to work against growing a local teaching workforce in that neighborhoods in inner-city schools are perceived as unsafe). These are no small tasks, however, and we do not want to imply that teacher leaders and building principals in urban schools can do this alone. They need partners and "allies," for example city managers who, like in the city of Anaheim, California, have made Community Development Block Grant funds available to local school districts to support after school programs (Mirón, Riel, and Schwarz 1997).

On the other hand, we believe that planning for school-community partnerships must proceed sequentially, beginning with *improvement from within*. This sequence seems in direct violation of the school-community "social relation" paradigm we postulated above. The reason is that in order to transform the culture and teacher ideology of professionalism, leaders in the school must set in motion an inquiry process (Levin 1988) to assess and strategically plan to reach out to their local communities. As we saw in the Chicago case, community empowerment is problematic when mandated in state law. Even the boldest of urban school reform efforts—federal desegregation—has apparently experienced widespread failure. Choice must prevail, and school leaders must learn to develop an "ethics of the heart" (Mirón 1997). Realistically such noble values can only be nurtured developmentally when classroom teachers in particular feel secure in their own work and able to trust students and their families for the mutual betterment of each.

Finally, we cannot ignore the increasingly regulatory role of state government. The desired end of the process of community-making is the institutionalization of deep participatory democracy in inner-city schools. This process, we argue, is not tangential to the process of urban school reform. It is integral to it. Yet at the same time public, inner-city schools can only embrace these radical democratic values in their professional lives to the extent allowable under state laws and public policies. We want to end this section by extending Spencer Maxcy's (1995) call for enacting democracy to the process of urban school reform. For reform without attention to the meaning of community may be doomed to failure, yet again. We interpret Maxcy's perspective as defining the new school-community relation in inner city schools as one that both

> . . . have as their goal individual human beings participating and providing mutual recognition. Through the everyday practice of dialogue, conversation, phronesis [practical wisdom], practical discourse and judgment, the goal of community solidarity and unity would be sought. (1995, cited in Mirón 1997, 17)

An Agenda for Future Research

In summary, in this volume we have sought to present research findings and theoretical arguments to shed light on a historical dilemma: after nearly fifty years of intense urban school reform, why has student achievement been so uneven in inner city public schools? More to the point with so much money (see chapters 2 and 3) and perhaps even more in the way of political and policy resources, why have urban schools failed or has school reform failed urban schools? From the voluminous evidence mounted we offer the following tentative hypothesis and invite commentary and empirical analysis to confirm (or disconfirm) this theoretical exploration. We tentatively hypothesize that perhaps a central explanation for the apparently large-scale failures of urban school reform is the lack of reconciliation of two fundamental, and ultimately competing values that seem to undergird school reform in urban centers. These are the cultural values (principally community "empowerment") and technical values (mainly student achievement).

Community empowerment generally is made subordinate to student achievement. This volume has produced studies of the dynamics of urban school reform. We conclude that urban school reform architects might wish to mount future reform efforts simultaneously along these twin value lenses. Urban school reform should be purposively and strategically redesigned so as to reconcile their predictable ideological conflicts. Urban school reform practitioners and policy elites must be trained in what we shall call "practical deconstruction" so as to intellectually and pragmatically interrupt the historical tendencies to cast these value premises in binary opposition. On the contrary we believe they are mutually constitutive. In future studies, researchers should consider using these two guiding value lenses. For example, they might consider using case study approaches, complemented with statistical analysis and innovative analytical tools such as Geographic Information System (GIS) software to explore the relationships among the residence of teachers and the location of neighborhood schools to test the hypothesis that these historically competing values, unless resolved, will nearly always lead to failed school reform or the continuation of academic or social inequalities in the inner city (Sarason 1990; Tyack 1974; Smith 2001).

References

Apple, M., and J. Beane, eds. 1995. *Democratic schools*. Alexandria, Va.: Association of Supervision and Curriculum Development.

Baldwin, 2001. In *Advances in research and theories in school management and educational policy*, edited by R. Crowson. Stamford, Conn.: JAI Press.

Baum, H. S. 1997. *The organization of hope: Communities planning themselves*. Albany: State University of New York Press.

Crowson, R., and W. Boyd. 2001. In *Advances in research and theories in school management and educational policy*, ed. R. Crowson. Stamford, Conn.: JAI Press.

Driscoll, M. E. (2001). In *Advances in research and theories in school management and educational policy*, edited by R. Crowson. Stamford, Conn.: JAI Press.

Driscoll, M. E., and C. T. Kerchner. 1999. The implications of social capital for schools, communities, and cities. In *Handbook of Research on Educational Administration*, 2nd Edition, edited by J. Murphy and K. S. Louis. San Francisco: Jossey-Bass.

Green, P. E. 1999. Separate and still unequal: Legal challenges to school tracking and ability grouping in America's public schools. In *Race is . . . race isn't: Critical race theory and qualitative studies in education*, edited by L. Parker, D. Deyhle, and S. Villenas. Boulder, Colo.: Westview Press.

Habermas, J. 1970. Toward a theory of communicative competence. *Inquiry* 13: 205–18.

Harvey, D. 1990. *The condition of postmodernity*. Oxford: Blackwell Publishers.

Holloway, L. 2001. Temporary housing sought to help recruit teachers. *New York Times*, March 8, A20.

Laclau, E. 2000. What's in a name. Paper presented to the Critical Theory Institute. University of California, Irvine, November.

Lauria, M., et al. 2000. Panel on schools and Community Development. Annual meeting of American Schools and Colleges for the Study of Planning. Atlanta, Georgia, November.

Levin, H. M. 1988. *Accelerated schools for at-risk students*. New Brunswick, N.J.: Center for Policy Research in Education.

Maxcy, S. 1991. *Educational leadership: A critical-pragmatic perspective*. New York: Bergin and Garvey.

———. 1995. *Democracy, chaos and the new school order*. Thousand Oaks, Calif.: Corwin Press.

Mirón, L. F. 1995. Pushing the boundaries of urban school reform: Linking student outcomes with community development. *Journal for a Just and Caring Education* 1(1): 98–114.

———. 1997. *Resisting discrimination: Affirmative strategies for principals and teachers*. Thousand Oaks, Calif.: Corwin.

———. 2001. The cultural images of public schooling and the emergence of plurality in research. *Educational Researcher*.

Mirón, L. F., I. Bogotch, and G. Biesta. 2001. Students constructions of morality in inner city schools and implications for educational leadership. *Cultural Studies-Critical Methodologies*.

Mirón, L. F., and M. Lauria. 1998. Student voice as agency: Resistance and accommodation in inner city schools. *Anthropology & Education Quarterly* 29(2): 189–213.

Mirón, L F., M. Riel, and J. Schwartz. 1997. Anaheim Achieves. Grant funded through the Community Development Block Funds, Anaheim, California.

Noblit, G. W., and V. O. Dempsey. 1996. *The social construction of virtue: The moral life in schools*. Albany: State University of New York Press.

Popkewitz, T. 1999. Educational research as the production of memory/forgetting: Ethnography and the politics of knowledge. Paper presented at the "Reclaiming Voice II": Ethnographic Inquiry and Qualitative Research in a Postmodern Age. University of California, Irvine, California.

St. John, E. P., A. I. Griffith, and L. Haynes. 1997. *Families in schools: A chorus of voices in restructuring*. Portsmouth, N.H.: Heinemann.

Sarason, S. 1990. *The Predictable Failure of Educational Reform*. San Francisco: Jossey-Bass.

Sassen, S. 1991. *The global city*. Princeton, N.J.: Princeton University Press.

Sergiovanni. T. 1994. *Moral leadership: Getting to the heart of school improvement*. San Francisco: Jossey-Bass.

Smith, M. P. 2001. *Transnational urbanism*. Oxford: Blackwell Publishers.

Starratt, R. 1991. Building an ethical school: A theory for practice in educational leadership. *Educational Administration Quarterly* 27(2): 185–202.

———. 1994. *Building an ethical school: A practical response to the moral crisis in schools*. Washington, D.C.: Falmer.

Teacher next door. 2001. *http://www.hud.gov/offices/hsg/teacher/index.html*. 20 March 2001.

Torres, R., and L. F. Mirón. 2001. Economic geography of Latino Los Angeles. In *Advances in research and theories in school management and educational policy*, edited by R. Crowson. Stamford, Conn.: JAI Press.

Tyack, D. 1974. *The one best system*. Cambridge, Mass.: Harvard University Press.

Weber, M. 1968. *On charisma and institutional building*. Chicago: University of Chicago Press.

Wilson, W. 1987. *The truly disadvantaged: The inner city, the underclass, and public policy*. Chicago: University of Chicago Press.

Contributors

Choong-Geun Chung is a statistician at Indiana Education Policy Center, Indiana University, Bloomington. He is interested in statistical models for school reform, access and persistence in higher education, and issues in minority representation in special education.

Richard Fossey is a professor in the Department of Educational Leadership at the University of Houston and a senior consultant at the Center for Reform of School Systems in Houston, Texas. His research interests are education law and policy. Before beginning an academic career, he practiced education law in Alaska, representing Alaska Native school districts in Inuit, Athabaskan, and Aleut communities.

Barry Franklin is professor and head of the Department of Education at Utah State University where he teaches courses in curriculum and educational policy. His research interests and writings are in the areas of curriculum reform policy and urban education.

Leeta Allen-Haynes is Dean of the Graduate Studies Program at Southern University at New Orleans. Several years ago she served as a trainer and action researcher in the Louisiana Accelerated Schools Project at the University of New Orleans where she worked with schools in a few southern states. Prior to that, Dr. Allen-Haynes worked in the New Orleans Public Schools. More recently Dr. Allen-Haynes has directed her students in research comparing the academic outcomes of African American students in pre and post desegregation classrooms in New Orleans through the reflections of teachers who taught in both.

Carol-Anne Hossler is an assistant professor of Education at Indiana University Purdue University Columbus. A former classroom teacher and elementary school principal, her research interests focus on professional development, creating professional learning communities, and school improvement.

Kim M. Manoil is a school psychology doctoral student at Indiana University–Bloomington. She received her bachelor of science degree in psychology and social work at the University of Wisconsin–Madison.

Louis F. Mirón is professor of Educational Policy Studies and Social Theory at the University of Illinois, Urbana–Champaign. He is one of the nation's leading scholars in the application of interpretive and postmodern theories to educational issues and public policy. Having provided extensive commentary to the national print and broadcast media, Mirón is a powerful voice on urban school reform. Professor Mirón is the author of the *Social Construction of Urban Schooling: Situating the Crisis*.

Glenda Droogsma Musoba is a policy analyst at the Indiana Education Policy Center and is a doctoral student in the Higher Education Administration program at Indiana University. Her research interests include access and equity in higher education and other social justice issues.

Kathryn Nakagawa is an assistant professor in lifespan development, Division of Psychology in Education, at Arizona State University. Her specializations are family-school relationships and the social/cultural context of education. She is the co-author (with Dan A. Lewis) of the book, *Race and Educational Reform in the American Metropolis: A Study of School Decentralization*.

Carolyn S. Ridenour is professor in the Department of Educational Leadership at the University of Dayton. She teaches graduate courses in research methodology, program evaluation, and issues of diversity in schools. She has published most recently in the areas of school choice and issues of diversity. Prior to 1998 she published as Carolyn R. Benz.

Edward P. St. John is professor of Education at Indiana University. His research focuses on policy issues, school reform and higher education finance.

Neil Theobald is professor of education finance and Vice Chancellor for Budget and Administration at Indiana University–

Bloomington. He is a Past-President of the American Education Finance Association.

Sandy Washburn is a research assistant for the Indiana Institute on Disability and Community, Indiana's University Center for Excellence on Disabilities. She is currently pursuing a doctoral degree in special education and educational psychology at Indiana University. Sandy's areas of interest include educational reform, school practices that support students with diverse abilities, community building, and positive behavioral supports.

Genevieve Manset-Williamson is an associate professor of special education at Indiana University, where she teaches courses in mild disabilities, instructional methods, and assessment. Her research interests include learning disabilities, literacy, and school reform.

Kenneth K. Wong is professor in the Department of Leadership, Policy, and Organizations, Professor in the Department of Political Science, and Associate Director of the Peabody Center for Education Policy at Vanderbilt University. His research interests include urban school reform, educational policy and federalism. He currently serves as the president of the Politics of Education Association.

Index